MW01259054

God, Time, and Knowledge

A volume in the Series

Cornell Studies in the Philosophy of Religion

EDITED BY WILLIAM P. ALSTON

A full list of titles in the series appears at the end of the book.

William Hasker

God, Time, and Knowledge

Cornell University Press, *Ithaca and London*

dedicated to Robert and Kevin

Copyright © 1989 by Cornell University

All rights reserved. Except for brief quotations in a review, this book, or parts thereof, must not be reproduced in any form without permission in writing from the publisher. For information, address Cornell University Press, Sage House, 512 East State Street, Ithaca, New York, 14850.

First published 1989 by Cornell University Press
First printing, Cornell Paperbacks, 1998

Printed in the United States of America

Library of Congress Cataloging-in-Publication Data

Hasker, William, 1935–
God, time, and knowledge.
(Cornell studies in the philosophy of religion)
Includes index.
ISBN 978-0-8014-8545-9 (pbk. : alk. paper)
1. God—Omniscience.   2. Free will and determination.
3. Time (Theology)   I. Title.   II. Series.
BT131.H18   1989   231'.4   88-43294

Cornell University Press strives to use environmentally responsible suppliers and materials to the fullest extent possible in the publishing of its books. Such materials include vegetable-based, low-VOC inks and acid-free papers that are also either recycled, totally chlorine-free, or partly composed of nonwood fibers.

For further information visit our website at www.cornellpress.cornell.edu

Paperback printing   10 9 8 7 6 5 4 3

Contents

Preface

This book explores some questions concerning divine knowledge in relation to time and human free will. The philosophical fascination of these questions is undeniable, and I trust it will become sufficiently evident in the following pages. The religious and theological importance of the issues is seldom denied, but I think this aspect of the matter is often not given the attention it deserves; if I am right, furthermore, the theological bearing of some common views on these topics is often misconstrued.

Since I have tried to provide a fairly comprehensive treatment of some aspects of the topic, it may be well to mention some things this book does not do. First of all, this is a work of philosophical argument rather than philosophical scholarship. The first chapter does, it is true, provide a brief historical survey, but only to provide a proper context for the contemporary discussion; readers in search of original historical insights must look elsewhere. And of course I have made no attempt to cover all of the historically important figures. Even when commenting on the more recent discussion, I have by no means mentioned every important book or article, though I hope I have considered those which are most relevant to my own line of argument.

Proceeding in the same vein, I need to point out that I have done little to display the relevance of scriptural exegesis for my arguments or vice versa. Clearly, for those who approach the issues from within a context of faith, exegetical questions cannot be ignored, but an exploration of this dimension of the subject would exceed both the limits of this book and the competence of the author.

Although I argue in these pages for a definite position, I do not consider that any one position, including my own, comes anywhere close to being obviously definitive and correct. At the same time, all of the positions on these matters which have been embraced by serious thinkers seem to me to merit respectful consideration. Nevertheless, at least two important classes of positions have not been considered. Those views which hold that, for example, the relationship between divine foreknowledge and human freedom is an ultimate, humanly irresolvable paradox are omitted because of a simple but, for me, decisive consideration: once we admit that both of two mutually inconsistent propositions can be true, I simply do not know how to go about doing philosophy. And views based on a compatibilist or "soft determinist" view of free will are also largely ignored. This is not because I regard such a conception of free will as untenable, though I do tend to think so. But if one takes a compatibilist view of free will, most of the problems considered here are rather readily resolved and a whole battery of new problems arises to take their places; thus a book that considered those problems as well would be approximately twice as long as this one.

The writing of a book such as this would be unthinkable apart from the contributions of a great many other philosophers. Many of these debts are acknowledged in the footnotes, but I wish to include here a more personal word of appreciation to several friends. Thomas Talbott and David Basinger have both contributed immensely through personal discussions and the exchange of letters and papers over the past several years. Alfred J. Freddoso has assisted in several ways—through occasional personal conversations, through a mutual exchange of published and unpublished papers, by giving me an advance copy of his important introduction and translation of Molina, and finally by writing a remarkably detailed, generous, and helpful reviewer's report on this book for

Cornell University Press, and giving me permission to quote from it in revising the book. Alvin Plantinga has contributed greatly to my philosophical growth in many ways; perhaps his most important contribution to this book came through his 1978 National Endowment for the Humanities Seminar, "Evil and Foundationalism," which laid the foundation for such understanding as I possess of the counterfactuals of freedom and the modern theory of middle knowledge. And last but by no means least there is George Mavrodes, whose correspondence with me about the topics of this book, carried on over several years, is about equal in its combined length to the book itself. And without it the book would not have been written.

WILLIAM HASKER

Huntington, Indiana

Preface to the Cornell Paperbacks Edition

My response to the release of a paperback edition of *God, Time, and Knowledge* is one of thankfulness that, after a decade, the book is still sufficiently relevant to warrant a new (and slightly emended) edition.[1] This preface is devoted to a brief review of the progress of the discussion in the intervening years.

The principal theme of the book is a sustained argument for theological incompatibilism, the view that comprehensive divine foreknowledge is inconsistent with libertarian free will for creatures. It would seem that the debate over this issue has now reached a degree of maturity. The various strategies for defending theological compatibilism discussed in chapters 5 through 7 continue to be pursued, but without notable breakthroughs; and no major new strategies have emerged. Two significant books on this theme published in the meantime are *God, Foreknowledge, and Freedom*, edited by John Martin Fischer, and *The Dilemma of Freedom and Foreknowledge*, Linda Zagzebski.[2] Fischer's anthology collects a number of important essays on theological compatibilism and incompatibilism. Zagzebski's engaging book pursues an unusual approach: she gives trenchant criticisms of the usual strategies for defending theological compatibilism, then suggests several novel strategies of her own. So far none of these new strategies seems to have attracted a following, but it is too early for a final judgment on their prospects.

The Molinist theory of divine middle knowledge is subject to the usual arguments for theological incompatibilism. But the distinctive metaphysical commitments of Molinism—in particular, the "counterfactuals of freedom"—create issues peculiar to this theory, and about these issues there has been vigorous continuing debate.[3] Thomas Flint has emerged as the leading contemporary defender of Molinism, and I have profited greatly from his prodding and critiques. With regard to the "refutation of middle knowledge" featured in chapter 2, it has become clear that the main point of resistance for Molinists lies in the premise that, assuming there are true counterfactuals of freedom, these counterfactuals are more fundamental features of the world than are particular facts. I still believe this to be true, and I find the arguments in support of it cogent, but at this stage there seems to be no way to resolve the disagreement. It is fortunate, then, that Robert Adams, in his "An Anti-Molinist Argument," has presented an argument in some ways parallel to mine, which does not depend on this premise. I in turn have combined his argument with aspects of my earlier version to produce, in "Middle Knowledge: A Refutation Revisited," what may be the strongest anti-Molinist argument yet. Also of significance are the development of explicit definitions of the expressions 'explanatorily prior' and 'bring about', and, based on the latter definition, a formal proof of the power entailment principle.[4]

In addition to the debate about the metaphysical assumptions of Molinism, there has also been discussion about the consequences of Molinism for our understanding of divine providence. My own contribution to this discussion is found in "Providence and Evil: Three Theories." A major emphasis of Thomas Flint's fine book *Divine Providence* is on the detailed application of Molinism to various aspects of divine providential governance.

A third topic that deserves mention in this preface is the emergence of the view of divine knowledge and divine providence sketched in chapter 10 as a live issue in contemporary theological debate. The precipitant for this development was *The Openness of God*, authored by Clark Pinnock and others; other significant contributions include Pinnock and Brow's *Unbounded Love*, David Basinger's *The Case for Freewill Theism*, Greg Boyd's *God at War*, and John Sanders's *The God Who Risks*.[5] There has, to be sure, been sharp opposition to this view in various quarters.[6] The importance of this discussion lies in the fact that a way of understanding God, divine knowledge, and divine providential action in the world that formerly was peripheral and marginalized has come to be recognized as a viable theological option deserving of serious consideration. Trusting in divine providence, I believe that a vigorous discussion of this option can be of great benefit, not only for a lively and relevant theology but for a living faith.

WILLIAM HASKER

Huntington, Indiana

[1] The only substantive change is noted in n. 15 on p. 88; the numbering of propositions on pp. 94–95 has also been corrected.

[2] John Martin Fischer, ed., *God, Foreknowledge, and Freedom* (Stanford: Stanford University Press, 1989); Linda Trinkaus Zagzebski, *The Dilemma of Freedom and Foreknowledge* (New York: Oxford University Press, 1991).

[3] See Thomas P. Flint, "Hasker's *God, Time, and Knowledge*," *Philosophical Studies* 60 (1990): 103–15; William Hasker, "Response to Thomas Flint," *Philosophical Studies* 60 (1990): 117–26; Robert M. Adams, "An Anti-Molinist Argument," *Philosophical Perspectives* 5 (1991): 343–53; William Hasker, "Providence and Evil: Three Theories," *Religious Studies* 28 (1992): 91–105; William Lane Craig, "Robert Adams' New Anti-Molinist Argument," *Philosophy and Phenomenological Research* 54 (December 1994): 857–61; William Hasker, "Middle Knowledge: A Refutation Revisited," *Faith and Philosophy* 12:2 (April 1995): 223–36; William Hasker, "Explanatory Priority: Transitive and Unequivocal, A Reply to William Craig," *Philosophy and Phenomenological Research* 52 (June 1997): 389–93; Thomas P. Flint, *Divine Providence: The Molinist Account* (Ithaca: Cornell University Press, 1998); William Hasker, "Review of Flint's *Divine Providence*," to appear in *Faith and Philosophy*.

[4] For details, see Hasker, "Middle Knowledge: A Refutation Revisited," my reply to Craig, and my review of Flint's *Divine Providence*. For Flint's present views on these topics, see chapters 6 and 7 of *Divine Providence*.

[5] Clark Pinnock, Richard Rice, John Sanders, William Hasker, and David Basinger, *The Openness of God: A Biblical Challenge to the Traditional Understanding of God* (Downers Grove, Ill.: InterVarsity Press, 1994); Clark Pinnock and Robert Brow, *Unbounded Love: A Good News Theology for the Twenty-first Century* (Downers Grove, Ill.: InterVarsity Press, 1994); David Basinger, *The Case for Freewill Theism: A Philosophical Assessment* (Downers Grove, Ill.: InterVarsity Press, 1996); Gregory Boyd, *God at War: The Bible and Spiritual Conflict* (Downers Grove, Ill.: InterVarsity Press, 1997); John Sanders, *The God Who Risks: A Theology of Divine Providence* (Downers Grove, Ill.: InterVarsity Press, 1998).

[6] For example, R. K. McGregor Wright, *No Place for Sovereignty: What's Wrong with Freewill Theism* (Downers Grove, Ill.: InterVarsity Press, 1996); Norman Geisler, *Creating God in the Image of Man?* (Minneapolis: Bethany House, 1997).

The Historical Matrix

It seems probable that whenever theistic belief encounters or engenders a tradition of philosophical reflection, questions will arise about the relation between divine knowledge and power and human freedom. The Stoics wrestled with such problems, and Cicero framed what may have been the first argument for the incompatibility of foreknowledge and free will, in the form of an argument against divination. The Jewish and Moslem traditions have contributed their share of reflection on these matters. But the fullest and richest development of these questions has occurred in the Christian theological tradition, beginning at least as early as Origen and reaching a climax in the debates of the sixteenth and seventeenth centuries.

According to Anthony Kenny, "nineteenth- and twentieth-century treatments of these matters have added very little to the work of earlier philosophers and theologians."[1] It is to be hoped that this is not strictly true; if it were, there would be little excuse for the spate of recent writings on the subject, including Kenny's own, or for this book. I believe, in fact, that the insights and techniques of contemporary analytic philosophy offer the opportunity for gen-

---

[1]Anthony Kenny, *The God of the Philosophers* (Oxford: Oxford University Press, 1979), p. 8.

uine and important gains in the understanding of these topics; in this sense, philosophy does make progress, though here as elsewhere consensus and the ultimate resolution of disagreements remains an elusive goal. It does seem to be true, however, that all of the major alternative positions on the underlying issues had been formulated by about the end of the sixteenth century; recent discussion may have added to our understanding of these options, but it has contributed no major new ones.

These major theoretical options, with their context in the tradition of theistic reflection, form the framework or matrix within which contemporary discussion must find its place. So it seems fitting that a work such as this one, a book of argument rather than scholarship, should nevertheless begin by establishing this framework, in the process acknowledging several of the giants on whose shoulders we hope to stand. Five major figures have been selected for brief treatment here; each played a major role in the development of the tradition, and between them they articulate most of the major alternatives with which we must deal.[2]

Augustine

Augustine of Hippo (354–430) has the distinction of having occupied, and perhaps created, three distinct positions that are relevant to our topic. In the early book *On Free Will* he discusses the classical problem of foreknowledge and free will, and offers some answers that still resonate today:

> *Euodius* . . . I still do not see why these two things—God's foreknowledge of our sins, and our free choice in sinning—are not opposed to one another. . . .
> *Augustine* Why then do you think that our free choice is opposed to God's foreknowledge? Is it because it is foreknowledge, or because it is God's foreknowledge?
> *E.* Rather because it is God's.

---

[2]An excellent survey of the later medieval developments is given in Calvin Normore, "Future Contingents," in *The Cambridge History of Later Medieval Philosophy*, ed. N. Kretzmann et al. (Cambridge: Cambridge University Press, 1982), pp. 358–81.

A. Well, if you foreknew that someone was going to sin, would it
not be necessary that he should sin?

E. Surely it would be necessary that he should sin, for it would not
be foreknowledge, if I did not foreknow a certainty.

A. Therefore, it is necessary that what God foreknows must happen, not because it is God's foreknowledge, but simply because it is
foreknowledge; for if what He foreknew were not certain it would
be no foreknowledge.

E. I agree: but why are you making these points?

A. Because if I am not mistaken you would not necessarily compel a
man to sin who you foreknow was going to sin; although without
doubt he will sin, for otherwise you would not foreknow that it will
be so. And so, just as these two are not opposed, that you know by
your foreknowledge what another is going to do of his own will: so
God, while compelling no one to sin, nevertheless foresees those
who will sin of their own volition.[3]

Here Augustine deploys two of the classical arguments for the
compatibility of foreknowledge and free will—or, as we shall say
henceforth, for compatibilism: Knowledge as such does not compel, and human beings are able to foreknow the free actions of
others without removing their freedom. Nevertheless, there remains the implication, accepted by both Euodius and Augustine,
that if a person's sin is foreknown, whether by God or by another
person, it is necessary that the person should sin;[4] the necessity
involved here, however, is held not to be incompatible with free
will.

The second major position occupied—and in this case, we can
say confidently, created—by Augustine, is the doctrine that God is
timelessly eternal and has timeless knowledge of temporal events.[5]
In his famous words from the *Confessions:*

[3]*St. Augustine on Free Will*, trans. Caroll Mason Sparrow (Charlottesville, Va.:
University of Virginia Press, 1947), bk. 3, chap. 4, pp. 93–94.

[4]Since Augustine accepts the classical view that knowledge as such must be
certain in order to be knowledge, he does not distinguish between human knowledge and God's with regard to their certainty.

[5]Several of the Greek philosophers had what might be described as a doctrine of
divine timelessness. But in their view contingent temporal events are so lacking in
inherent dignity as to be beneath God's notice. The combination of divine timelessness with comprehensive divine knowledge of temporal events constitutes
Augustine's distinctive contribution.

Nor dost Thou by time, precede time: else shouldest Thou not precede all times. But Thou precedest all things past, by the sublimity of an ever-present eternity; and surpassest all future because they are future, and when they come, they shall be past; but Thou art the Same, and Thy years fail not. Thy years neither come nor go; whereas ours both come and go, that they all may come. Thy years stand together, because they do stand; nor are departing thrust out by coming years, for they pass not away; but ours shall all be, when they shall no more be. Thy years are one day; and Thy day is not daily, but To-day, seeing Thy To-day gives not place unto tomorrow, for neither doth it replace yesterday. Thy To-day, is Eternity.[6]

What may puzzle us is that this conception, destined to play such a momentous role in the controversy over divine foreknowledge, was so far as we can tell never employed to this end by Augustine himself. It may be that Augustine was fully satisfied with the answers he had given in On Free Will and thus felt no need for further illumination on this topic. And on the other hand it is possible that the connection between divine eternity and the foreknowledge problem, which seems so evident since it was made by Boethius, is in itself neither evident nor inevitable. My favorite solution to the puzzle, however, goes in another direction: I surmise that by the time Augustine wrote the Confessions his commitment to belief in free will in anything approaching the libertarian sense[7] had been sufficiently weakened that he was no longer disposed to feel the foreknowledge problem as a pressing one. It is acknowledged that Augustine reached a turning point in his thought about grace and free will in the first of his two books To Simplician—On Various Questions.[8] Of this book he said in his Retractions, "In answering this question [concerning Romans 9:10–29] I have tried hard to maintain the free choice of the human will,

[6]The Confessions of St. Augustine, trans. Edward B. Pusey (New York: Random House, 1949), bk. 11, pp. 252–53.
[7]We must of course be wary of reading modern definitions of various philosophical positions into ancient texts. Nevertheless, it is abundantly clear that Augustine's early thoughts on free will were closer to what is now termed "libertarianism" than were those he entertained later in life.
[8]In Augustine: Earlier Writings, trans. John H. S. Burleigh (Philadelphia: Westminster Press, 1953), pp. 370–406.

but the grace of God prevailed."[9] Evidence for the effect of this change on Augustine's thinking about foreknowledge will be drawn from a passage in *The City of God* in which he once again addresses that topic. The occasion is an argument of Cicero's against foreknowledge,[10] which Augustine summarizes as follows:

What is it, then, that Cicero feared in the prescience of future things? Doubtless it was this—that if all future things have been foreknown, they will happen in the order in which they have been foreknown; and if they come to pass in this order, there is a certain order of things foreknown by God; and if a certain order of things, then a certain order of causes, for nothing can happen which is not preceded by some efficient cause. But if there is a certain order of causes according to which everything happens which does happen, then by fate, says he, all things happen which do happen. But if this be so, then is there nothing in our own power, and there is no such thing as freedom of will; and if we grant that, says he, the whole economy of human life is subverted.[11]

Augustine replies:

We assert both that God knows all things before they come to pass, and that we do by our free will whatsoever we know and feel to be done by us only because we will it. . . . But it does not follow that, though there is for God a certain order of all causes, there must therefore be nothing depending on the free exercise of our own wills, for our wills themselves are included in that order of causes which is certain to God, and is embraced by His foreknowledge, for human wills are also causes of human actions; and He who foreknew all the causes of things would certainly among those causes not have been ignorant of our wills.[12]

Note Augustine's assertion that "we do by our free will whatsoever we know and feel to be done by us only because we will it"; no concern is evinced here about prior, determining *psychological*

[9]Ibid., p. 370.
[10]Cicero's argument is found in *De divinat.*, bks. 2 and 3.
[11]*The City of God by Saint Augustine*, trans. Marcus Dods (New York: Random House, 1950), bk. 5, chap. 9, p. 153.
[12]Ibid., p. 154.

causes, and the statement is strongly suggestive of what would now be termed a "soft determinist"[13] conception of free will. Even more revealing, however, is Augustine's response to Cicero's charge that, given foreknowledge, there is "a certain order of causes according to which everything happens which does happen." In responding to this claim, with its powerful evocation of determinism, Augustine does not say, as a modern libertarian would say, that the free will functions as an uncaused or undetermined cause and that the "order of causes" is thus not deterministic. Nor does he object to Cicero's assumption that it is only through such a deterministic order that God could foreknow the future. What he says, rather, is that the will is *included in* the order of causes. But a "free will" that can be part of a deterministic order of causes is surely a soft determinist free will, not one that is free in the libertarian sense. Augustine's answer to Cicero is a rather clear statement of theological determinism.

Boethius

Augustine's influence on subsequent theology and philosophy was immense, but his deterministic position on grace and free will did not become normative in any branch of the church until the Reformation. So the problem of foreknowledge and free will remained on the agenda, and Boethius (480–524) took the important step of viewing, and indeed resolving, the issue in terms of Augustine's conception of divine eternity. For the definition of eternity, we turn to *The Consolation of Philosophy*:

> Now, eternity is the complete possession of an endless life enjoyed as one simultaneous whole; this will appear clearer from a comparison with temporal things. For whatever is living in time proceeds in the present from times past to times future; and nothing existing in time is so constituted as to embrace the whole span of its life at once, but it has not yet grasped tomorrow, while it has already lost yesterday. In this life of today you are living in no more than a fleeting, transitory moment. . . . What is rightly called eter-

---

[13]Or, "compatibilist"—but we are reserving *that* term for a position on the foreknowledge controversy.

nal is that which grasps and possesses simultaneously the entire fullness of an unending life, a life which lacks nothing of the future and has lost nothing of the fleeting past. Such a being must necessarily always be its whole self, unchangingly present to itself, and the infinity of changing time must be as one present before him.[14]

He states the implications for God's knowledge:

Since, then, every judgment comprehends the objects of its thought according to its own nature, and since God has an ever present and eternal state, His knowledge also, surpassing every temporal movement, remains in the simplicity of its own present and, embracing infinite lengths of past and future, views with its own simple comprehension all things as if they were taking place in the present. If you will weigh the foresight with which God discerns all things, you will rightly esteem it to be the knowledge of a never fading instant rather than a foreknowledge of the "future." It should therefore rather be called *provision* than *prevision* because, placed high above all lowly things, it looks out over all as from the loftiest mountain top.[15]

Boethius also addresses the "necessity" that, according to Augustine, attaches to anything that is foreknown, either by God or by human beings. He distinguishes two kinds of necessity:

One is simple: for instance, it is necessary that all men are mortal. The other is conditional: for instance, if you really know that a man is walking, he must be walking. For what a man really knows cannot be otherwise than it is known to be. But the conditional kind of necessity by no means implies the simple kind. . . . Therefore free acts, when referred to the divine intuition, become necessary in the conditional sense because God's knowledge provides that condition; on the other hand, viewed by themselves, they do not lose the perfect freedom of their nature. Without doubt, then, all things which God foreknows do come to pass, but certain of them proceed from free will.[16]

[14]Boethius, *The Consolation of Philosophy*, ed. James J. Buchanan (New York: Frederick Ungar, 1957), bk. 5, prose 6, pp. 62–63.
    [15]Ibid., p. 64.
    [16]Ibid., pp. 65–66.

The point, I take it is, this: Once we have distinguished conditional necessity from simple necessity (what Aquinas was to call "absolute" necessity), it is evident that only the latter is inconsistent with free will. It is clear, furthermore, from our own case, that *present* knowledge does not imply simple necessity: If I know that you are walking, this does not imply that your walking is necessary. It might, however, be thought that *fore*knowledge implies simple necessity—for instance, because (as Cicero and the late Augustine agree) foreknowledge requires a "certain order of causes." But given divine timelessness, *fore*knowledge is precisely what we do not have.

Aquinas

Thomas Aquinas (1225–1274), as is well known, embraced the Boethian doctrine of divine timelessness, and by doing so he contributed greatly to its continued popularity down to the present. He is noted here, however, rather for his statement of one of the *objections* to God's knowledge of future contingent things: By a more penetrating statement of the argument for incompatibilism, he also brought about new insight into the character of the answer provided by the doctrine of timelessness. To set the stage for this, we return briefly to Euodius's statement of the argument for incompatibilism, a statement that is typical of many others: "But I would like to know . . . how it is that [sins] do not have to be, when He foreknows that they will be."[17] Now this argument is not completely stated, but it may seem reasonable to suppose that it is an instance of the form:

> Necessarily, if God knows that *P,* then *P.*
> God knows that *P.*
> Therefore, necessarily *P.*

But of course, this argument is invalid, which may lead us to suppose that Augustine could, and should, have dealt with it even more summarily than he actually did. Now, I am by no means

---

[17]*St. Augustine on Free Will,* bk. 3, chap. 4, p. 93.

certain that the argument is correctly and perspicuously represented by the form suggested above, though it does undeniably
leave itself open to this interpretation. Still, it may reasonably be
doubted whether the foreknowledge problem has been done justice to by murmuring "Sleigh's fallacy" and turning back to the
baseball scores.

If you do doubt this, then you are ready for Thomas's formulation of the argument, which is as an objection to his claim that God
knows future contingent things:

> Every conditional proposition of which the antecedent is absolutely
> necessary, must have an absolutely necessary consequent. For the
> antecedent is to the consequent as principles are to the conclusion:
> and from necessary principles only a necessary conclusion can fol-
> low, as is proved in *Poster*. i. But this is a true conditional proposi-
> tion, *If God knew that this thing will be, it will be,* for the knowledge of
> God is only of true things. Now the antecedent of this is absolutely
> necessary, because it is eternal, and because it is signified as past.
> Therefore the consequent is also absolutely necessary. Therefore,
> whatever God knows, is necessary; and so the knowledge of God is
> not of contingent things.[18]

Here the missing ingredient for Euodius's argument is supplied,
namely, the fact that God's knowledge is itself absolutely (or simply) necessary, "because it is eternal, and because it is signified as
past." Given this, the form of the argument becomes:

> Necessarily, if God has known that *P,* then *P.*
> Necessarily, God has known that *P.*
> Therefore, necessarily *P.*

Thomas has thereby formulated a really powerful argument for
incompatibilism, one that tests his mettle to the limit.[19]

---

[18]Thomas Aquinas, *Summa Theologica*, trans. Fathers of the English Dominican
Province, 2d ed. (London: Burnes Oates & Washbourne, 1920), I, 14, 13, Obj. 2.
[19]For an excellent discussion of this objection, see A. N. Prior, "The Formalities
of Omniscience," in *Papers on Time and Tense* (Oxford: Oxford University Press,
1968), pp. 31–38.

In responding to this objection Thomas first mentions and then sets aside several unsatisfactory answers, but he finally replies:

> When the antecedent contains anything belonging to an act of the soul, the consequent must be taken not as it is in itself, but as it is in the soul: for the existence of a thing in itself is different from the existence of a thing in the soul. For example, when I say, *What the soul understands is immaterial;* this is to be understood that it is imma-terial as it is in the intellect, not as it is in itself. Likewise if I say, *If God knew anything, it will be,* the consequent must be understood as it is subject to the divine knowledge, that is, as it is in its pres-entiality. And thus it is necessary, as also is the antecedent: *for everything that is, while it is, must necessarily be,* as the Philosopher says in *Periherm.* i.[20]

Further light is shed by his answer to the next objection:

> Things reduced to act in time, are known by us successively in time, but by God (are known) in eternity, which is above time. Whence to us they cannot be certain, forasmuch as we know future contingent things as such; but (they are certain) to God alone, whose understanding is in eternity above time. Just as he who goes along the road, does not see those who come after him; whereas he who sees the whole road from a height, sees at once all travelling by the way. Hence what is known by us must be necessary even as it is in itself; for what is future contingent in itself, cannot be known by us. Whereas what is known by God must be necessary according to the mode in which they are subject to the divine knowledge, as already stated, but not absolutely as considered in their own causes.[21]

The answer, then, goes something like this: What God knows *is* necessary, simply and absolutely necessary, *as it is known by God;* for it is known by God *as present,* and *everything* that is present is necessary—by the time something *is,* it is then *too late* for it not to be! But this, of course, does not remove either the freedom of a free action or the contingency of a contingent event. What *would* interfere with freedom and contingency would be a necessity of the

---

[20]Ibid., I, 14, 13, Reply Obj. 2.
[21]Ibid., I, 14, 13, Reply Obj. 3.

action or event *as they are coming to be*—or, as Thomas says, "in their own causes." Now, certain and infallible foreknowledge on *our* part *would* imply such a prior necessity of an occurrence, and so Thomas, unlike Augustine, denies that we ever do have advance knowledge of what is truly contingent.

Whether Thomas's position on this matter is coherent and correct remains, of course, a debatable question. If the reader will be patient for the next 150 pages or so, the matter will be addressed. What can be said at this point, however, is that Thomas has raised both the argument for incompatibilism and the response in terms of divine eternity to new heights of precision and penetration.

Before leaving Thomas, it may be of interest to consider briefly one of his rejected answers to the objection discussed above. He writes:

> Some say that this antecedent, *God knew this contingent to be future*, is not necessary, but contingent; because although it is past, still it imports relation to the future. This however does not remove necessity from it; for whatever has had relation to the future, must have had it, although the future sometimes does not follow.[22]

It would be most interesting to know *who* said this[23] because it is not difficult to see in this reply an anticipation of the Ockhamist solution to the foreknowledge problem, a solution that will occupy us in the next section and indeed repeatedly throughout this book. God's knowledge does indeed lie in the past, the reply states, but it does not partake of the necessity that attaches to the past in general, because "it imports relation to the future." As we have learned to say, facts about God's past knowledge are "soft facts" about the past and not "hard facts." Unfortunately, Thomas's reason for rejecting this reply is not as clearly stated as the reply itself.[24] But it is, I think, of considerable interest to note that

---

[22]Ibid., I, 14, 13, Reply Obj. 2.

[23]Calvin Normore cites Robert Grosseteste and Peter Lombard as having held views similar to this, so it is possible that Aquinas had either or both of them in mind ("Future Contingents," p. 370).

[24]I hazard as a conjecture the following interpretation of the claim "Whatever has had relation to the future, must have had it, although the future sometimes

Thomas was aware of this solution, and had considered and rejected it.

Ockham

William of Ockham (c. 1285–1349) may have given more sustained attention, and almost certainly devoted more literary effort, to the problem of free will and foreknowledge than any of the earlier thinkers we have considered.[25] Yet in the view of many contemporary philosophers his important contribution to the topic is focused in a single idea, or perhaps in a pair of closely related ideas. To set the stage for this contribution, recall for a moment the powerful objection to God's knowledge of future contingents which was formulated by Aquinas and discussed in the last section. By introducing the notion that the past, as such, is necessary, Thomas transformed what might have appeared to be a trivially fallacious argument into a formidable objection to his position. Thomas is able finally to rebut the objection only by appealing to his doctrine that God, and God's knowledge, are timelessly eternal.

Now, Thomas's argument was if anything even more formidable for William of Ockham than for Thomas himself, because Ockham rejected the notion of divine timelessness. He did not, however, reject the notion of the past as being necessary; rather, he distinguished a special sort of necessity that pertains to the past,

---

does not follow." I take "whatever has had relation to the future" to be an intentional attitude of some sort—say, expectation, or belief, or hope, or fear, or knowledge. If the occurrence of the intentional attitude is now past, then it is *now* necessary that that attitude was directed to the anticipated future, even though the future may actually turn out differently than expected. (In the fall of every year, it is still true that Ernie Banks hoped that spring that the Cubs would win the pennant—the truth of *that* lies in the past, and is thus immutable and necessary, regardless of whether the Cubs do or don't fulfill Ernie's hopes.) To be sure, when the intentional attitude in question is one of *knowledge*, whether divine or human, then the failure of the future to correspond cannot occur. But Aquinas strengthens his point by considering the more general case.

[25]See William Ockham, *Predestination, God's Foreknowledge, and Future Contingents*, trans. Marilyn McCord Adams and Norman Kretzmann (New York: Appleton-Century-Crofts, 1969).

called by him necessity *per accidens*, "accidental necessity."[26] But given this, it looks as though the argument

> Necessarily, if God has known that *P*, then *P*.
> Necessarily, God has known that *P*.
> Therefore, necessarily *P*.

is going to be, not only valid, but also sound. And if so, then incompatibilism is triumphant and the divine foreknowledge of future contingents is impossible.

Ockham's reply is both ingenious and subtle. He writes:

> Some propositions are about the present as regards both their wording and their subject matter (*secundum vocem et secundum rem*). Where such [propositions] are concerned, it is universally true that every true proposition about the present has [corresponding to it] a necessary one about the past—e.g., "Socrates is seated," "Socrates is walking," "Socrates is just," and the like.
>
> Other propositions are about the present as regards their wording only and are equivalently about the future, since their truth depends on the truth of propositions about the future. Where such [propositions] are concerned, the rule that every true proposition about the present has [corresponding to it] a necessary one about the past is not true.[27]

The idea that a "true proposition about the present has corresponding to it a necessary one about the past" is further clarified when Ockham says, "If 'Socrates is seated' is true at some time, 'Socrates was seated' will be necessary ever afterwards."[28] The necessity of the latter proposition is of course necessity *per accidens*, accidental necessity.[29] But, and this is the important point, not all present-tense propositions generate or correspond to accidentally

[26]An excellent recent discussion of this notion is found in Alfred J. Freddoso, "Accidental Necessity and Logical Determinism," *Journal of Philosophy* 80 (1983): 257–78.

[27]Ockham, *Predestination*, pp. 46–47.

[28]Ibid., p. 92.

[29]The necessity is "accidental" because, unlike the necessity of the truths of logic, it is not essential to the proposition that possesses it; it is something a proposition has at one time but not at another.

necessary propositions about the past. Consider, for instance, the following proposition: "The bride-to-be is trying on her wedding dress." This proposition, though grammatically present tense, is at least in part of the sort Ockham would describe as "equivalently about the future"; since it implies that the young woman in question will in fact become a bride, its truth "depends on the truth of a future [proposition]," and thus "it is not required that a necessary proposition about the past correspond to the true proposition about the present."[30] So the proposition "The bride-to-be was trying on her wedding dress" will *not* be necessary *per accidens* beginning from the time of the trying on.[31]

But now that we have this apparatus in place, the application to the foreknowledge problem is straightforward. In the case where "*P*" is a future contingent proposition, "God knows that *P*" is a proposition whose truth "depends on the truth of a future proposition," namely, "*P*" itself, so the proposition "God has known that *P*" is not accidentally necessary, and the argument taken from Aquinas, though valid, is unsound. Propositions about God's past knowledge of future events do not partake of the necessity of the past.

Ockham believed that this argument was successful in removing any incompatibility between foreknowledge and free will. Nevertheless, he admitted to great difficulty in understanding *how* God could foreknow free actions. In order to appreciate his difficulty, it will be helpful to have before us his definition of free will, which is a rather exact (and exacting) libertarian definition: Freedom is "that power whereby I can do diverse things indifferently and contingently, such that I can cause, or not cause, the same effect, when all conditions other than this power are the same."[32]

We have already noted his rejection of Boethian timelessness, but he also objected to the teaching of Duns Scotus according to which God knows future contingent propositions by knowing his own will. He writes:

[30]Ibid., p. 92.
[31]It will, however, be thus necessary *after the wedding.*
[32]*Quod.* I, q. 16, cited by Ernest A. Moody, "William of Ockham," *Encyclopedia of Philosophy,* 8: 315.

I ask whether or not the determination of a created will necessarily follows the determination of the divine will. If it does, then the will necessarily acts [as it does], just as fire does, and so merit and demerit are done away with. If it does not, then the determination of a created will is required for knowing determinately one or the other part of a contradiction regarding those [future things that depend absolutely on a created will]. For the determination of the uncreated will does not suffice, because a created will can oppose the determination [of the uncreated will]. Therefore, since the determination of the [created] will was not from eternity, God did not have certain cognition of the things that remained [for a created will to determine].[33]

In the end, Ockham is forced to a rather unsatisfactory conclusion: "I maintain that it is impossible to express clearly the way in which God knows future contingents. Nevertheless it must be held that He does so, but contingently."[34]

Molina

In a sense, Luis de Molina (1535–1600) began his investigation at the point at which Ockham ended his. Like Ockham, he was persuaded that there was no logical inconsistency between divine foreknowledge and human freedom,[35] but he sought to understand the *way* in which God is able to know future free actions. Like Ockham, he rejected the Boethian-Thomistic solution in terms of timeless knowledge, and he also rejected as inconsistent with free will the view of contemporary Thomists, such as Báñez, according to which "God knows the future free acts of men, even conditional future free acts, in virtue of His predetermining decrees, by which He decides to give the 'physical premotion' which is necessary for any human act."[36] (It will be noted that this is quite similar to the view of Scotus that was rejected by Ockham.)

[33]Ockham, *Predestination*, p. 49.
[34]Ibid., p. 50.
[35]His reasons for affirming consistency, however, are not the same as Ockham's. See chapter 6 for a discussion of this point.
[36]Frederick Copleston, S.J., *A History of Philosophy*, vol. III: *Ockham to Suarez* (London: Burns and Oates, 1968), p. 343.

Molina's solution to the problem was formulated in terms of divine *scientia media* or "middle knowledge." This type of divine knowledge is so called, because it is, as it were, intermediate between God's "natural knowledge" by which he knows antecedently all possibilities, and his "free knowledge" by which "*after* the free act of His will, God knew *absolutely and determinately, without any condition or hypothesis,* which ones from among all the contingent states of affairs were *in fact* going to obtain and, likewise, which ones were not going to obtain."[37] In addition to these two types, there is according to Molina yet another: "Finally, the third type is *middle* knowledge, by which, in virtue of the most profound and inscrutable comprehension of each free will, He saw in His own essence what each such will would do with its innate freedom were it to be placed in this or in that or, indeed, in infinitely many orders of things—even though it would really be able, if it so willed, to do the opposite."[38]

It is easy to see how middle knowledge enables God to know future free actions. He knows by middle knowledge what each possible free creature *would* do if placed in any possible situation; then he decides which possible creatures to make actual, and which situations they shall be placed in; and, in virtue of his having decided this, his middle knowledge again informs him concerning what the *actual* free creatures will *in fact* do. In addition to explaining the way God knows the future, middle knowledge offers many apparent advantages in understanding God's providential governance of the world, advantages that will be explored at length in later chapters.

In spite of these advantages, Molina's theory was not well received by the Thomists, who accused Molina and his fellow Jesuits of weakening divine sovereignty. The controversy became so heated that Pope Clement VIII convened the Congregatio de auxiliis in Rome (1598–1607) in an attempt to resolve it. The upshot was that "both opinions were permitted," but "the Jesuits were

---

[37]Luis de Molina, *On Divine Foreknowledge (Part IV of the Concordia)*, trans. Alfred J. Freddoso (Ithaca, N.Y.: Cornell University Press, 1988), Disputation 52, par. 9 (emphasis in original). My thanks to Professor Freddoso for allowing me to use a manuscript copy of his forthcoming translation.
    [38]Ibid.

forbidden to call the Dominicans Calvinists, while the Dominicans were told that they must not call the Jesuits Pelagians."[39] It is at least ironic, and perhaps significant, that the theory of middle knowledge, which was then under suspicion because it conceded too much to free will, should now be viewed with concern by a number of philosophers because it comes too close to determinism.[40]

[39]Copleston, *Ockham to Suarez*, p. 344. I am told that in principle a decision from the Holy See on this controversy is still pending.

[40]For an excellent overview of this controversy, see Freddoso's Introduction to Molina, *On Divine Foreknowledge*.

[2]

Middle Knowledge

Beginning this set of problems with the issue of middle knowledge may seem an eccentric choice. As we have seen, the theory of middle knowledge was the last of the major positions on these issues to make its appearance. It has never been close to a majority opinion, and even today it commands only a relatively small group of adherents. Furthermore, a direct attack on middle knowledge may be redundant. The theory of middle knowledge, in all its historical forms, presupposes the compatibility of divine foreknowledge and human freedom, so a successful argument for incompatibilism, if one can be mounted, would render superfluous a separate refutation of middle knowledge.

All this is true, yet middle knowledge has much to recommend it as a starting point. For one thing, the complexities of this theory lend it an almost irresistible philosophical fascination. With regard to redundancy, it is clear that in a controversy as heated as this one it is a merit and not a defect to assemble multiple independent arguments for the same conclusion; a single argument, even if apparently unimpeachable, is too likely to be treated with suspicion when it contravenes strong inclinations. Furthermore, the theory of middle knowledge, though dependent on the truth of compatibilism, also serves to strengthen compatibilism in at least two ways. For one thing, it offers an account of *how* God is able to know future free actions, and the account of this given by middle knowledge is free of some of the difficulties—for instance, retroactive causation—that plague other accounts of the matter. More important, middle knowledge provides the key to a uniquely powerful conception of the operation of divine providence, almost certainly the strongest view of providence that is possible short of complete theological determinism. In contrast with this, it will be argued in the next chapter that foreknowledge *without* middle knowledge—simple foreknowledge—does *not* offer the benefits for the doctrine of providence that its adherents have sought to derive from it. In view of this it could be argued that a good many theists who are not explicit adherents of middle knowledge nevertheless hold to a conception of divine providence that implicitly commits them to this theory.[1] And if this is so, a refutation of middle knowledge substantially weakens the doctrine of foreknowledge by removing one of its principal motivations. Finally, it should be noted that a structural possibility exists (not to my knowledge exploited by anyone as yet) of combining middle knowledge with the theory of divine timelessness, thus gaining the benefits of middle knowledge for the doctrine of providence without incurring the difficulties of foreknowledge. In view of these considerations, a refutation of middle knowledge which is independent of the foreknowledge issue can hardly be considered superfluous.

Our procedure in this chapter will be as follows: First, we shall consider the doctrine as it emerged in the sixteenth-century controversy and mention briefly some of the arguments pro and con that were put forward at that time. Then, we shall turn to the modern form of the doctrine as it has been revived—or rather, reinvented[2]—by Alvin Plantinga. Finally, a series of objections to this theory will be considered, leading up to one that I consider decisive.

[1]On this point, see David Basinger, "Middle Knowledge and Classical Christian Thought," *Religious Studies* 22 (1986): 407–22.

[2]Plantinga developed his view independently; it was Anthony Kenny who pointed out to him the similarity between this view and the classical theory of middle knowledge. See Plantinga, "Self-Profile," in James E. Tomberlin and Peter van Inwagen, eds., *Alvin Plantinga*, Profiles vol. 5 (Dordrecht: D. Riedel, 1985), p. 50.

The Classical Theory

The theory of middle knowledge holds that, for each possible free creature that might exist, and for each possible situation in which such a creature might make a free choice, there is a truth, known to God prior to and independent of any decision on God's part, concerning what definite choice that creature would freely make if placed in that situation. In effect, middle knowledge extends the doctrine of divine foreknowledge to include knowledge of the outcome of choices that *might have been* made but in fact were not.

On casual consideration, middle knowledge may appear to be simply an obvious implication of divine omniscience: If God knows everything, how could he fail to know *this*? And by the same token, it may seem relatively innocuous. Both impressions, however, are mistaken. Middle knowledge is not a straightforward implication of omniscience, because it is not evident that the truths postulated by this theory exist to be known. In ordinary foreknowledge, it may be argued, what God knows is the agent's *actual decision* to do one thing or another. But with regard to a situation that never in fact arises, no decision is ever made, and none exists for God to know. And if the decision in question is supposed to be a *free* decision, then all of the circumstances of the case (including the agent's character and prior inclinations) are consistent with any of the possible choices that might be made. Lacking the agent's *actual* making of the choice, then, there is nothing that disambiguates the situation and makes it true that some one of the options is the one that *would be* selected. This line of argument indicates the single most important objection that the proponent of middle knowledge must seek to answer.

But the very same feature that makes middle knowledge problematic (viz., that God can know the outcome of choices that are never actually made) also makes it extraordinarily useful for theological purposes. Consider the following counterfactual: "If A were in circumstances C, she would do X." According to middle knowledge, God knows the truth of this *whether or not* A ever actually *is* placed in circumstances C; indeed, God knows this whether or not A even exists, so that his knowledge about this is entirely independent of any of *God's own decisions* about creation and providence. But this, of course, makes such knowledge ideal for God to use in *deciding* whether or not to create A, and, if he does create her, whether or not to place her in circumstances *C*. As Molina says:

> God in his eternity knew by natural knowledge all the things that he could do: that he could create this world and infinitely many other worlds . . . [and] given his complete comprehension and penetrating insight concerning all things and causes, he saw what would be the case if he chose to produce this order or a different order; how each person, left to his own free will, would make use of his liberty with such-and-such an amount of divine assistance, given such and such opportunities, temptations and other circumstances, and what he would freely do, retaining all the time the ability to do the opposite in the same opportunities temptations and other circumstances.[3]

Another way to look at the matter is this: It is evident that, if God had created a thoroughly deterministic world, his creative plan would have involved no risks whatsoever; all of the causal antecedents of such a world would be set up to produce exactly the results God intended. But it seems extremely plausible that in a world involving libertarian free choice, some risks are inevitable: God in creating such a world makes it possible for us to freely bring about great good, but also great evil—and which we in fact choose is up to us, not to God. Thus, the frequently heard statement that God "limits his power" by choosing to create free creatures. But according to the theory of middle knowledge, this is not quite correct. To be sure, it is still the creatures, not God, who determine their own free responses to various situations. But God, in choosing to create them and place them in those situations, knew exactly what their responses would be; he views the future, not as a risk taker seeking to optimize probable outcomes, but as a planner who knowingly accepts and incorporates into his plan

[3]L. Molina, "De Scientia Dei," quoted by Anthony Kenny, *The God of the Philosophers* (Oxford: Oxford University Press, 1979), pp. 62–63.

exactly those outcomes that in fact occur—though, to be sure, some of them may not be the outcomes he would most prefer. The element of risk is entirely eliminated.

As we have already seen, the chief difficulty that the proponent of middle knowledge must confront is the contention that the truths God is alleged to know, commonly called "counterfactuals of freedom," do not exist to be known. Most of the arguments *for* counterfactuals of freedom seem to depend on general considerations of philosophical plausibility, but in the medieval controversy there were also arguments based on Scripture. A favorite text for this purpose is found in I Samuel 23, which recounts an incident in the troubled relationship of David with King Saul.[4] David, currently in occupation of the city of Keilah, consults Yahweh by means of the ephod about the rumors that Saul intends to attack the city:

> "Will Saul come down, as thy servant has heard? O Lord, the God of Israel, I beseech thee, tell thy servant." And the Lord said, "He will come down." Then said David, "Will the men of Keilah surrender me and my men into the hand of Saul?" And the Lord said, "They will surrender you." (I Samuel 23:11–12, RSV)

The advocates of middle knowledge took this passage as evidence that God knew the following two propositions to be true:

(1) If David stayed in Keilah, Saul would besiege the city.
(2) If David stayed in Keilah and Saul besieged the city, the men of Keilah would surrender David to Saul.

But (given the assumption that Saul and the men of Keilah would act freely in performing the specified actions), these two propositions are counterfactuals of freedom, and the incident as a whole is a dramatic demonstration of the existence and practical efficacy of middle knowledge.

But this argument is hardly compelling. As Anthony Kenny

---

[4]For my discussion of this passage I rely chiefly on R. M. Adams, "Middle Knowledge and the Problem of Evil," *American Philosophical Quarterly* 14 (1977): 109–117. See also Kenny, *The God of the Philosophers*, pp. 63–63.

points out, the ephod seems to have been a yes-no device hardly possessing the subtlety required to distinguish between various possible conditionals that might have been asserted in answer to David's questions. Kenny, indeed, suggests that we may understand material conditionals here,[5] but that seems hardly likely, since on that construal both conditionals would be true simply in virtue of the fact that their antecedents are false. Much more plausible candidates are given by Robert Adams:

(3)   If David stayed in Keilah, Saul would *probably* besiege the city.
(4)   If David stayed in Keilah and Saul besieged the city, the men of Keilah would *probably* surrender David to Saul.

As Adams points out, "(3) and (4) are enough for David to act on, if he is prudent, but they will not satisfy the partisans of middle knowledge."[6] The prospects for a scriptural proof of middle knowledge, therefore, do not seem promising.

But of course, the argument just given shows only that the responses to David's questions *need not* be taken as asserting counterfactuals of freedom, not that they *cannot* be so understood. And there are not lacking situations in everyday life in which it seems plausible that we are taking counterfactuals of freedom to be true. Plantinga, for example, says he believes that "If Bob Adams were to offer to take me climbing at Tahquitz Rock the next time I come to California, I would gladly (and freely) accept."[7] And Adams notes that "there does not normally seem to be any uncertainty at all about what a butcher, for example, would have done if I had asked him to sell me a pound of ground beef, although we suppose he would have had free will in the matter."[8]

So the discussion of examples seems to end in a stand-off. Still, the proponent of middle knowledge needs to address the question mentioned earlier: How is it possible for counterfactuals of free-

[5]Kenny, *The God of the Philosophers*, p. 64.
[6]Adams, *"Middle Knowledge,"* p. 111.
[7]"Reply to Robert M. Adams," in Tomberlin and van Inwagen, eds., *Alvin Plantinga*, p. 373.
[8]Adams, "Middle Knowledge," p. 115.

dom to be *true*? What is the truth maker for these propositions? At
this point the advocate of middle knowledge is presented with an
attractive opportunity, but one that it is imperative for her to
resist. The opportunity is simply to claim that counterfactuals of
freedom are true in virtue of the *character and psychological tendencies*
of the agents named in them. The attractiveness of this is evident in
that in nearly all of the cases where we are disposed to accept such
counterfactuals as true, the epistemic grounds for our acceptance
would be found precisely in our knowledge of such psychological
facts—Saul besieging Keilah, Adams's compliant butcher, and
Plantinga climbing Tahquitz Rock are all cases in point. But the
weakness of the suggestion becomes apparent when the following
question is asked: Are the psychological facts about the agent,
together with a description of the situation, plus relevant psychological laws, supposed to *entail* that the agent would respond as
indicated? If the answer is yes, then the counterfactual may be *true*
but it is not a counterfactual of *freedom*; the agent is not then free in
the relevant (libertarian) sense.[9] If on the other hand the answer is
no, then how can those psychological facts provide good grounds
for the assertion that the agent *definitely would* (as opposed, say, to
very probably would) respond in that way?

Probably the best line for the proponent of middle knowledge to
take here is the one suggested by Suárez: When a counterfactual of
freedom is true, it is simply an ultimate fact about the free agent in
question that, if placed in the indicated circumstances, she would
act as the counterfactual states; this fact requires no analysis or
metaphysical grounding in terms of further, noncounterfactual
states of affairs. (Or, if the agent in question does not actually
exist, it is a fact about a particular *essence* that, if it were instantiated

---

[9]There are complexities in our use of such expressions as "acting freely" that are
not always sufficiently taken note of. For example, it may happen that an action is
"psychologically inevitable" for a person, based on that person's character and
dispositions, yet we say that the person acts "freely" *if the character and dispositions
are thought to be the result of previous freely chosen actions of the person.* Thus, it is said of
the redeemed in heaven both that they freely serve and worship God, and that they
are not able to sin; this happy inability is the result of their own free choices and is
not typically seen as a diminution of freedom. But acts of this sort are *not* free in
the very strict sense required by libertarianism. If we are exacting in our *definition*
of "free" but lax in *applying* the term, trouble is inevitable.

and its instantiation were placed in such circumstances, the instantiation would act as stated.) Adams, commenting on this, says, "I do not think I have any conception . . . of the sort of . . . property that Suárez ascribes to possible agents with respect to their acts under possible conditions. Nor do I think that I have any other primitive understanding of what it would be for the relevant subjunctive conditionals to be true." Nevertheless, he admits that Suárez's view on this is of the "least clearly unsatisfactory type," because "It is very difficult to refute someone who claims to have a primitive understanding which I seem not to have."[10]

The Modern Theory

The modern theory of middle knowledge[11] differs from the classical version in virtue of the application to the counterfactuals of freedom of the powerful possible-worlds semantics for counterfactuals developed by Robert Stalnaker, David Lewis, and John L. Pollock.[12] The central idea of this semantics is that a counterfactual is true if some possible world in which the antecedent and the consequent are both true is more similar to the actual world than any in which the antecedent is true and the consequent false.[13] Thus (1) above is correctly analyzed as

(5)   The actual world is more similar to some possible world
        in which David stays in Keilah and Saul besieges the city

[10]Adams, "Middle Knowledge," p. 112.

[11]The basic source for the modern theory of middle knowledge is Alvin Plantinga, The Nature of Necessity (Oxford: Oxford University Press, 1974), chap. 9.

[12]See Robert Stalnaker, "A Theory of Conditionals," in N. Rescher, ed., Studies in Logical Theory (Oxford: Blackwell, 1968); David Lewis, Counterfactuals (Cambridge: Harvard University Press, 1973); and John L. Pollock, Subjunctive Reasoning (Dordrecht: D. Riedel, 1976). It should be noted, however that some contemporary adherents of middle knowledge have reservations about this semantics. Alfred J. Freddoso, for example, writes: "I repudiate the claim that the standard semantics applies to [counterfactuals of freedom] or to any other 'simple' conditionals that involve causal indeterminism" (personal communication).

[13]Pollock argues that the relevant notion is not that of comparative similarity but rather that of a possible world "minimally changed" from the actual world so as to make the antecedent of the counterfactual true. (See Subjunctive Reasoning, pp. 17–23.) Pollock's argument seems to be correct, but the difference between the two formulations is not significant for present purposes, so we shall continue to employ the more familiar terminology.

than to any possible world in which David stays in Keilah
and Saul does not besiege the city.[14]

At this point it will be well to get a bit clearer about the exact
positions both of the advocate and of the opponent of middle
knowledge. First of all, it may be noted that the term "counterfactual," though customary and convenient, is not strictly accurate as
a designation of the propositions in question. In some cases (namely, those whose antecedents God decides to actualize) both the
antecedent and the consequent of the conditionals will be *true*, and
so not *counter*factual at all. A better term, therefore, would be, as
Adams suggests, "deliberative conditionals." Having said that,
however, we shall continue to refer to them as "counterfactuals of
freedom."

But just what kind of conditionals are these? Both Lewis and
Pollock distinguish "would" conditionals from "might" conditionals; the "might" conditional corresponding to (1) would be

(1m) If David stayed in Keilah, Saul *might* beseige the city.

But Pollock goes further and distinguishes three different kinds of
"would" conditionals; these distinctions are not explicitly made by
Lewis.[15] There are "simple subjunctives"; these are the conditionals most frequently, and most naturally, expressed by English sentences of the form "If it were the case that *P*, it would be the case
that *Q*." Second, there are "even if" conditionals, of the form
"Even if it were the case that *P*, it would (still) be the case that *Q*."
These are the conditionals Nelson Goodman calls "semi-factuals";
they are asserted when their consequents are believed to be true,
whereas their antecedents may or may not be true, and their force
is to deny that the truth of the antecedent would bring about the
falsity of the consequent. Finally, there are "necessitation conditionals"; according to Pollock, "the notion of necessitation that I
am trying to analyze here is that of the truth of one statement
'bringing it about' that another statement is true,"[16] so an appro-

[14]Adams, *"Middle Knowledge,"* p. 112.
[15]See Pollock, *Subjunctive Reasoning,* chap. 2, "Four Kinds of Conditionals."
[16]Ibid., pp. 35–36. Pollock says, "Perhaps the term 'necessitation' is inappropri-

priate formula might be "Its being the case that P would bring it about that Q."

Now, into which of these categories do we place the counterfactuals of freedom? Evidently they cannot be "might" conditionals. "Even if" conditionals are true only in (some of) those possible worlds in which their consequents are true, but the truth of the counterfactuals of freedom must be known to God quite independently of whether or not their consequents are true in the actual world. Pollock shows that a simple subjunctive is equivalent to the disjunction of a necessitation conditional and an "even if" conditional. If, then, we were to equate counterfactuals of freedom with simple subjunctives, it would follow that in those cases where the necessitation conditional is false the counterfactual of freedom would be equivalent to an "even if" conditional, which we have seen to be impossible. So if the counterfactuals of freedom are to be found among the varieties discussed by Pollock, they must be necessitation conditionals. As he says, "All counterfactual conditionals express necessitation."[17]

Now that we have clarified the nature of the counterfactuals of freedom, how exactly shall we characterize the view taken of such counterfactuals by the opponents of middle knowledge? There seem to be three alternatives: One may deny that such propositions exist at all; one may concede their existence but deny that they possess truth-values; or one may hold that all such propositions are false. The denial that there are such propositions as counterfactuals of freedom does not seem to have much to recommend it; as Plantinga says, he may conceivably be *wrong* in believing that if Adams were to invite him to climb Tahquitz Rock he would accept, but it would be passing strange to deny that *there is* such a proposition as the one he claims to believe. I think, in fact, that this view may best be understood as arising from an exigency; if one thinks (as the second view holds) that there is no way to assign

---

ate for the notion I have in mind here, but I have been unable to find a better term" (p. 36). Pollock does not identify any single English locution that is customarily used in stating necessitation conditionals, though he thinks the force of such conditionals may be captured by the formula "If it were true that P, it would be true that Q *since* it was true that P" (p. 27).

[17]Ibid, p. 34.

truth-values to counterfactuals of freedom, and if one is also convinced that every proposition must be either true or false, then one is virtually forced to deny that there are such propositions—that is, one is forced to deny that the relevant sentences express any propositions at all.

The second view, according to which counterfactuals of freedom lack truth-values, probably arises from the reflection that there is no way to assign the truth-values because (where the consequent expresses a free choice to be made in hypothetical circumstances) there is in principle no way of knowing whether the consequent would be true if the antecedent were true. This, however, overlooks the possibility that we might be able to know whether the counterfactual is true *without* knowing this.

But how is this possible? The general relationship between counterfactuals and libertarian free will is something that still needs to be worked out. (Indeed, it is really the central theme of the present discussion.) But an extremely plausible view to take is the following: A situation in which an agent makes a libertarian free choice with respect to doing or not doing something is a situation in which the agent *might* do that thing but also might refrain from doing it. Suppose that A, if she found herself in circumstances C, would freely decide whether or not to do X. Then both of the following counterfactuals will be true:

(6)   If A were in C, she might do X.
(7)   If A were in C, she might refrain from doing X.

But if this is so, then there is no true counterfactual of freedom with respect to A's doing X in C. For (6) is inconsistent with

(8)   If A were in C, she would refrain from doing X.

Likewise, (7) is inconsistent with

(9)   If A were in C, she would do X.

If propositions like (6) and (7) properly characterize a situation of libertarian free choice, then all counterfactuals of freedom are false.

In the ensuing discussion, this is the position which we shall assume the opponent of middle knowledge to be asserting and defending.

Objections to Middle Knowledge

Now that the opposition between proponents and opponents of middle knowledge has been delineated, how can we make progress on resolving the issue? As noted, proponents seem willing to rest their case on general considerations of plausibility, perhaps buttressed by allusions to the alleged theological necessity of the doctrine. Opponents can do the same, of course, and many do, but if the discussion is to be advanced, more substantial arguments are needed. And, in fact, such arguments are available. In this section three brief arguments against the theory will be spelled out, and in the next a somewhat more detailed argument will be developed.

The first objection to be considered is one we have already alluded to: What, if anything, is the *ground* of the truth of the counterfactuals of freedom? It is important to see that the question here is metaphysical, not epistemological. The question is not, How can we *know* that a counterfactual of freedom is true? It may be that we cannot know this, except perhaps in a very few cases, and although it is claimed that *God* knows them, it is not clear that the friend of counterfactuals (or any other theist, for that matter) is required to explain *how* it is that God knows what he knows. The question, rather, is What *makes* the counterfactuals true—what is the *ground* of their truth? As Adams says, "I do not understand what it would be for [counterfactuals of freedom] to be true."[18]

In replying to this Plantinga finds this notion of a requirement that there be something that "grounds" the truth of a proposition to be obscure. But insofar as the requirement does hold, he thinks the counterfactuals of freedom are no worse off with respect to it than are other propositions whose credentials are unimpeachable.

Suppose, then, that yesterday I freely performed some action *A*. What was or is it that grounded or founded my doing so? I wasn't

18Adams, "*Middle Knowledge*," p. 110.

caused to do by anything else; nothing relevant *entails* that I did so. So what grounds the truth of the proposition in question? Perhaps you will say that what grounds its truth is just that in fact I did *A*. But this isn't much of an answer; and at any rate the same kind of answer is available in the case of Curley. For what grounds the truth of the counterfactual, we may say, is just that in fact Curley is such that if he had been offered a $35,000 bribe, he would have freely taken it.[19]

This answer of Plantinga's appears to be an endorsement of the view already attributed to Suárez: When a counterfactual of freedom is true, it is simply an ultimate fact about the free agent in question that, if placed in the indicated circumstances, she would act as the counterfactual states; this fact requires no analysis or "grounding" in terms of further, noncounterfactual states of affairs.[20] It seems to me, however, that there is something seriously wrong about this answer. In order to bring this out, I want to try and formulate a certain intuition—an intuition that, I believe, underlies Adams's objection even though Adams does not explicitly formulate it. The intuition is this: In order for a (contingent) conditional state of affairs to obtain, its obtaining must be grounded in some categorical state of affairs. More colloquially, truths about "what *would be the case* . . . *if*" must be grounded in truths about what *is in fact* the case. This requirement seems clearly to be satisfied for the more familiar types of conditionals. The truth of a material conditional is grounded either in the truth of its consequent, or the falsity of its antecedent, or both.[21] More interestingly, the truth of causal conditionals, and of their associated counterfactuals, are grounded in the natures, causal powers, inherent tendencies, and the like, of the natural entities described in them.[22] The lack of anything like this as a basis for the counterfac-

---

[19]"Reply to Robert M. Adams," p. 374. Plantinga here alludes to an example found in *The Nature of Necessity*, pp. 173–74.

[20]That this is Plantinga's view is clearly implied by the argument given on pp. 177–79 of *The Nature of Necessity*.

[21]Some would deny that these are genuinely *conditionals*, in the interesting sense of that term.

[22]I am assuming that whereas these natures, causal powers, etc., may, because of our limitations, have to be *described* in terms of conditional statements, the *truth* of

tuals of freedom seems to me to be a serious problem for the theory.[23]

Perhaps it is worthwhile to repeat here that the grounding *cannot* be found in the character, psychological tendencies, and the like of the agent. This point is, in effect, conceded by the defenders of middle knowledge; they recognize that such psychological facts are insufficient as a basis for the counterfactuals. And yet there is the following point: *In virtually every case where we seem to have plausible examples of true counterfactuals of freedom, the plausibility is grounded precisely in such psychological facts as these.* (Again we recall Saul besieging Keilah, Plantinga climbing Tahquitz Rock, and Adams's butcher selling him a pound of hamburger.) And this, I think, ought to make us very suspicious of those examples. If the basis for the plausibility of the examples is in all cases found in something that has no tendency to show that the examples are correct—no tendency, that is, to show that the propositions in question really *are* true counterfactuals of freedom[24]—then the examples lose all force as support for the theory. And without the examples, there is very little in sight that even looks like supporting evidence.[25]

---

these conditionals is itself grounded in occurrent states of affairs—for example, in the microstructures of physical materials. It is noteworthy that Humeans, who deny the existence of causal powers, natures, etc., have great difficulty in dealing with counterfactuals generally.

[23]Freddoso points out that middle knowledge "cuts against the spirit, if not the letter, of the standard possible worlds semantics for subjunctive conditionals. For it is usually assumed that the similarities among possible worlds invoked in such semantics are conceptually prior to the acquisition of truth-values by the subjunctive conditionals themselves. . . . On the Molinist view the dependence runs in just the opposite direction when the conditionals in question are conditional future contingents. . . . If the standard possible worlds semantics for subjunctive conditionals presupposes otherwise, then Molinists will have to modify it or propose an alternative capable of sustaining realism with respect to conditional future contingents" (Introduction to Luis de Molina, *On Divine Foreknowledge (Part IV of the Concordia)*, trans. Alfred J. Freddoso [Ithaca, N.Y.: Cornell University Press, 1988], sec. 5.6).

[24]Note, however, that such psychological facts might very well provide grounding for conditionals such as (3) and (4), asserting that under given conditions the agents would *probably* act in a certain way.

[25]Plantinga says, "Surely there are many actions and many creatures such that God knows what he would have done if one of the latter had taken one of the former. There seem to be true counterfactuals of freedom about God; but what

The second difficulty to be considered—one, so far as I know, not noticed in the literature to date—concerns the *modal status of* counterfactuals of freedom. To do the job required of them, these counterfactuals must be logically contingent—but I shall argue that, based on the assumptions of the theory of counterfactual logic, certain crucial counterfactuals should be regarded rather as necessary truths, if indeed they are true at all.[26]

The examples of counterfactuals considered so far (e.g., "If David stayed in Keilah, Saul would besiege the city") are in a certain way notoriously incomplete. The antecedent specifies a single crucial fact but leaves unstated many other facts about the situation which would undoubtedly be relevant to Saul's decision—facts about Saul's character and state of mind, but also facts about the strength and readiness of Saul's own military forces, about other threats to the kingdom, and so on. Now, it cannot seriously be supposed that the counterfactuals God considers in deciding about his own activity in creation and providence are incomplete in this way. Surely, the antecedents of the conditionals *he* considers must include *everything* that might conceivably be relevant to Saul's deciding one way or the other. In order to have some grasp on this sort of counterfactual, I suggest that we think in terms of *initial-segment counterfactuals,* in which the antecedent specifies a *complete initial segment of a possible world*[27] up to a given point in time, and the consequent an event that may or not take place at that time. (Of course, the antecedent will include any relevant causal laws that have held up until that time in that possible

---

would *ground* the truth of such a counterfactual of freedom?" ("Reply to Robert M. Adams," p. 375) The answer to this, however, is obvious: The truth of such a counterfactual about God's action is grounded in God's *conditional intention* to act in a certain way. But humans, for the most part, have no such conditional intentions about choices they might be called upon to make—or, when they do have them, the intentions at best ground *"would probably"* counterfactuals.

[26]Jonathan Kvanvig actually holds that the counterfactuals of freedom are contained in the *essence* of the free creature, (see Jonathan L. Kvanvig, *The Possibility of an All-Knowing God* [New York: St. Martin's, 1986], pp. 124–25). But this is fatal to the theory: No individual chooses, or is responsible for, what is contained in that individual's essence.

[27]In order fully to explicate the notion of an "initial segment" of a possible world, we need the distinction between hard facts and soft facts about the past; for this distinction see chapter 5.

world.) If now we symbolize such counterfactuals using a capital letter followed by an asterisk to stand for the antecedent, then the initial-segment counterfactual corresponding to (1) would be:

(10) $A^* \rightarrow$ Saul besieges Keilah,

where 'A^*' represents a proposition specifying the entire initial segment of the possible world envisaged by God as the one in which Saul makes his decision. The contrary counterfactual then would be

(11) $A^* \rightarrow$ Saul does not besiege Keilah.

If, as we have been assuming all along, (1) is true, then (10) also will be true, and (11) false.

The interesting question, however, is whether (10) is a *contingent* or a *necessary* truth. Clearly, the theory of middle knowledge requires that it be contingent; if on the contrary it is necessary, then Saul's decision is *entailed* by a complete statement of antecedent conditions and his action is not free. (10), in fact, is to be evaluated in the same way as any other counterfactual proposition: To assert (10) is in effect to assert that some world in which "A^*" is true and Saul besieges Keilah is more similar to the actual world than any in which "A^*" is true and Saul does not do this. But, we may ask, if (10) is contingent, then under what possible circumstances would it be false? The answer is that (10) might be false if the actual world were different than it is; what is crucial is the similarity of envisaged possible worlds to the actual world, and so if the actual world were a different world (in ways we need not attempt to specify) than the one which is in fact actual, it might turn out that the world specified in (11) would be more similar to *that* world than is the world specified in (10), in which case (11) would be true and (10) false.

But this, I want to say, violates the fundamental idea that underlies the possible-worlds semantics for counterfactuals. For why exactly is it that counterfactuals are to be evaluated in terms of comparative similarity of possible worlds to the actual world? The answer to this is crucially related to the incompleteness, noted above, which attaches to the antecedents of the counterfactuals we use in everyday discourse. We simply do not have the resources to specify in the antecedents of our counterfactuals everything that might be relevant to the occurrence of the consequent, and even when we are clear in our own minds what the circumstances should be, we often do not take the trouble to state them. The notion of similarity to the actual world, then, removes what would otherwise be the ambiguity of our counterfactuals by specifying how the unstated conditions are to be understood: We are to think of the actual world as being modified *as little as possible* so as to accommodate the counterfactual antecedent. Thus, David Lewis states that the point of his "system of spheres representing comparative similarity of worlds" is "to rule out of consideration many of the various ways the antecedent could hold, especially the more bizarre ways."[28] He also says

> A counterfactual $\phi \mathbin{\Box\!\!\rightarrow} \psi$ is true at world i if and only if ψ holds at certain ϕ-worlds; but certainly not all ϕ-worlds matter. "*If kangaroos had no tails, they would topple over*" is true (or false, as the case may be) at our world, quite without regard to those possible worlds where kangaroos walk around on crutches, and stay upright that way. Those worlds are too far away from ours. What is meant by the counterfactual is that, things being pretty much as they are—the scarcity of crutches for kangaroos being pretty much as it actually is, the kangaroos' inability to use crutches being pretty much as it actually is, and so on—if kangaroos had no tails they would topple over.[29]

So the point of the notion of comparative similarity between possible worlds is to place limits on the worlds that are relevant for the evaluation of a given counterfactual. But of course, (10) is already maximally limited in this way; it already includes *everything* about the envisaged world up until the time when Saul makes his decision. With regard to initial-segment counterfactuals, then, comparative similarity has no work left to do. Ask yourself this question: In evaluating (10), *why* should it make a difference

[28]Lewis, *Counterfactuals*, p. 66.
[29]Ibid., pp. 8–9.

whether the actual world is as it is, or is a world different in various ways from this one? After all, if A^* *were* actual, then *neither* "our" actual world nor that other one would *be* actual—so why should the truth of (10) depend in any way on which of those worlds is actual as things now stand? This contrasts sharply with the situation as regards Lewis's kangaroos: If, for instance, we lived in a world in which a large and active Animal Friendship League was assiduously providing prosthetic devices for "handicapped" animals, then we would "fill in" these conditions as we evaluate his counterfactual and would very likely judge it to be false. But with initial-segment counterfactuals there is just no room for this to happen; there are no spaces left to *be* filled in.

The situation, then, is as follows: The theory of middle knowledge is obliged to hold that some initial-segment counterfactuals are logically contingent. But in order to do this, the theory must apply to these counterfactuals the notion of comparative similarity to the actual world, and I have argued that this notion has no legitimate application here—which is to say, the notion is *misapplied*. The correct conclusion to be drawn from counterfactual logic, then, is that if initial-segment counterfactuals are true at all, they are true in *all* worlds and thus are *necessarily* true. But this conclusion is fatal to middle knowledge.

There is another, closely related point, one that connects this second argument with the first one given. Plantinga admits that "We can't look to similarity, among possible worlds, as *explaining* counterfactuality, or as *founding* or *grounding* it. (Indeed, any founding or grounding in the neighborhood goes in the opposite direction.)"[30] This means that (in some cases at least) of two worlds W and W', one is more similar to the actual world *precisely because it shares counterfactuals* with the actual world—it is *not* the case that, because one of those worlds is more similar to the actual world *in other respects*, certain counterfactuals are true. But this, as I have argued above, violates the reason for introducing the comparative-similarity notion in the first place—that reason being, as explained by Lewis, to secure that counterfactuals are evaluated in worlds sufficiently similar to the actual world *in noncounterfactual*

[30]"Reply to Robert M. Adams," p. 378.

respects. How can Plantinga justify relying on the principles of counterfactual logic when at the same time he undercuts the rationale for accepting those same principles?

The third (and final) objection of this group is one that was discovered independently by Robert Adams and Anthony Kenny.[31] This difficulty arises as we bring together the account given of the truth-conditions for counterfactuals and the use God is said to make of them. As Kenny says, "If it is to be possible for God to know which world he is actualizing, then his middle knowledge must be logically prior to his decision to actualize; whereas if middle knowledge is to have an object, the actualization must already have taken place."[32]

Let's spell this out a bit more. We will suppose, contrary to the argument in the preceding section, that some initial-segment counterfactuals (namely, those whose consequents involve freely chosen actions) are contingently true. Their truth, according to the theory, depends on the similarity of various possible worlds to the actual world, and thus it depends on which world *is* the actual world. But, which world is actual depends, in part at least, on God's decision about what to create: It is only by deciding to create that God settles which world is actual, and therefore which counterfactuals are true. So rather than the counterfactuals providing *guidance* for God's decision about what to create, the fact is that their truth is determined only as a consequence of that very decision!

Plantinga's answer to this is spelled out in his reply to Adams. In order for the truth of the counterfactuals to be "available" to God as he makes his creative decisions, it need not be already settled *in every respect* which world is the actual world. What needs to be settled, in order for the truth of a given counterfactual to be determinate and knowable, is only that the actual world is a member of the *set of worlds* in which that particular counterfactual is true. Now, why shouldn't this be the case, even prior to God's decision about which particular world to actualize? Why shouldn't it be the

[31]See Adams, "Middle Knowledge," pp. 113–14; Kenny, *The God of the Philosophers,* pp. 70–71.
[32]*The God of the Philosophers,* p. 71.

case, in other words, that *the same counterfactuals of freedom are true in all the worlds God could actualize?*[33] Why shouldn't the truth of the counterfactuals of freedom be *"counterfactually independent* of the various courses of action God could have taken"?[34] If this is so, then the truth of the counterfactuals *is* settled prior to God's decision about which world to actualize, and the Adams-Kenny objection collapses.[35]

[33]Plantinga seems to say that an even weaker requirement than this will suffice to enable the theory to work. He says:

It isn't at all clear that if (8) ["If God created Adam and Eve, there would be more moral good than moral evil in the history of the world"] could be God's reason for creating Adam and Eve, then there was nothing he could do to make it the case that (8) is false. For suppose (8) would have been false if God had created no free creatures. We can still imagine God reasoning as follows: "If I were to create *no* free creatures there would not, of course, be more moral good than moral evil; and it would be better to have more moral good than moral evil. But if I were to create free creatures, (8) would be true, in which case if I were to create Adam and Eve, there would be more moral good than moral evil. So I shall create Adam and Eve." Thus even if God could bring it about that (8) was false, (8) could perfectly well serve as his reason, or part of his reason, for creating Adam and Eve. ("Reply to Robert M. Adams," p. 377)

I believe this suggestion to be incoherent. For consider the following supposition, which on Plantinga's principles ought to be possible: Suppose, as Plantinga hypothesizes, (8) would be true if God created free creatures but false if he did not create free creatures. Suppose, furthermore, that God decided *not* to create free creatures. (Possibly he is more repelled by the prospect of moral evil than attracted by the prospect of moral good.) Then God, looking back on his decision to create a world that lacks free creatures, can truthfully say, "I'm glad I decided not to create Adam and Eve, for if I had created them there would have been more moral evil than moral good." But this contradicts the supposition of the example, which is that if God were to create free creatures, (8) would have been true. So the example is incoherent, and the correct requirement for the theory of middle knowledge is the one stated in the text: the same counterfactuals of freedom must be true in all the worlds God can actualize.

[34]Ibid. p. 376.

[35]It should be pointed out that Adams anticipated the possibility of a reply along these lines but rejected it because it seemed implausible to him that (for example) a world in which there are no free creatures at all would be "more like a world in which most free creaturely decisions are good ones than like a world in which most free creaturely decisions are bad ones" ("Middle Knowledge," p. 114). Plantinga, however, is unmoved by this—as we have already noted, he sees no reason why the similarities between worlds that are relevant for the truth of counterfactuals must have anything to do with similarities in noncounterfactual characteristics of those worlds.

It must be acknowledged that this reply suffices as a formal answer to the objection, but I think it leaves us with a further, major problem. *How are we to explain* the alleged fact that the same counterfactuals of freedom are true in all the worlds God could actualize? These counterfactuals, according to the theory, are not necessary truths. Their truth, furthermore, is not due to *God's* decision; on the contrary, they constitute an *absolute limit* on which worlds God is able to actualize. For example: There are possible worlds, plenty of them, in which it is true that, if God had created Adam and placed him in Eden just as he did in the actual world, Adam would freely have refrained from sinning. (We will symbolize this initial-segment counterfactual as "$E^* \rightarrow$ Adam refrains from sinning.") Now, why didn't God actualize one of *those* worlds in preference to this one? The answer is, that *in fact* the true counterfactual, the one true in all the worlds God could actualize, is "$E^* \rightarrow$ Adam sins." But *why* is this counterfactual true? Not because of God's decision, and not because of any noncounterfactual truths about the creatures God has created. We will see in the next section that a very few of these counterfactuals are said to be true in virtue of the free choices made by created beings, but even if this answer proves tenable, it can account only for a tiny proportion of the whole. So we are confronted with this vast array of counterfactuals—probably, thousands or even millions for each actual or possible free creature—almost all of which simply *are true* without any explanation whatever of this fact being given. Is this not a deeply puzzling, even baffling state of affairs?

The three objections in this section have been developed independently, yet on close inspection they reveal a common theme. The first objection complained about the lack of a *ground* for the truth of counterfactuals in nonhypothetical, noncounterfactual reality. The reply is, that no such ground is needed. The second objection points out that if this is so, then the rationale is cut from under the principles of counterfactual logic on which the theory relies, thus making such reliance dubious at best. In the third objection, the groundlessness of counterfactuals reappears at a higher level, not concerned this time merely with individual counterfactuals but rather with the whole vast array of them, all allegedly true in all the worlds God could have actualized, and true without there being any ground for this either in the nature and actions of God, or in the natures of created beings, or (except for a tiny fraction) in the choices of created free agents. Without doubt, we are here confronted with something deeply mysterious—but is this the mystery of God's creation, or simply the mysteriousness of a misguided philosophical theory?[36]

A Refutation of Middle Knowledge

We turn now to a final, and slightly more complex, argument.[37] In this argument we shall not, as previously, argue directly against the counterfactuals of freedom. Instead, we shall concede, provisionally, that there are true counterfactuals of freedom and ask about them the question suggested in the last section: Who or what is it (if anything) that *brings it about*[38] that these propositions are true?

In order to give the discussion a touch of concreteness, imagine the following situation: Elizabeth, a doctoral student in anthropology, is in the concluding phase of her course work and is beginning to make plans for her dissertation field research. Her advisor has been asked to make a recommendation for a foundation grant to be awarded for observation of a recently discovered tribe in New Guinea. This assignment offers exciting prospects for new

[36]It is evident that many (though not all) of these difficulties result from the applications to counterfactuals of freedom of the possible-worlds semantics. Thus, the proponent of middle knowledge may be tempted to dispense with the semantics, perhaps agreeing with Freddoso that "we might wonder why it wasn't perfectly obvious from the start that comparative similarity wouldn't help us if the conditionals in question involve genuine causal indeterminism" (personal communication). It is true that getting rid of the semantics makes the theory somewhat harder to attack, but it also eliminates a good deal of the theory's philosophical substance. Those philosophers (their name is legion) who are disposed in any case to be suspicious of counterfactuals can only have their suspicions confirmed if we are deprived of any systematic account of their semantics.

[37]See William Hasker, "A Refutation of Middle Knowledge," *Noûs* 20 (1986): 545–57.

[38]The concept of *bringing about* employed here and elsewhere throughout the book will be discussed in detail in chapter 6. For the present, suffice it to say that the concept is of an asymmetrical relation of dependence of what is brought about on the action or event that brings it about; the dependence in question may be, but is not necessarily, causal.

discoveries but would also involve considerable hardship and personal risk. The advisor asks himself whether Elizabeth would choose to undertake this study, or whether she would prefer to continue with her present plans to study a relatively placid group of South Sea islanders. He wonders, in other words, which of the following two counterfactuals of freedom is true:

(12)   If Elizabeth were offered the grant, she would accept it (in symbols, $O \rightarrow A$).

(13)   If Elizabeth were offered the grant, she would not accept it ($O \rightarrow {\sim}A$).

Now, Elizabeth's advisor may find himself unable to decide which counterfactual is true, or he may reach the wrong conclusion about this. But according to the theory of middle knowledge, one of the two counterfactuals *is* true, and God, if no one else, knows which one. For the sake of our discussion, we will assume it is (12) that is true rather than (13); we shall assume, moreover, that Elizabeth is in fact offered the grant and she accepts it. All this, however, is merely preparatory to raising the question already suggested: Who or what is it that *brings it about* that this proposition is true?

In the previous section we have considered the reasons why it cannot be *God* who brings it about that counterfactuals of freedom are true; we shall not rehearse those reasons here. The answer to this question that is in fact given by the friends of middle knowledge is that it is the *agent named in the counterfactual* who brings it about that the counterfactual is true. More precisely, it is the agent who brings this about *in those possible worlds in which the antecedent is true*.[39] It is this claim, then, that will be the principal subject of discussion throughout this section.

How might it be possible for the agent to bring it about that a given counterfactual of freedom is true? It would seem that the only possible way for the agent to do this is to perform the action specified in the consequent of the counterfactual under the condi-

---

[39]This is a view I have heard stated in discussion by Plantinga; I know of no written source. In any case, the attribution is not crucial, since we shall also be discussing the consequences for middle knowledge if this claim is *not* made.

tions stated in the antecedent. That is to say: In the case of a genuinely free action, the only way to insure the action's being done is to do it. I believe the proponents of middle knowledge accept this, which is why they claim that the agent brings about the truth of the counterfactual *only in those possible worlds in which the antecedent is true*. It is in other words an accepted principle that

(14)   It is in an agent's power to bring it about that a given counterfactual of freedom is true, only if its truth would be brought about by the agent's performing the action specified in the consequent of the conditional under the conditions specified in the antecedent.

But is it possible for the agent to bring about the truth of a counterfactual of freedom in this way? What is required if it is to be the case that a particular event brings it about that a proposition is true? It seems initially plausible that

(15)   If E brings it about that "Q" is true, then "Q" would be true if E occurred and would be false if E did not occur ((E occurs) $\rightarrow$ Q and $\sim$(E occurs) $\rightarrow$ $\sim$Q).[40]

But this cannot be quite right, as is shown by the following examples: I knock on your door at ten o'clock, Sam knocks on your door at eleven o'clock, and no one else knocks on your door all day. It seems clear that my knocking on your door brings it about that "Someone knocks on your door today" is true, in spite of the fact that this would still be true even if I did not knock on your door. Or suppose we are bowling against each other, and you need a count of 5 or better on your last ball to win the game. If you roll a 9, your doing so brings about that you win the game, even though it need not be true that if you had not rolled a 9 you would not have won. (It may be that if you had not rolled a 9 you would have

[40]I speak both of an *event* as bringing about the truth of a proposition, and of a *person* as doing so. Thomas Flint ("Hasker's 'Refutation' of Middle Knowledge," unpublished, n. 12) correctly points out that there is a need for a principle to connect these two uses. The required principle is as follows: A person brings it about that a proposition is true just in case that person's performance of some action brings it about.

rolled a 7 or an 8.) In each case the problem arises because the event in question is a token of a type of event such that the occurrence of any event of that type (someone's knocking on the door, your rolling a 5 or better on your last ball) would bring about the truth of the proposition in question. With this in mind, we revise (15) as follows:

(16)   If E brings it about that "Q" is true, then E is a token of an event-type T such that (some token of T occurs) $\rightarrow Q$ and $\sim$(some token of T occurs) $\rightarrow \sim Q$, and E is the first token of T which occurs.

If then we add the simplifying assumption that if E were not to occur, no other token of T would occur, we get (15) as a special case. When, on the other hand, we have an event and a proposition such that the conditions specified in (15) and (16) are not satisfied, we will say that the truth of the proposition is *independent* of the event in question.

Applying this to our example, what we need to know is whether Elizabeth brings about the truth of the counterfactual of freedom "$O \rightarrow A$" by accepting the grant, or whether its truth is *independent* of her action, in the sense just specified. In order to determine this, we need to know whether the following propositions are true:

(17)   If Elizabeth were to accept the grant, it would be true that $O \rightarrow A$ (i.e., $A \rightarrow (O \rightarrow A)$).

(18)   If Elizabeth were not to accept the grant, it would be true that $O \rightarrow A$ (i.e., $\sim A \rightarrow (O \rightarrow A)$).

There can be no question about the truth of (17); if both "O" and "A" are true in the actual world, the counterfactual will be true. It might seem equally obvious that (18) is false: If Elizabeth does not accept the grant, how can it be true that, if offered it, she would accept it? This, however, is a mistake. If (18) seems to us to be obviously false, we are probably misreading (18) as

(19)   If Elizabeth were to reject the grant, it would be true that $O \rightarrow A$ (i.e., $(O \,\&\, \sim A) \rightarrow (O \rightarrow A)$).

This is indeed obviously false, but it is not the same as (18); the antecedent of (18) says, not that Elizabeth rejects the offer, but merely that she does not accept it. It is consistent both with her rejecting the offer, and with the offer's never having been made. If she rejects it, then "$O \rightarrow A$" must be false, but if no offer is made, "$O \rightarrow A$" will still be true. So now we have to evaluate the counterfactuals

(20) If Elizabeth does not accept the offer it will be because she rejected it (i.e., $\sim A \rightarrow (O \ \& \sim A)$).[41]

(21) If Elizabeth does not accept the offer, it will be because the offer was not made (i.e., $\sim A \rightarrow (\sim O \ \& \sim A)$).

If (20) is true, (18) will be false, but if (21) is true, so is (18).

How shall we decide this question? According to our semantics for counterfactuals, the question about (20) and (21) comes down to this: Is a world in which Elizabeth received the offer and rejected it more or less similar to the actual world (in which the offer was accepted) than a world in which the offer was neither made nor accepted?

One's first thought might be that the world specified in (20), which differs from the actual world with respect to Elizabeth's acceptance of the offer, is more similar to the actual world than the world specified in (21), which differs with respect both to the making of the offer and to its acceptance. If so, however, then one's first thought (as is so often the case in matters counterfactual) would have overlooked important considerations. To see why, consider the following example: I have been hard at work making a poster announcing an upcoming event, and just as the poster is nearly completed I knock over my ink bottle, spilling ink on the poster and forcing me to start all over again. As I do this, I pause from cursing my clumsiness long enough to wonder what it would have been like not to have had my poster ruined in this way. Two possibilities occur to me: I might have refrained from knocking

---

[41]The verbal formulations in (20) through (23) represent my attempts to express in natural-sounding ways some propositions that under normal circumstances we would seldom if ever have any occasion to state. No special emphasis is to be laid on the "because" language; the logically relevant content of the propositions is what is contained in the symbolic formulations.

over the ink bottle in the first place, or, I might have knocked it over just as I did in the actual world, but instead of spilling any ink, the bottle spontaneously righted itself and come to rest again in its original position. I then wonder which of these scenarios would have occurred if I had not gotten the ink spilled on my poster. I am wondering, in other words, which of the following counterfactuals is true:

(22)   If no ink had been spilled on my poster, it would have been because I did not knock over my ink bottle ($\sim S \rightarrow (\sim K \& \sim S)$).

(23)   If no ink had been spilled on my poster, it would have been because I knocked over my ink bottle but no ink spilled ($\sim S \rightarrow (K \& \sim S)$).

I puzzle over this for a few moments, but my question is quickly answered along the same lines already suggested for (20) and (21). The (22)-world would have differed from the actual world with respect both to the bottle's being knocked over and the ink's spilling, whereas the (23)-world differs from it only in the latter respect. So the (23)-world is more similar to the actual world than the (22)-world; it is (23) that is true and not (22), and I realize that if my poster had not been ruined, the reason for this would have been, not that I was careful about my ink bottle, but that after I knocked over the bottle it miraculously righted itself without spilling any ink. And that makes me feel a little better about my clumsiness.

Of course this is absurd, but why is it absurd? What exactly is wrong with the reasoning that led me to conclude that (23) is true rather than (22)? The answer seems to be this: In the actual world certain counterfactuals are true, among them

(24)   If I were to knock my ink-bottle in such-and-such a way, the bottle would fall over and spill ink on my poster.

This counterfactual is true in the actual world (as events have shown), and it is also true in the (22)-world, but not in the (23)-

world. And in weighing the comparative similarity to the actual
world of the (22)-world and the (23)-world, the truth in the
(22)-world of the counterfactual (24) counts far more heavily than
the slightly greater similarity of the (23)-world with respect to
factual content. So as we thought all along, it is (22) that is true
rather than (23).

But of course exactly similar considerations apply in the case of
(20) and (21). In the actual world, it is true that

(12)   If Elizabeth were offered the grant, she would accept it.

This counterfactual is true in the actual world, and also in the (21)-
world, but not in the (20)-world. And in a comparison of the latter
two worlds, the truth of the counterfactual (12) outweighs the
slight difference with respect to similarity in factual content, so
that the (21)-world is indeed more similar to the actual world than
the (20)-world, and it is (21) that is true rather than (20).

It might be suggested that the reason (24) is decisive with respect
to the decision between (22) and (23) is that (24) is backed by laws
of nature; counterfactuals of freedom such as (12) do not have such
backing and are therefore not decisive with regard to the choice
(for example) between (20) and (21). But this really will not do.
For one thing, Plantinga himself is pretty clearly committed to the
view that, in deciding the comparative similarity of possible
worlds, counterfactuals outweigh differences in matters of fact
whether or not they are backed by laws of nature.[42] And there are
reasons that make it very difficult to justify weighting counterfactuals of freedom less heavily than laws of nature. First, there is the
contention, noted in the last section, that the same counterfactuals
of freedom are true in all the worlds God can actualize and constitute *absolute limitations* on God's power to bring about states of
affairs. (Laws of nature, clearly, do *not* limit God's power in this
way; he could have created a world in which different laws obtained.)

The proponent of middle knowledge, however, may object to

[42]I take this to be the upshot of the argument given in *The Nature of Necessity*,
pp. 177–78.

this piece of reasoning. He may point out that, although *God* cannot control which counterfactuals of freedom are true, the *human
beings* in question—the agents named in the counterfactuals—*do*
have control over this, since it is they who, by making the choices
that they do, bring about that those counterfactuals are true. Now,
of course, whether or not the agent brings about the truth of the
counterfactual is the very point at issue in the present discussion. In
view of this, one might tend to consider it question-begging to
introduce this point on *either* side at this stage of the argument.[43]
But the proponent of middle knowledge may feel this is unfair to
him. The claim that the agent brings about the truth of counterfactuals of freedom is, he points out, an integral part of his position,
one that he should be permitted to appeal to until and unless it is
refuted by his opponent.[44] Suppose we concede this point and
agree to evaluate the immediate point in question—the question,
that is, whether it is (20) or (21) that is true—in the light of the
claim that the agent decides which of the counterfactuals about her
actions are true. How will this affect the outcome of the discussion?

   A natural view to take would seem to be that this point made by
the proponent of middle knowledge tends to balance off, and thus
to neutralize, the last point made in the previous paragraph. There
it was pointed out that God has control over which laws of nature
obtain, but not over which counterfactuals of freedom are true.
The rejoinder is that human beings have control over some counterfactuals of freedom, but not over natural laws. If, as would seem
to be the case, these considerations weight about equally on either

---

[43]Flint accuses me of begging the question (in my "Refutation of Middle
Knowledge") by assuming that "since *God* has no control over which counterfactuals of creaturely freedom are true, neither do *we*" ("Hasker's 'Refutation' of
Middle Knowledge," p. 20). But this is just false. I do not *assume* this; I *argue* for it,
and the reader will search in vain to find this proposition, or anything equivalent to
it, among the premises of my argument. What is true, however, is that I fail to
consider this point (viz., the proponent's claim that agents control the truth of the
counterfactuals of freedom) in my discussion of whether counterfactuals of freedom outweigh laws of nature, or vice versa.

[44]The position then would be similar to the one that obtains in discussions of the
problem of evil, where the burden of proof is assumed by the nontheist and the
theist is entitled to invoke all of her theistic beliefs unless and until the nontheist
has refuted them.

side of the argument, the upshot would seem to be that we cannot decide, on the basis of these considerations alone, whether counterfactuals of freedom are more fundamental than laws of nature, or vice versa. If anything, what seems to be suggested is that the two are roughly at a parity. If we wish for a more definitive answer to our question, we must look further.

Now, what is at issue is whether it is counterfactuals backed by laws of nature or counterfactuals of freedom that have counterexamples in possible worlds "closer" to the actual world. It is relevant in this connection that we now know with virtual certainty that the fundamental laws of nature are probabilistic rather than strictly deterministic; thus, the counterfactuals backed by the laws of nature (such as [24]) are in fact *would-probably conditionals* rather than true necessitation conditionals. Surely, however, necessitation conditionals (such as the counterfactuals of freedom are supposed to be) have to be weighted *more* heavily than "would–probably" conditionals in determining the relative closeness of possible worlds. There is also the important point that God, according to Christian belief, can and does work miracles. If this is so, then some counterfactuals backed by laws of nature have counterexamples *in the actual world itself,* and therefore also in possible worlds as close to the actual world as you please. In view of all this, the counterfactuals of freedom seem to be considerably more fundamental, with respect to explaining why things are as they are, than the laws of nature; *a fortiori,* they are more fundamental than particular facts such as that Elizabeth is offered the grant.[45]

[45]Freddoso, commenting on the version of this argument given in the article "A Refutation of Middle Knowledge," claims that the argument is "seriously flawed" because of my claim that "the proponents of middle knowledge hold, or should hold, that the truth of a counterfactual of freedom is as fixed in the worlds closest to the actual world as is the truth of a law of nature" (Introduction to Molina, *On Divine Foreknowledge,* sec. 5.7 and n. 96).

Now, since I do not think any counterfactuals of freedom are true *at all,* I have no views of my own concerning *when* they are true; I must therefore rely on inferences from principles that are or should be accepted by the proponents of middle knowledge. If the particular conclusion criticized by Freddoso turned out to be stronger than warranted, this would not create serious difficulties for my overall argument. What is required for my argument is only the much weaker claim that, in determining the relative similarity of possible worlds, counterfactuals of freedom outweigh particular facts such as that Elizabeth is offered the

But if (21) is true, then so is (18), and (since [17] is also true) it follows that the truth of the counterfactual "$O \rightarrow A$" is independent of whether or not Elizabeth actually accepts the grant. (It is not true if she *rejects* the grant, but that is another matter.) And it also follows (by [16]) that Elizabeth's acceptance of the offer does *not* bring it about that the counterfactual "$O \rightarrow A$" is true. And in general, it is not true that the truth of a counterfactual of freedom is brought about by the agent.[46]

---

grant. Plantinga's argument cited in note 42 above seems to commit him to holding that they do, and in view of this the difficulty here does not seem especially serious.

But I am by no means convinced that the conclusion I have drawn is too strong. I believe that the arguments given in the text provide cogent reason for holding that, *if* there are true counterfactuals of freedom, they outweigh laws of nature in determining the relative similarity of possible worlds. If the friends of counterfactuals disagree with this, they are invited to present (at least) equally cogent arguments for the contrary conclusion.

[46]I am indebted to Alvin Plantinga for an extremely interesting objection to this argument. He suggests that the argument cannot be general in its force, because it will not work if we change the original supposition slightly. Suppose that in the actual world it is true that (14) $O \rightarrow \sim A$, rather than that (13) $O \rightarrow A$, and suppose furthermore that Elizabeth is offered the grant, and she rejects it. We then ask what it would have been like had she *accepted* the grant. And here, it may seem, the only reasonable answer is that, if she had accepted the grant, it would have been true that $O \rightarrow A$, and from this it is but a short step to say that she would *bring about* the truth of "$O \rightarrow A$" by accepting the grant. If we do not say that, what can we say? Surely not, that she accepted the grant because she was not offered it!

No, we can't say *that*! Rather, we proceed as follows: Starting with the assumption that "$O \rightarrow \sim A$" is true, and she in fact rejects the grant, we ask ourselves this question: What is the minimal change that would be needed in the actual world, such that if things were different in that way, Elizabeth would accept the grant? It may not be obvious what the answer is, but surely there must *be* an answer. Possibly the minimal change would be that all her other opportunities for field research have fallen through, so that if she does not accept the grant, her research, and the granting of her degree, will be postponed indefinitely. (If we represent the proposition saying that she is offered the grant under those modified circumstances as '$O\#$', then it follows from what has been said that "$O\# \rightarrow A$" is true even though "$O \rightarrow A$" is false.) Supposing this to be the case, we then ask, If Elizabeth were to accept the grant, would it be because "$O\#$" was true rather than "O," or because "$O \rightarrow A$" was true? And for the reasons already discussed, the correct answer will be that if she were to accept it this would be because the circumstances were different than they are in the actual world (in which she rejects it), and not because the counterfactual "$O \rightarrow A$" would be true. So it still is not true that Elizabeth brings about the truth of a counterfactual of freedom. The beauty of Plantinga's objection is that it brings out the generality of the argument in a way in which the original example does not.

Does the conclusion we have reached constitute a serious problem for middle knowledge? Perhaps not. David Basinger has recently argued that the proponent of middle knowledge need not and should not hold that the truth of the counterfactual of freedom is brought about by the agent.[47] To be sure, the view that the truth of these counterfactuals is brought about by God must also be excluded, for the reasons already discussed. Rather, these counterfactuals simply *are true* without their truth having been brought about either by God or by anyone else. "Who is responsible for the truth of [the counterfactuals of freedom] in the actual world? The answer is that no one is responsible."[48]

This proposal, however, creates serious difficulties for middle knowledge. On the proposed view, Elizabeth is not responsible for the fact that, if she were offered the grant, she would accept it (i.e., for the truth of the counterfactual "$O \to A$"). Nor, we may assume, is she responsible for the truth of the antecedent—that is, for the fact that she is offered the grant. But if she is responsible for neither of these things, it is difficult to see how she can be responsible for accepting the grant—a conclusion that is entirely unwelcome to the proponents of middle knowledge.

But there is another, even more fundamental, difficulty. We have learned that Elizabeth does not bring it about that the counterfactual "$O \to A$" is true. What effect, if any, does this have on the question of what is in her power when the grant offer is made? In order to investigate this, we need what I call *power entailment principles*, principles that state that an agent's possessing the power to perform a certain kind of action entails that the agent also possesses the power to perform another kind of action. More will be said about power entailment principles in chapter 6, but a principle that will suffice for our present purposes is

(PEP) If it is in A's power to bring it about that P, and "P" entails "Q" and "Q" is false, then it is in A's power to bring it about that Q.

[47]"Divine Omniscience and Human Freedom: A Middle Knowledge Perspective," *Faith and Philosophy* 1 (1984): 291–302.
[48]Ibid., p. 300.

A little thought will show this principle to be correct. If "*P*" entails
"*Q*", it cannot be the case that *P* unless it is also the case that *Q*. If
"*Q*" is already true, then the entailment presents no obstacle to A's
being able to bring it about that *P*. (Since the sun is in fact rising, it
is in your power to bring it about that you see the sunrise, even
though you completely lack the power to bring about the sunrise
itself.) But if "*Q*" is not true, it is not possible for you to bring it
about that *P* unless it is also possible for you to bring it about that
Q. (I approach your house with the intention of ringing your
doorbell, only to discover that you do not have a doorbell. Unless
it is in my power to bring it about that you have a doorbell—e.g.,
by installing one myself or having one installed—it is not in my
power to ring your doorbell.)[49]

How does this principle apply to the matter in hand? In order to
proceed we will make the assumption, which is sanctioned by the
theory of middle knowledge, that of any pair of counterfactuals
such as (12) and (13) one or the other is true; this implies that the
disjunction of the two is necessarily true, true in all possible
worlds. Given this assumption, we have the following as necessary
truths:

(25) If Elizabeth is offered the grant and accepts it, it is true that
      $O \rightarrow A$ $((O \ \& \ A) \Rightarrow (O \rightarrow A))$.
(26) If Elizabeth is offered the grant and rejects it, it is true that
      $O \rightarrow \sim A$ $((O \ \& \ \sim A) \Rightarrow (O \rightarrow \sim A))$.

That is to say, Elizabeth's acceptance or rejection of the grant
entails the truth of the corresponding counterfactual of freedom.[50]

---

[49]Freddoso (Introduction to Molina, *On Divine Foreknowledge*, sec. 5.7) rejects
this principle, and with it the conclusion of the present argument. For his objection
to (PEP), see chapter 6.

[50]If the inference-rule

(A)   *P* & *Q*; therefore, *P* → *Q*

is accepted as valid, (25) and (26) can be derived without recourse to the assumption made in the text. But (A) may occasion some discomfort. Lewis admits that
"it would seem very odd to pick two completely unrelated truths φ and ψ and, on
the strength of their truth . . . to assert the counterfactual φ $\square\rightarrow$ ψ " (*Counterfactuals*, p. 28). Lewis suggests a semantics on which (A) would not hold, but in his
own, "official" theory (A) is accepted.

I believe the right solution here is to be found in the distinctions made by

Now we are ready to consider what is in Elizabeth's power when the offer is made. First of all, is it in her power to accept the grant? One would suppose that it is, since in fact she actually does so. And (PEP) places no obstacle in the way of this conclusion. Her accepting the offer entails the truth of the counterfactual "$O \rightarrow A$," but that counterfactual is in fact true, and so the question of whether it is in her power to *bring about* its truth does not arise.

But now let us ask, does she have it in her power to *reject* the grant? Her rejecting the grant entails that the counterfactual "$O \rightarrow \sim A$" be true, but this counterfactual is in fact false. So—according to (PEP)—she can have the power to reject the grant only if it is in her power to bring it about that this counterfactual is true. If she does not have this power, then she lacks power to reject the grant.

And now the situation becomes serious. We have seen that it would be in Elizabeth's power to bring it about that the counterfactual "$O \rightarrow \sim A$" is true only if the truth of this counterfactual would be brought about by her rejecting the offer. But we have also seen that the truth of a counterfactual of freedom is *not* brought about in this way. It follows that Elizabeth does *not* have it in her power to bring it about that $O \rightarrow \sim A$, and lacking this, she also—by (PEP)—lacks the power to reject the offer.

It is time to summarize. In this section we are investigating the question, Who or what brings it about that the counterfactuals of freedom are true? We first considered the possibility that it is the agent named in the counterfactual who does this—in terms of our example, that Elizabeth by accepting the grant offer brings it about that $O \rightarrow A$. It turns out, however, that this counterfactual is true independently of whether or not she accepts the offer: It would be true if she were to accept the offer, and it would also be true were she not to accept the offer. To be sure, it would not be true if she were to *reject* the offer, but this turns out not to be relevant; if she did not accept the offer, this would be because the offer was never made and not because it was made and she rejected it. But since the

---

Pollock between various kinds of subjunctive conditionals. (A) is valid for simple subjunctives, and also for "even if" conditionals. But as we have seen, the counterfactuals of freedom are necessitation conditionals, and for these conditionals (A) is invalid. (See Pollock, *Subjunctive Reasoning*, chap. 2.) (A), then, is not valid for the counterfactuals of freedom.

counterfactual is true independently of whether or not she accepts the offer, it cannot be the case that she *brings about* the truth of the counterfactual by her acceptance of the grant.

We then went on to consider what Elizabeth has it in her power to do when the grant is offered to her. Clearly, she has it in her power to accept the grant, and she demonstrates this by doing so. But does she also have the power to reject the grant? Of particular importance here is the fact that (given the truth of the theory of middle knowledge) her rejection of the grant entails the truth of the counterfactual "$O \rightarrow \sim A$." But this counterfactual is not true, so it can be in her power to reject the grant only if it is also in her power to bring about the truth of this counterfactual. But we have already seen that this is impossible. She could have the power to bring about the truth of the counterfactual "$O \rightarrow \sim A$" only if its truth could be brought about by her rejection of the offer, but we have seen that the agent *cannot* in this way bring about the truth of a counterfactual of freedom. So it is not in her power to reject the grant.

The conclusion to be drawn from this is that the concession made earlier—that some counterfactuals of freedom are true—was unwarranted. It turns out from our consideration of the case of Elizabeth that insofar as such counterfactuals are *true*, they are not counterfactuals of *freedom*: If the counterfactual "$O \rightarrow A$" is true, it is not in Elizabeth's power to reject the offer, and she is not free in the required sense. And, on the other hand, insofar as an agent is genuinely free, there *are* no true counterfactuals stating what the agent would definitely do under various possible circumstances. And so the theory of middle knowledge is seen to be untenable: *There are no true counterfactuals of freedom.*

[3]

Simple Foreknowledge

This chapter is in the nature of an interlude. The preceding chapter dealt with the possibility of middle knowledge; the next several chapters will be occupied with the logical possibility of comprehensive divine foreknowledge in a world containing free choices. But there is another important question about foreknowledge which has received much less attention than it deserves—namely, what would be the use of foreknowledge if it existed? Why, in other words, is foreknowledge important? This is the topic for the present chapter.

One answer to our question which comes readily to mind is the following: That God has foreknowledge of all things whatever is an inescapable implication of divine *omniscience*—and, since omniscience is recognized as an essential attribute of the theistic God, what is at stake in the foreknowledge controversy is nothing less than theism itself. This answer, however, will not withstand investigation. It is clear that there are versions of the doctrine of divine omniscience which are compatible with God's having less than complete knowledge of future events; this would be the case, for instance, if certain propositions about the future lack truth-values, and a similar result follows if omniscience is defined by saying that an omniscient being is one that knows everything that it is logically possible to know. Now, theists who feel strongly about the necessity of foreknowledge may be less than enthusiastic about these sorts of definition of omniscience—but if this is so, the definition of omniscience is itself in part a *result* of the importance ascribed to the foreknowledge issue; it cannot therefore, be used to *explain* that importance.

I believe that the importance attached to foreknowledge finds its explanation in certain aspects of theism which are more "religious," and closer to the actual experience and concerns of religious persons, than are the somewhat arid topics with which philosophers of religion usually concern themselves. It is a part of theistic religions such as Judaism and Christianity that certain persons, speaking in God's name and with his authority, *foretell the future*. But (it may be asked) if God does not *know* what is going to happen, how can he tell the prophets what to *say* about it? Furthermore, theistic religions make extensive claims—claims that are experientially important to religious persons—about God's providential guidance and control of worldly affairs. And many times these claims seem to "cash out" in terms of the doctrine of foreknowledge: Since God *already knows* everything that is going to happen—especially, perhaps, he knows of some severe testing I am going to have to face—he *has already arranged things* so as to work out in the best possible way, say, by developing my character to meet the anticipated challenge, and perhaps by prearranging other circumstances so as to provide a solution for otherwise unsurmountable difficulties.[1] Of a piece with this, though perhaps less common in practice, is the belief that *answers to prayer* can be understood along these same lines—that God, knowing beforehand that one of his children will ask in faith for a certain blessing, may prearrange things long in advance (perhaps even as early as the initial state of the entire universe) in such a way that, in the natural course of things and without further direct divine intervention, the desired answer will result.

Prayer, providence, and prophecy—these are matters of intense concern to many ordinary religious believers, though they are less common in the books of philosophers. But then, some of the

[1]For an extensive development of these topics, see David Basinger, "Middle Knowledge and Classical Christian Thought," *Religious Studies* 22 (1986): 407–22.

philosophers are themselves religious believers, and if it seems to these philosophers that vital religious concerns are at stake in the foreknowledge controversy, they may see compatibilism as a position to be defended to the last ditch.

All this is entirely understandable, and it sheds light on the intensity with which the foreknowledge issue is pursued. But I want to say, nevertheless, that all of this is misguided—that the doctrine of divine foreknowledge, in its most widely held form, is of *no importance whatever* for the religiously significant concerns about prayer, providence, and prophecy. If I am right about this, then compatibilist and incompatibilist alike can return to their discussion with lighter hearts and lowered pulse rates. They will continue, and rightly so, to pour their best philosophical efforts into a fascinating logical and conceptual problem. But they need not fear that central religious interests will be vitally affected by the way the controversy comes out.

The Theory of Simple Foreknowledge

What has been said above does not apply to all versions of the belief in foreknowledge. It does not apply to versions of theism which are straightforwardly deterministic,[2] but neither does it apply to the theory of middle knowledge. Rather, it relies on the refutation of middle knowledge given in the previous chapter—and on the other hand, philosophers unconvinced by those arguments may welcome the present chapter as a demonstration of how essential middle knowledge really is. This chapter is concerned with *simple foreknowledge,* foreknowledge that embraces all *actual* free choices, including those that are yet to be made, but not

---

[2]I would include under this rubric such views as those of Scotus and Bañez, as set forth in the previous chapter. Freddoso points out, however, that "the Bañezian conception of human freedom . . . denies that free actions can occur by a necessity of nature. . . . [The] Bañezian conception is at least not the crass sort of naturalistic determinism that is so fashionable nowadays" (personal communication). This is certainly true, and perhaps this is as good a place as any to acknowledge that the various views I call "determinism" are distinguished from each other in ways that have seemed significant to their proponents. Speaking personally, however, I have never been able to see that a determinism of divine decrees is any more benign than one of natural causation.

(as in middle knowledge) those choices that *might have been* made but in fact never are.

It is possible to be a bit more precise about the nature of simple foreknowledge by asking the following question: Just *how is it* that God is able to know future events? It seems clear that the notion of a mere accidental correlation between God's beliefs about the future and the actual events when they occur is inadequate here. Evidently, one way God could know the future is by knowing the *causal antecedents* that will lead to the future events in question; this view is open to soft determinists but not to libertarians. Another way is given by the theory of middle knowledge: God, by knowing both the conditions in which a choice would be made and the relevant counterfactual of freedom, knows infallibly which choice would be made under those circumstances. But if, as has been argued, there are no true counterfactuals of freedom, this possibility also is eliminated. It seems, then, that the only way left for the adherent of simple foreknowledge is to claim that God *directly knows the actual future event*; that God's belief about the matter in question is somehow brought about *by the future event itself.* Thus, advocates of foreknowledge speak of God as having "direct vision" of the future as if in a crystal ball or a telescope.[3] This of course involves something very much like retroactive causation; the advocate of simple foreknowledge, if she is wise, will cheerfully admit this and challenge her opponent to prove that retroactive causation is impossible. It may be tempting to suppose that this also means that the future must in some way *already exist*; otherwise, how could it have effects in the present (and past)? But perhaps this temptation can be resisted. The inference will hold only if we assume that causes must exist at the time at which their effects are produced, and proponents of foreknowledge and retroactive causation may decline to accept this. They may rather maintain, pending proof to the contrary, that the future event can have effects in the present *even though it does not yet exist.*

[3]For the crystal ball comparison, see Stephen T. Davis, *Logic and the Nature of God* (Grand Rapids, Mich.: Eerdmans, 1983), p. 66; for the telescope, see Jonathan Edwards, *The Freedom of the Will* (Indianapolis: Bobbs-Merrill, 1969), p. 126. (It should be noted that Edwards himself does not subscribe to this way of viewing foreknowledge.)

What sort of understanding of providence can emerge from this conception of foreknowledge? In order to make this question concrete, let's consider an example suggested by Basinger concerning a young woman deciding which of two men to marry. If she is devout, she will very likely seek divine guidance on the matter; our question is, what sort of guidance might be available? To begin with, God will have full and complete knowledge of the physical and personality characteristics of each of the three people involved, including hopes, ambitions, and commitments, latent fears and cravings, and the like. He knows, in short, a great deal more than even the wisest and best informed marriage counselor could hope to find out. All of this, however, comes from God's *present knowledge*, whereas our question concerns what benefit can be derived from God's knowledge of the *future*. What difference, if any, does this make to the sort of guidance God is able to give?

In seeking to answer this question, it may be helpful to remind ourselves how it would be answered from the standpoint of middle knowledge. If God has middle knowledge, he has no need to base his guidance on the *potential* for happiness and success of the two envisioned marriages. Rather, he knows in full detail *exactly* what would happen to the young woman if she married either of these men or if she refused both of them. The guidance, in this case, is based on full and complete knowledge.

The situation if God has simple foreknowledge, however, is quite different. An immediate, and striking, result, is that God *cannot* use his foreknowledge in guiding the young woman about her marriage decision. For the future situation which God foreknows is, of course, a situation in which she *already* is married to one of the two men (or, perhaps, to neither)—and since the decision's *actually having been made* is presupposed by God's *knowledge* of the future, he cannot possibly *use* that knowledge in deciding how to *influence* that decision. And in general, it is clear that God's foreknowledge cannot be used either to *bring about* the occurrence of a foreknown event or to *prevent* such an event from occurring. For what God foreknows is *not* certain antecedents which, unless interfered with in some way, will *lead to* the occurrence of the event; rather, it is *the event itself* that is foreknown as occurring, and it is contradictory to suppose that an event is *known* to occur but then also is *prevented* from occurring. In the logical order of dependence of events, one might say, by the "time" God knows something will happen, it is "too late" either to *bring about* its happening or to *prevent* it from happening. God's guidance of the young woman with respect to her marriage must be *independent* of God's knowledge of her actual future.

What may seem to be possible, however, is this: God, because he foreknows that a certain event will occur, may prearrange *other factors* in the situation in such a way as to produce the best overall result. Such "prearrangement" is really what is involved in the concrete applications of foreknowledge mentioned earlier. In prophecy, God prearranges the *announcement* of the foreknown event; this announcement may serve any of a number of purposes, including the accreditation of God's spokesman (when the prophecy is fulfilled) as well as influencing hearers of the prophecy to conduct themselves in the ways God intends for them. In answering prayers, God can prearrange circumstances in such a way that when the prayer is made (as he knows it will be), the answer comes, not as a result of any immediate intervention by God at that moment, but as a consequence of the circumstances that have been prearranged months or millennia before. The general case of providence differs from this only in that the foreknown event for which the circumstances are prearranged is not specified as a prayer that will at some future time be offered. And to return to our example, although God cannot use his foreknowledge of the young woman's marriage decision to influence that decision itself, it would seem that he may use it to arrange other aspects in the situation in such a way as to improve the outcome of the choice she actually makes.

To make this still more concrete, let us consider an actual example. In a famous World War II battle the Allied armies were encircled by the Germans at Dunkirk in June 1940. The military balance heavily favored the Germans, and the situation of the Allied forces was desperate. However, unusually calm weather on the English Channel and a fog that inhibited dive bombing by the Luftwaffe made possible the evacuation by sea of most of the Allied troops with far fewer losses than could have been expected. If we assume (as many of us would) that the Allied cause was just and that God desired an Allied victory in the war, we can interpret these events along the following lines: God, having foreknowledge of the encirclement, prearranged the causal factors that would determine the weather at the time of the evacuation, thus making possible the relatively favorable outcome instead of the annihilation or mass surrender of the Allied forces. This example, I believe, gives a fair picture of the way in which simple foreknowledge can be incorporated into an understanding of providence.

The Uselessness of Simple Foreknowledge

I now argue that this conception of divine providence is incoherent and that, in fact, simple foreknowledge is *entirely useless* for the doctrine of providence. Let us begin with a distinction concerning the way God knows the future. The distinction I have in mind is between knowing *propositions* about the future and knowing the *concrete events* of the future—that is, the actual *space-time processes* that will occur. The distinction may be illustrated by the story of King Croesus, who upon consulting the Delphic Oracle was told, "If you cross the Halys River, a great empire will be destroyed." He knew, let us assume, the truth of this proposition, but he was not acquainted with the *concrete events* that would make the proposition true—in particular, he did not know that the that empire that was to be destroyed was his own.

Now, it is not to be thought of that, in knowing the future, God knows merely the truth of certain propositions. All accounts of God's knowledge stress that past and future events are for God *no less vivid or complete in their epistemic presence* than those that are presently occurring. (This is at least one of the points made by the crystal ball and telescope metaphors.) God, we may say, not only knows *that* a given proposition about the future is true; he also knows in the fullest detail exactly *how* it is true, down to the minutest fact that might remain forever inaccessible to even the most assiduous human investigator. We may, say, then, that if God has simple foreknowledge, he knows the *concrete events* of the future, and not merely propositions about the future.

With this in mind, let us return to the example of the young woman's marriage. God, we may assume, knows the truth of the

proposition "One year hence Susan will be married to Kenneth."
But he not only knows *that* this is true, he knows in full detail *how*
it is true—he knows, in other words, the full complex pattern of
mutual interactions that will constitute Susan and Kenneth's married life together one year hence. (Let's call this pattern, the concrete event of Susan and Kenneth's marriage, *M*.) Now, let us
suppose that God, on the basis of this foreknowledge, acts in the
present in some way so as to improve the eventual happiness of the
marriage—for example, he influences Kenneth to work on over-
coming his tendency toward impatience so as to become a more
sympathetic and understanding husband. It is evident, given the
description of the situation to date, that God's so acting will have a
distinct effect on the concrete event *M*. God's intervention will
not, of course, have the effect of bringing it about that Kenneth
and Susan are *not* married in a year; to suppose that it would is
incoherent, given that God's action is *based on* his foreknowledge
of their marriage. Nor will God's intervention *change* the pattern *M*
of their marriage. Since God's intervention is based on his foreknowledge of *M*, it would be incoherent to assume that the actual
pattern of their married life, as it is influenced by the intervention,
is something *other* than *M*. Nevertheless, it is quite inevitable that
God's intervention will *affect M*—that the pattern *M*, which is the
pattern of Susan and Kenneth's marriage that eventuates following
God's intervention, is a *different pattern* than some pattern (call it
M') that might have been the pattern of their marriage *without* this
intervention of God's.[4]

A little reflection will show that a similar situation obtains in the
Dunkirk example. God, we suppose, knew in advance the concrete
event *E* of the Allied encirclement at Dunkirk. On the basis of this
knowledge, God at some earlier time prearranged the weather
patterns in a way he would not have done but for his knowledge of
E, so as to provide favorable weather for the evacuation. God's
intervention, of course, cannot *change E*; to suppose that it does
leads to incoherence. But this intervention surely must *affect E*: The

---

[4] I say "might have been" because, lacking the counterfactuals of freedom, there
is no single pattern that *would have been* the pattern of their lives if things had been
different in a specific respect.

weather modifications that result in calm weather for the evacuation must inevitably affect the weather patterns in the area *before* that time, and of course weather patterns are the sorts of things that profoundly influence military campaigns; they determine visibility, the feasibility of aerial support, the possibility of transporting men and equipment over various terrains, and so forth. So the pattern E, which comes about in the actual world subsequent to God's modification of weather patterns, is different from some pattern E' that might have resulted in the absence of such modification.

But now consider the implications of this. In each case we have a future concrete event—M or E—that is foreknown by God. God, we say, knows the *actual space-time processes* comprised in M or E *in their totality*, down to the smallest detail. But God's knowledge of these processes must also involve complete knowledge of their *causal antecedents*; it is out of the question to think of God as knowing M, for example, but *not* knowing how M comes about. So God's knowledge must also embrace all of the immediate antecedents of the processes comprised in M—and again, we must suppose that he knows these in their full concreteness and particularity. But this, in turn, implies knowledge of *their* causal antecedents—and so on. So God knows not only the proposition "One year hence Susan will be married to Kenneth"; he also knows the concrete event M that is the entire pattern of their married life, and in knowing this he knows its *complete causal antecedents*—and this means, he knows all of the previous events that *in any way* contributed causally to the pattern M, which means in effect that he knows *the entire causally relevant past history of the universe* leading up to the space-time processes that constitute M.

Now, let us see what follows from this. Earlier it was argued that God cannot use his foreknowledge of the marriage either to *bring about* or to *prevent* the marriage, because God's foreknowledge presupposes the decision about the marriage *having actually been made*. But given that what God knows is the *concrete event* of the marriage, a great deal more is presupposed. God's knowledge of M, we have seen, involves the *entirety of the causally relevant past history of the universe* leading up to M—and since all of this is *presupposed* in God's knowledge of M, *none of it* is left to be *decided*

by God *on the basis of* his knowledge of *M*. It follows from this that
God cannot *use* his knowledge of *M* as a basis for *any prior action*
occurring within the relevant past sector of space-time; the *entire*
history of the sector is presupposed in God's knowledge, and God
can no more *use* the knowledge either to change or to bring about
that history than he can use his knowledge of Susan and Kenneth's
marriage either to bring about or prevent the marriage. Nor, furthermore, can God on the basis of this knowledge cause a *prophecy*
to be made concerning *M*, for such a prophecy would itself constitute an intervention *on the basis of his knowledge of M*, and we have
seen this to be impossible.[5]

What emerges from all this is that the account of divine providence given above, an account of how God's management of the
world is facilitated by simple foreknowledge, is incoherent. But if
this is so, why has the point been so largely overlooked? My
conjecture is that the reason for this is that the implications of
God's foreknowledge of concrete events are not seen. We are inclined to think, albeit unconsciously, of God's foreknowledge
along the lines of the limited foreknowledge we ourselves sometimes have, when we see certain events coming that are *not* contingent upon anything we may choose to do or to refrain from
doing. In such cases the actions that we take in view of our foresight lead to no paradox. But if we could foresee *everything,* then
for us, as for God, it would be too late to do anything about it.

I have argued that the notion of divine providence based on
simple foreknowledge is incoherent. But there is yet a final question that may be asked about this: Just where, in particular, does
the incoherence arise? For the incompatibilist, the answer may
appear simple; what is incoherent is simply the notion that God can
have comprehensive foreknowledge of free human actions. The
discussion in this chapter, however, does not presuppose *either*
compatibilism or incompatibilism about foreknowledge. It should
be noted, furthermore, that the demonstration given of incoherence given above does *not* depend at any essential point on the

[5]It may be that this reasoning does not apply to those space-time processes, if
any, that undergo *entire causal extinction*—that is, that are such that they have *no
causal consequences whatever*. It is evident, however, that if total causal extinction is
possible, it is of no help to the doctrine of providence.

assumption that human beings have libertarian free will. So we arrive at the following, rather striking, result: *Whether or not there are creatures endowed with libertarian free will, it is impossible that God should use a foreknowledge derived from the actual occurrence of future events to determine his own prior actions in the providential governance of the world.* If simple foreknowledge did exist, it would be useless.

[4]

Two Arguments
for Incompatibilism

The modern controversy over the compatibility of divine foreknowledge and human freedom, begun in the 1960s by Nelson
Pike and A. N. Prior, has so far failed to reach a satisfactory
conclusion.[1] It is not immediately apparent why the issue should
be so difficult to resolve. There do not appear to be any systematic
differences in philosophical style or methodology between the op-
posing sides which might explain their differing conclusions. Nor
does the issue seem to be one that marks the difference between
major competing world-views—like, for example, the controversies over scientific determinism or mind-body dualism.

It is clear that differences concerning religious belief play a role
in sustaining the controversy, but just what that role is, is less
clear. There are theists and nontheists on both sides of the issue.
And incompatibilism is hardly a potent weapon against theism,
since it is evident that there are versions of theism which can
coexist happily with it. To be sure, there are also theists to whom
these versions of theism are unacceptable, and for those theists

---

[1]Some of the material in this and the next three chapters is derived from my
"Foreknowledge and Necessity," *Faith and Philosophy* 2 (1985): 121–157. See
Nelson Pike, "Divine Omniscience and Voluntary Action," *Philosophical Review*
74 (1965): 27–46; A. N. Prior, "The Formalities of Omniscience," *Philosophy* 32
(1962): 119–29.

religious belief may be a powerful motive for resistance to incompatibilism. But it would be unjust both to the participants in the discussion and to the quality of their arguments to suggest that the controversy is kept alive only by religious dogma.

What does seem to be true, however, is that the issues of religious belief which are involved have strongly motivated the development of more and more complex positions on both sides of the debate. And in view of this complexity it is unlikely that any simple, straightforward argument will be able by itself to move the controversy toward resolution. Such an argument might capture effectively what one side perceives as the grounds for its position, but in view of the complexity of the discussion it is not likely to convince those who need to be convinced.

I believe, therefore, that an illuminating treatment of this topic must take a more subtle and dialectical approach. The aim must be to strip away, one by one, the complexities that envelop the controversy in order to lay bare the core disagreements. Formal arguments will have their role to play in this, but only as a part of a larger process that seeks to elucidate the total philosophical context within which the arguments must function.

But what *are* the core disagreements—the central points on which the controversy at last will hinge? The only sure way to answer this is to let the controversy take its course and thus discover empirically which issues emerge as primary. I offer, however, some conjectures about this, based on my own reading of the discussion to this point. First, I suggest that the *power entailment principles*, discussed extensively in chapter 6, will play a central role in future discussions of the topic. These principles are called upon at a crucial juncture in the best argument for incompatibilism, and a compatibilist who succeeds in refuting them will have advanced her cause significantly. Second, and perhaps more fundamental, there is the matter of the *necessity of the past*—or, if one prefers, its fixity or unalterability. In any case, the notion that the past is somehow fundamentally different than the future, with respect to the possibilities for human action, is deeply entrenched in ordinary language and common sense, as well as in much philosophy. But all fatalists, and at least one professed libertarian,[2] deny this. And

[2]George Mavrodes.

among those who concede that *in some sense* the past is necessary, fixed, or inalterable, the interpretations placed on this and the implications drawn from it vary considerably. Third, and most basic of all, this controversy leads us to the question of *the nature of free will*. For though libertarianism is a presupposition of the controversy, it turns out, I believe, that the difference between compatibilists and incompatibilists is in the final analysis a difference in the meanings attached to free will and free choice.

But all this, if correct, must be shown to be so by the future development of the discussion. In the meantime, we shall proceed as follows: The next section begins with a clarification of the notion of free will presupposed in the present discussion and proceeds to set out two arguments for incompatibilism. We then turn to a consideration of some of the simpler objections to incompatibilism, and the chapter concludes with a reformulation of the second incompatibilist argument. The most formidable replies to this argument are treated in the next three chapters.

Two Arguments

It is incumbent on the incompatibilist to make clear what it is that divine foreknowledge is incompatible *with*. The notion of free will involved here is nicely expressed by David Basinger when he says that when a person is free to perform an action, she "has it in her power to choose to perform A or choose not to perform A. *Both A and not A could actually occur*; which *will* actually occur has *not yet been determined*."[3]

For a formal definition of this notion, we have the following:

(FW) N is free at T with respect to performing $A =_{df}$ It is in N's power at T to perform A, and it is in N's power at T to refrain from performing A.

Some comments may help to clarify this definition. It should be noted that the power in question is the *power to perform a particular*

[3]"Middle Knowledge and Classical Christian Thought," *Religious Studies* 22 (1986): 416.

act under given circumstances, and not a *generalized* power to perform acts of a certain kind. (Thus, if Thomas has the skill to perform on the parallel bars, but at T_1 his arms are tied behind his back, we shall say that he *lacks* the power at T_1 to perform on the parallel bars.) In general, if it is in N's power at T to perform A, then there is nothing in the circumstances that obtain at T which *prevents or precludes* N's performing A at T. Here "prevent" applies especially to circumstances that are *causally* incompatible with N's performing A at T, and "preclude" to circumstances that are *logically* incompatible with N's doing so. (The tied hands *prevent* Thomas from performing on the parallel bars; he is *precluded* from marrying Edwina at T by the fact that at that time she is already married to someone else.)[4]

A further point that should be noted is the following: The ascription of powers to finite agents *is always subject to the possibility of interference*. If I bump your elbow while you are shaving and cause you to cut yourself, this does not show that, on that occasion, you lacked the power to shave without cutting yourself. You had the power, but my interference prevented its exercise. (This assumes that my bumping your arm is not *causally inevitable*—if it were, then you *would* lack the power in question under those circumstances.)[5]

As has become customary, the arguments for incompatibilism will be presented in terms of a specific example, the results from which can then be generalized. But philosophers who have become weary of Jones's interminable project of mowing his lawn will rejoice to learn that a new example is in the offing: our concern will be with Clarence, an aficionado of cheese omelets, and with the question, Will Clarence have such an omelet for breakfast tomorrow morning, or won't he?

The first argument begins by assuming that Clarence will, in

[4]But what counts as a circumstance? The answer is that the circumstances that obtain at T include all and only the *hard facts* with respect to T. For the explication of hard facts, see the next chapter.

[5]These considerations, I believe, suffice to free my definition from the dreaded "Frankfurt counterexamples." (See Harry G. Frankfurt, "Alternate Possibilities and Moral Responsibility," *Journal of Philosophy* 66 [1969]: 829–39.) But a full discussion of this point must wait for another occasion.

fact, have a cheese omelet tomorrow morning, and it argues that
Clarence's eating that omelet is necessary, hence not a matter of
free choice. The argument goes like this:

(A1) Necessarily, God has always believed that Clarence will
     have a cheese omelet tomorrow morning. (Premise: the
     necessity of the past)
(A2) Necessarily, if God has always believed that a certain thing
     will happen, then that thing will happen. (Premise: divine
     infallibility)
(A3) Therefore, necessarily, Clarence will have a cheese omelet
     tomorrow. (From 1,2)

This argument has impressive merits. It is complete, with no
suppressed premises, and as concise as one could ask. Its validity is
beyond reasonable doubt, and it will be sound if any incompatibilist argument for this conclusion is sound. Yet its very conciseness
works against its usefulness as a tool for analyzing the controversy.
The purpose of the argument, after all, is to say something about
free will and therefore about what Clarence has it in his power to
do—but these topics are present in argument (A) only by implication. Also, the first premise makes assumptions about the relation
of God's knowledge to events in time, and these assumptions need
to be made explicit so they can be examined. But the most serious
deficiency of argument (A) concerns the modal operator in the first
premise. 'Necessarily' here does not refer to logical necessity, as it
does in the second premise; it is not claimed that God has the belief
in question in all possible worlds. Rather, 'necessarily' in the first
premise refers to the "necessity of the past": God's having held this
belief is *now* necessary because it has *already happened*. And it is this
necessity that is, as it were, transmitted across the entailment stated
in the second premise so as to appear again in the conclusion. But it
is clear that this notion, the idea of the necessity of the past, is one
of the most crucial and difficult elements in the entire controversy.
Any argument that is to throw light on the dispute must do more
with this notion than baldly assert it.

With these considerations in mind, let us try another argument:

(B1) It is now true that Clarence will have a cheese omelet for breakfast tomorrow. (Premise)

(B2) It is impossible that God should at any time believe what is false, or fail to believe anything that is true. (Premise: divine omniscience)

(B3) Therefore, God has always believed that Clarence will have a cheese omelet for breakfast tomorrow. (From 1,2)

(B4) If God has always believed a certain thing, it is not in anyone's power to bring it about that God has not always believed that thing. (Premise: the unalterability of the past)

(B5) Therefore, it is not in Clarence's power to bring it about that God has not always believed that he would have a cheese omelet for breakfast. (From 3,4)

(B6) It is not possible for it to be true both that God has always believed that Clarence would have a cheese omelet for breakfast, and that he does not in fact have one. (From 2)

(B7) Therefore, it is not in Clarence's power to refrain from having a cheese omelet for breakfast tomorrow. (From 5,6) So Clarence's eating the omelet tomorrow is not an act of free choice.

No doubt this argument could be expanded still further; still, it can serve as a basis for analysis. It does meet the objections raised against argument (A): It speaks explicitly about what it is in Clarence's power to do, it makes explicit the conception of divine omniscience which the argument assumes, and it deals with the necessity (or unalterability) of the past in a way that is at least somewhat less opaque than (A).[6]

[6]It will be noted that arguments (A) and (B), though ostensibly about divine foreknowledge, refer explicitly to God's *beliefs*. On any standard analysis, "N knows at T that P" entails "(N believes at T that P) & P." Now, the necessity asserted in (A1) and the inalterability affirmed in (B4) both are held to attach to God's past beliefs *because they are past*. But to assert that God's past *knowledge* that P is necessary, is to imply that "P" itself is necessary *even if it is a proposition about the future*. But of course this is precisely what the arguments are trying to establish; it will not do simply to assume it as a premise.

Some Objections to the Arguments

At this point we will consider some of the commoner, and simpler, objections to these incompatibilist arguments and will also add some further clarifying remarks about the arguments themselves. First, we consider an objection that is raised rather frequently: Sometimes we ourselves know what another person is going to do (say, in anticipating a friend's reaction to some situation that has arisen), and we do not suppose that our knowing this is incompatible with the person's acting freely—so why suppose such an incompatibility when it is God who knows?

The short answer to this is that arguments (A) and (B) do not proceed from God's knowledge as a premise but from God's belief, and no one supposes that a human being's believing something necessitates the truth of what is believed. But there may be more to the objection than this. If Susan, his wife, knows that Clarence will have an omelet for breakfast tomorrow, it must be true not only that she believes this but also that she has *adequate evidence* for her belief (she knows about his addiction to cheese omelets, he came home yesterday with a new hunk of sharp cheddar, and so on). And (it may be supposed) this justifying evidence must be sufficient to exclude the possibility that Clarence will *not* have an omelet; otherwise, she could not be said to know that he will. In general, however, this need not be true. We often ascribe knowledge in situations where the justifying evidence is insufficient to warrant absolute certainty. And surely this is one of those situations: whatever evidence Susan may have is surely compatible with its being possible that Clarence will decide not to have an omelet tomorrow, and therefore with its being a matter of free choice whether he has one or not. If, on the other hand, the requirement for knowledge is strengthened to absolute certainty, then it is perfectly plausible to suppose that we never do have knowledge of future free actions.[7]

---

[7]As Jonathan L. Kvanvig says, "To claim that God is essentially omniscient implies that God is absolutely certain about everything which He believes. And that certainty entails that God bears a very different relation to the future than we do, for we cannot be certain in the relevant sense of much more than our own present mental states" (*The Possibility of an All-Knowing God* [New York: St. Martin's Press, 1986], p. 73).

Another important point about arguments (A) and (B) is that neither one raises the question of *how* God is able to know future actions. One might argue that God can do this only if sufficient causal conditions of the actions already exist; thus, a world in which such knowledge is possible for God is of necessity a deterministic one. Such an argument might possibly be sound, but its major premise is exceedingly difficult to establish. Alternative accounts of God's knowledge of future actions are available, accounts that do not involve the presence of sufficient causal conditions. As we have seen in the last two chapters, God's knowledge of the future might result by retroactive causation from the actual future events—and, there is also the theory of middle knowledge to be considered. The task of disposing of these alternative accounts of God's knowledge is formidable enough to make the suggested argument unattractive. But, to repeat the point, neither (A) nor (B) relies on assumptions about how God is able to know what he knows.

Another objection that deserves at least passing mention is the following: The incompatibilist claims that if God foreknows a person's action, then that action is not free. But if God foreknows that some person will *freely* choose a certain action, what follows is that the action will be done *freely*, which is the reverse of the conclusion desired by the incompatibilist. I mention this argument because I have heard it used by reputable philosophers, but it quite transparently begs the question. Certainly, "God believes that N will freely do *A*" entails "N will do *A* freely." But arguments (A) and (B) claim that this same premise also entails "N will do *A* of necessity." Now the new entailment does not cancel the old, nor does this maneuver do anything to undermine either (A) or (B). So unless some *independent* refutation of (A) and (B) is possible, adding the premise that *A* is done freely simply leaves us with an inconsistent premise and with two incompatible conclusions, both validly derived. (In general, whenever it is claimed that "*P*" entails "*Q*," one can truly assert that "*P* & ~*Q*" entails "~*Q*," but this has no tendency whatever to show that "*P*" does *not* entail "*Q*.")

Still another objection claims that incompatibilism wrongly assumes that God's prior knowledge of what a person will do *causes* the subsequent action. But if I know (for instance) that you are walking across the street, this does not *cause* you to walk across the street, so why assume it is different with God? This is true enough, but close examination will reveal that neither (A) nor (B) makes the claim that God's knowledge (or belief) causes the event that he knows. They merely assert that it is impossible that God should believe that an event will happen and yet the event not occur. And this is certainly true. But what, if anything, *causes* Clarence to eat the omelet is left as a problem for further study. (It should be noted also that both [A] and [B] are consistent with the assumption that God's belief is caused retroactively by the future action.)[8]

But this answer may be insufficient. Some philosophers, at least, seem strongly inclined to think that *if the future action is itself the cause of God's belief,* then the belief cannot create a problem with respect to the action's being free.[9] Now, it is certainly true that, if the action causes the belief, it cannot also be the case that the belief causes the action. (The causal relation is asymmetrical.) The mistake, however, lies in the assumption that it is only by causing the action that the belief can be relevant to the action's freedom. But as Jonathan Edwards pointed out, foreknowledge can perfectly well *show* an action to be necessary even if it is not the foreknowledge that *makes* it necessary.[10] And there is another point here, also noted by Edwards: The fact that a future event has an *already existing effect* shows the occurrence of that event to be necessary, *whether or not* the effect in question involves God's beliefs. For it is

---

[8]Compare the following from A. N. Prior: "For a conditional proposition such as 'If it has come to God's knowledge that X will be, then X will be', doesn't require for its truth, or for its conveying necessity from its antecedent to its consequent, that its antecedent should *causally bring about* its consequent. It is enough that the former cannot be the case without the latter being the case, regardless of why this is so. And in fact if we like to say that it is because X will be that it can be known that it will be, rather than vice versa, this means more than ever that X's future coming to pass is beyond prevention, since it has already *had consequences* which its opposite could not have . . . ." ("The Formalities of Omniscience," p. 37).

[9]According to Bruce Reichenbach, "We can freely bring about the future [which God foresees], for the ground of his foreseeing it is our bringing it about. . . . That is, there is nothing for him to foresee or believe with respect to Clarence's eating the omelet except what Clarence brings about" ("Hasker on Omniscience," *Faith and Philosophy* 4 [1987]: 91–92).

[10]Jonathan Edwards, *Freedom of the Will* (Indianapolis: Bobbs-Merrill, 1969), p. 123.

clearly absurd to suppose that a present fact exists which is the effect of some future event, yet that future event *may or may not* occur![11] (This point, I note in passing, should be attended to by the authors of stories about time travel.)

The Second Argument Revisited

So far the incompatibilist arguments—(B) in particular—have proved able to withstand the challenges raised against them. But in one respect these arguments are misleading. Both (A) and (B) conclude to a denial of libertarian free will. In fact, however, relatively few incompatibilists accept this conclusion. Rather, incompatibilists tend to adopt modified conceptions of omniscience so as to avoid the deterministic outcome. One such conception simply denies that propositions describing future contingent events can be true; this means that the first premise of each argument is rejected. Another alternative, to be explored in later chapters, is to maintain that God's knowledge is timeless rather than temporal. But the alternative most serviceable for present purposes is to hold that God's omniscience entails his knowing, not all true propositions whatsoever, but only those that it is logically possible for him to know. With this conception in place, we can construct a variant form of argument (B) as follows:

(C1) It is now true that Clarence will have a cheese omelet for breakfast tomorrow. (Premise)

(C2) It is impossible that God should at any time believe what is false, or fail to believe any true proposition such that his knowing that proposition at that time is logically possible. (Premise: divine omniscience)

(C3) God has always believed that Clarence will have a cheese omelet tomorrow. (Assumption for indirect proof)

(C4) If God has always believed a certain thing, it is not in anyone's power to bring it about that God has not always believed that thing. (Premise: the unalterability of the past)

(C5) Therefore, it is not in Clarence's power to bring it about

[11]Ibid., p. 126.

that God has not always believed that he would have a cheese omelet for breakfast. (From 3,4)

(C6) It is not possible for it to be true both that God has always believed that Clarence would have a cheese omelet for breakfast, and that he does not in fact have one. (From 2)

(C7) Therefore, it is not in Clarence's power to refrain from having a cheese omelet for breakfast tomorrow. (From 5,6) So Clarence's eating the omelet tomorrow is not an act of free choice.

(C8) Clarence will act freely when he eats the omelet for breakfast tomorrow. (Premise)

(C9) Therefore, it is not the case that God has always believed that Clarence will have a cheese omelet for breakfast tomorrow. (From 3–8, indirect proof)

This argument represents more faithfully than (B) the actual thinking of most incompatibilists. But it also suggests what may be a promising strategy for resolving the entire controversy. I submit that compatibilists and incompatibilists alike ought to be able to agree on the definition of omniscience given by (C2) as a framework for the discussion. (C2), after all, does not affirm or presuppose that there *are* truths that are logically impossible for God to know, but by leaving that possibility open it achieves a generality that is lacking in (B2). And on the other hand, compatibilists presumably do not want to claim that there are truths that God knows in spite of its being logically impossible for him to know them! So I would suggest that compatibilist and incompatibilist begin by agreeing to accept (C2) as a common definition of omniscience. They will then proceed to resolve their differences with regard to the validity of the incompatibilist arguments (B) and (C)—which, to be sure, may not be an easy thing to do! But once this has been done, essentially complete agreement will have been reached; there will be no occasion, in view of the prior agreement to (C2), for any further disputes about the meaning of "omniscient."

What remains, then, is to examine the most important answers given by compatibilists to the arguments for incompatibilism. To that task we now turn.

Hard and Soft Facts

The distinction between hard and soft facts is usually introduced in the context of the controversy over free will and divine foreknowledge, but the need for the distinction is by no means limited to this.[1] Consider the following three propositions:

(1) If event E occurs at T_2, then "E will occur at T_2" is true at any previous time T_1.

(2) Some propositions about the future are such that it is now in someone's power to determine whether or not they are true.

(3) No propositions about the past are such that it is now in someone's power to determine whether or not they are true. (When I say that it is in someone's power to determine whether or not a proposition is true, I mean that, if it is true, it is in someone's power to bring it about that it is false, and if it is false, it is in someone's power to bring it about that it is true.)

Propositions (1) through (3) can easily seem to generate a contradiction. Suppose, for example, that John had a cup of tea for lunch.

[1]Much of the material in this chapter is drawn from "Hard Facts and Theological Fatalism," *Noûs* 22 (1988): 419–36, as well as from "Foreknowledge and Necessity," *Faith and Philosophy* 2 (1985): 121–57.

It follows, according to (1), that "John will have a cup of tea for lunch" was true at any arbitrarily chosen past time—for instance, it was true at 6:00 this morning. So now we have:

(4) It was true at 6:00 this morning that John would have a cup of tea for lunch.

But from this it follows, according to (3), that

(5) It was not in anyone's power at 6:01 this morning to determine whether or not John would have a cup of tea for lunch.

And since the same reasoning can be followed for any time prior to lunch, and indeed for any arbitrarily chosen action or event, it follows that (2) is false; what is true instead is

(6) No proposition is ever such that it is in anyone's power to determine whether or not it is true.

This, of course, is the problem of logical determinism or fatalism, and it is clear what must be done to solve it: If one accepts both (1) and (3), then one must explicate the phrase "propositions about the past" in such a way that (4) does not qualify as being "about the past," so that the inference from (4) to (5) is blocked. That is to say: We need to be able to classify (4) as a soft fact about the past rather than as a hard fact.

So the distinction between hard and soft facts is needed for the solution of the problem of logical fatalism. But of course this same distinction is often invoked to resolve the problem of theological fatalism. What needs to be clearly seen, however, is that this is a *new* problem and not the same problem over again. To solve the problem of logical fatalism, it suffices that (4) be classified as a soft fact rather than a hard fact, but this is not enough to avoid theological fatalism. For philosophers concerned with theological fatalism typically accept not only (1)-(3) but also

(7) If event E occurs at T_2, then "God believes that E will occur at T_2" is true at any previous time T_1.

And from this, together with the fact that John has tea for lunch, it follows that

(8)   God believed at 6:00 this morning that John would have a cup of tea for lunch.

And from this, together with (3), it would seem to follow that

(9)   It was not in anyone's power at 6:01 this morning to determine whether or not God believed at 6:00 this morning that John would have a cup of tea for lunch.

But, given that God is essentially infallible, God's having believed this at 6:00 entails John's drinking the cup of tea, so that (9) entails (5). And by the process of generalization, we arrive once again at the fatalistic conclusion (6). So to avoid theological fatalism, it is essential that not only (4) but also (8) be classified as soft facts.

But can this be done? That is the question which it is the task of the present chapter to investigate. First, I shall take a general overview of the strategy followed by the compatibilist in classifying facts about God's past beliefs as soft facts. Then, I shall provide a careful and detailed explication of the distinction between hard and soft facts. Finally, I shall apply the distinction as we have explicated it to facts about God's past beliefs, with the aim of determining whether such facts are hard or soft—concrete or silly putty.

The Compatibilist Strategy

As we attempt to grasp the compatibilist's strategy in this discussion, it is important to see that he does recognize, in general, that facts about the past are beyond our control. According to Alvin Plantinga, for instance, there is

an important asymmetry between past and future. This asymmetry consists in part in the fact that the past is outside our control in a way in which the future is not. Although I now have the power to raise my arm, I do not have the power to bring it about that I raised my arm five minutes ago. Although it is now within my power to think about Vienna, it is not now within my power to bring it about

that five minutes ago I was thinking about Vienna. The past is fixed
in a way in which the future is open. It is within my power to help
determine how the future shall be; it is too late to do the same with
respect to the past.[2]

But, continues the compatibilist, not *all* propositions about the
past are thus outside our control. No doubt

(10) John had a cup of tea for lunch,

spoken at some time after lunch, would be beyond our control,
just as are the propositions alluded to by Plantinga. On the other
hand,

(4) It was true at 6:00 this morning that John would have a cup
of tea for lunch,

spoken at 6:01 of that same morning, does *not* seem to be beyond
our control in the way indicated: assuming it is true, there may still
be quite a number of people who have it in their power to bring it
about that it is false, by preventing that cup of tea from being
drunk.

Now, the claim made by the compatibilist here is that

(8) God believed at 6:00 this morning that John would have a
cup of tea for lunch

is like (4) in the relevant respect and unlike (10); this proposition,
contrary perhaps to our first impression, is *not* "about the past" in
such a way that its truth now lies beyond our control. Indeed, all of
the same people who might have some control over the truth of (4)
can also be said to control the truth of (8)—all those persons,
namely, who might be able to prevent that cup of tea from being
drunk.

Now, in order to settle this question, we shall need a careful and
exact explication of the hard fact–soft fact distinction; and this is a
task to which we shall turn presently. Before we go into this,

[2]Alvin Plantinga, "On Ockham's Way Out," *Faith and Philosophy* 3 (1986): 244.

however, I think it may be helpful to have before us an informal presentation of the compatibilist's argument, one that conveys, with a minimum of technical apparatus, the point that the compatibilist is trying to make. For our specimen, then, we turn to Bruce Reichenbach:

> The objector contends that no one has the power to act so that the past would be different than it was. Though this is true in a nonrelational sense—one cannot alter facts about the past which have no intrinsic relation to the present—it is not true in a relational sense. For example, I have the power to act so that Martin Luther was born exactly 502 years before I wrote this paragraph by writing it on November 10th, 1985. However, I also have the power to act so that Martin Luther was not born exactly 502 years before I wrote this by delaying my writing. Here I have the power to act so that the past is different than it was, because what is brought about is relationally dependent on the present. Of course, my power is limited. I do not have it in my power to act so that, by writing this now, Martin Luther landed on the moon 502 years before I wrote this. My power relates only to the part having to do with me. But this is what is involved with respect to God's foreknowledge. What God knows about the acts of a person is relationally dependent on what the person who is the object of that knowledge does. Thus in this relational sense a person has the power to act so that the past is what it is, that is, that God truly believes something about the present. Consequently, there is no contradiction between my human freedom and divine foreknowledge.[3]

Clearly, this argument depends on an analogy between the facts about God's past beliefs and the facts about Martin Luther's birth. Both of these kinds of facts are "relationally dependent" upon the future, and to the extent that they are so they can be affected, retroactively, by the actions of someone in the future. So if we accept the claim about Luther's birth (and how could we reject it?), we should also accept the claim about God's belief.

[3]Bruce Reichenbach, "God Limits His Power," in *Predestination and Free Will*, ed. David Basinger and Randall Basinger (Downers Grove, Ill.: InterVarsity Press, 1986), pp. 110–11. The same example is used by Reichenbach in "Hasker on Omniscience," *Faith and Philosophy* 4 (1987): 91; see my reply, "The Hardness of the Past: A Reply to Reichenbach," *Faith and Philosophy* 4 (1987): 337–42.

Unfortunately, there is an important ambiguity in this argument—an ambiguity hidden in the expression "relationally dependent." True, both Luther's birth and God's belief *are* relationally dependent on the future, in that each has a property in virtue of its relationship to future facts that it otherwise would not have. But Luther's birth is dependent on Reichenbach's writing only for a *relational property.* Luther's birth, surely, is not different in any *intrinsic* way because of Reichenbach's writing—Frau Luther, we may suppose, would hardly have noticed the difference one way or the other! God's belief, on the other hand *is* intrinsically different because of the person's future action. We can all readily understand that the *very same event* of Luther's birth, *without any change in its intrinsic characteristics,* can count either as Luther's-being-born-502-years-before-Reichenbach-writes or as Luther's-being-born-502-years-before-Reichenbach-does-not-write, depending on what happens 502 years later. But can we at all understand that the *very same event of God's believing* can, without change in any of *its* intrinsic characteristics, count *either* as God's-believing-that-John-will-drink-a-cup-of-tea *or* as God's-believing-that-John-will-*not*-drink-a-cup-of-tea? If we cannot, then the project of classifying God's beliefs as soft facts is harmed rather than helped by Reichenbach's analogy.[4]

But we can hardly expect the question to be settled by considerations of the sort developed in the last paragraph. For Reichenbach might recognize that the two facts are disanalogous in the way I have pointed out, yet insist that they are analogous in a more important way: namely, both are soft facts about the past, and both are capable of being different than they in fact are because of events in the future.[5] In order to deal with this, it is essential for us

[4]An essentially similar argument is given by John Martin Fischer in "Freedom and Foreknowledge," *Philosophical Review* 92 (1983): 67–79.

[5]Reichenbach, in fact, has said just this; he writes, "I don't see that I must claim that the very same event can count either way; in fact, it seems that this is what the compatibilist wants to deny in the case of God's belief" (personal communication). Widerker and Zemach, on the other hand, have claimed that the identical mental state of God's can be a belief that P in some possible worlds (namely, those in which "P" is true), and not in others. (See David Widerker and E. M. Zemach, "Facts, Freedom and Foreknowledge," *Religious Studies* 23 (1987): 19–28.) Zemach and Widerker's argument for this claim strikes me as ingenious but not convincing.

to become more rigorous in delineating the classes of hard and soft facts.

Hard and Soft Facts

Before we proceed with the main task of this section, several observations are in order. First, it should be evident from what has already been said that the hard fact–soft fact distinction, if it is to be used at all, must be carefully explicated and not just alluded to in a general way. Quite apart from the issue of foreknowledge, there are (as will become apparent) other complexities inherent in this distinction which need careful attention.[6]

Second, it should be observed that, if the distinction is to be of use in settling the foreknowledge debate, that distinction cannot itself be explicated in terms of the powers of agents.[7] To be sure, there is no formal, logical objection to explicating the notion in this way, and such an explication might be useful for some purposes. But the main objective in the foreknowledge controversy is to *settle* disagreements about the powers of the agents, and it is evident that if the hard fact–soft fact distinction is *explicated* in terms of powers, then disagreements about what is in our power will simply reappear as differences about the hard fact–soft fact distinction itself. Rather, what is needed is to explicate the idea of a proposition's "being about the past" *without* involving the notion of powers; the distinction thus explicated can then be *used* to settle questions about our powers.

---

[6]An early attempt at explicating the distinction was made by Marilyn McCord Adams ("Is the Existence of God a 'Hard' Fact?" *Philosophical Review* 76 [October, 1967]: 492–503); this explication has been decisively criticized by John Martin Fischer ("Freedom and Foreknowledge"). More recently, explications have been offered by Alfred J. Freddoso ("Accidental Necessity and Logical Determinism," *Journal of Philosophy* 80 [1983]: 257–78), by Joshua Hoffman and Gary Rosenkrantz ("Hard and Soft Facts," *Philosophical Review* 93 [1984]: 419–34), by William Hasker ("Foreknowledge and Necessity"), by Alvin Plantinga ("On Ockham's Way Out"), by Jonathan L. Kvanvig (*The Possibility of an All-Knowing God* [New York: St. Martin's Press, 1986]), and by David Widerker and E. M. Zemach ("Facts, Freedom and Foreknowledge"). My own explication owes most to Freddoso, though there are significant differences.

[7]The most serious attempt to explicate the distinction in this way is found in Plantinga, "On Ockham's Way Out."

As we pursue this thought, third, it becomes apparent that there are at least *two* important ideas involved in the distinction between hard and soft facts. There is, on the one hand, the notion of a proposition's being "really about the past," and, on the other, the notion of a proposition's being such that it cannot be in anyone's power to render it false. It is clear, furthermore, that these notions do not entirely coincide: The truths of logic, for example, are not "about the past" in any relevant sense, but they are indeed beyond our powers to render false. It seems likely, then, that an illuminating explication of the notion of a hard fact will distinguish between these two moments or aspects of that notion.

It should be noted, finally, that our discussion to this point already provides some useful guidelines for judging the acceptability of a proposed explication of the distinction between hard and soft facts. It is clear that, for example,

(10)   John had a cup of tea for lunch,

as uttered later in the afternoon, must qualify as hard on any acceptable analysis, whereas

(4)   It was true at 6:00 this morning that John would have a
        cup of tea for lunch,

uttered at 6:01, must qualify as soft. To be sure, there will be many cases more difficult than these, and in some of those cases we may find ourselves confronted with uncertainty and/or disagreement. But a distinction that does not give the right answers on these two cases (and others like them) is simply not the distinction we set out to explicate.

It may be helpful at this point to provide a few more examples of propositions against which our explication may be tested. It is clear that (10) must be hard whereas (4) will be soft, but what of

(11)   David said yesterday that Sandra will arrive tomorrow ?

This seems to be genuinely about the past, but then what about

(12)   David yesterday said truly that Sandra will arrive
       tomorrow ?

If (12) is true, should we conclude that Sandra's arrival is already
necessary, unpreventable, beyond anyone's control, and so on?
And what about

(13)   Everything David said yesterday was true ?

This, again, speaks about what happened yesterday, and—unlike
(12)—it does not entail any propositions about the future. Yet
when conjoined with (11), which intuitively should be a hard fact
about the past, it entails

(14)   Sandra will arrive tomorrow.

Just one other example will be considered here; what about

(15)   Either David has already arrived or he will arrive
       tomorrow ?

Assuming that this is true, is it a hard fact or a soft fact? The first
disjunct, considered by itself, is, if true, a hard fact; the second
disjunct, if true, is a soft fact. What then shall we say of the entire
disjunction?

Our procedure is to explicate the distinction between hard and
soft facts in a series of steps, with two main stages as suggested
above. First, we shall delineate a category of *future-indifferent* propositions—propositions that are wholly about the past and the present, and that are such that their truth or falsity cannot be affected
by anything that happens in the future.[8] From there we proceed to

---

[8]At this point I shall simply stipulate that propositions describing *timeless* events
and actions, the sorts of actions ascribed to God according to the theory of divine
timelessness, will not be considered as candidates for the status of future-indifferent propositions. The purpose of this is to enable us to postpone consideration
of the relationship between the doctrine of timelessness and free will; such consideration is, in fact, pursued in chapter 9.

the category of *hard facts*—facts, or true propositions, such that, with respect to a given time, it is impossible that anyone at or after that time should have the power to render them false. Each step of the exposition will be accompanied by a commentary designed to make clear the justification and the motivation for it.

We begin by identifying a set of propositions that are "elementary" or "atomic" roughly in the sense of the *Tractatus* or the early Russell—propositions that say of some individual that it has a certain property, or of two or more individuals that they stand in a certain relation. These propositions may be tensed, or they may be tenseless propositions indexed to a time. The elementary propositions will include those that express propositional attitudes ("Mary believes that John drank a cup of tea"), but not propositions whose most natural representation would be as quantifications or truth functions. (It is evidently possible to contrive complex predicates whereby extremely complicated propositions can be represented in what appears to be simple subject-predicate form. Such contrived predicates can simply be rejected on an *ad hoc* basis—or, they may be dealt with in a way described in the commentary on [H4] below.)

The first step of our explication identifies as future-indifferent those elementary propositions that are wholly about the past and present, rather than the future. As a first approximation, consider

(16)   An elementary proposition is future-indifferent IFF it is consistent with there being no times after the present, and also with there being times after the present.

The intuitive idea here is that a future-indifferent proposition must permit, but not require, that the entire universe should disappear and there be nothing at all after the present moment. But (16) remains ambiguous at a crucial point, and the ambiguity must be removed if we are to have a workable principle. The term "consistent" refers, of course, to logical consistency, which is one of a group of related, and interdefinable, concepts including logical necessity, possibility, inconsistency, contingency, and entailment. If for convenience we take logical necessity as primitive, we can indicate the ambiguity by a question: What concept of logical necessity is being invoked here?

In one sense, a proposition may be said to be logically necessary if it is *conceptually necessary*, or true in virtue of the meanings of the terms in which it is expressed. In another sense, a proposition is logically necessary if it is *metaphysically necessary*, or true in all possible worlds.[9] It has often been assumed that the two concepts of necessity are coextensive; thus, a few philosophers still refer to all logically necessary propositions as "analytic." It has recently become clear, however, that in certain cases the two concepts diverge. Consider, for example, Kripke's example, "This table is not made of ice."[10] Clearly, this statement is not analytic or conceptually necessary; no amount of skill at logic and conceptual analysis will enable us to recognize its truth. But if it *is* true, Kripke says (and I agree) that it is necessarily true; in no possible world does *this table* exist made of ice.[11] The statement is metaphysically necessary but not conceptually necessary. (So far as I know, all statements for which the two kinds of necessity diverge involve the *essential properties* either of individual entities or of kinds of entities.)

Which kind of necessity is relevant to (11)? It seems not to have been noticed that this question is absolutely crucial to the correct explication of the notion of a future-indifferent proposition.[12] The answer, however is clear: the notion of a future-indifferent proposition must be explicated in terms of conceptual necessity, not metaphysical necessity. And the reason for this is also clear: if this notion is explicated using metaphysical necessity, the distinction collapses as all, or virtually all, propositions become non-future-indifferent.

---

[9]See my "Hard Facts and Theological Fatalism." In "Foreknowledge and Necessity" I spoke of *de re* and *de dicto* necessary truths, but in view of the confusing variety of ways in which the *de re–de dicto* distinction is being used, I now prefer to speak of "conceptually necessary" and "metaphysically necessary" propositions.

[10]Saul Kripke, "Naming and Necessity," in Donald Davidson and Gilbert Harman, eds., *Semantics of Natural Language* (Dordrecht: D. Riedel, 1972), pp. 332–33.

[11]Perhaps I should rather write "in no possible world does this table exist having been originally made of ice" in order to circumvent puzzles based on the gradual replacement of parts.

[12]None of the other philosophers referred to in n. 6 discusses this distinction. Freddoso, and also Hoffman and Rosenkrantz, have informed me that they intended their theories to be understood in the sense of metaphysical necessity (personal communications).

The *argument* for this reason, however, is complicated by the fact that there is considerable disagreement about what sorts of essential properties are had by various kinds of entities. The best I can do, under the circumstances, is to give a series of examples; my hope is that the examples will be striking enough to make my general thesis seem extremely plausible. If God is a metaphysically necessary being (i.e., exists in all possible worlds) and is also essentially everlasting (as compatibilists suppose), then we immediately get the result that no proposition whatever is future-indifferent, for any proposition metaphysically entails "God exists," which in turn entails the existence of times after the present. If, on the other hand, God's existence is not thought to be logically necessary, it is still reasonable to suppose that in a theistic universe *every contingent being has essentially the property, "being created by God."* And so, given God's essential everlastingness, we get the result that any proposition entailing the existence of contingent beings likewise metaphysically entails the existence of God and hence of future time. Furthermore, any proposition describing an event of the past, present, or future entails that God will *remember* that event for all time to come—so, no such proposition can be future-indifferent.[13] Finally, I propose as a plausible opinion the view that, once God has undertaken to create a world of contingent beings and, in particular, a world containing rational spirits capable of

---

[13]The Hoffman-Rosenkrantz explication presents a special problem, because, as they say, "on our view it's not enough merely for a state of affairs about a time t to entail a state of affairs about a later time to prevent it from being a hard fact; it must entail the right sort of state of affairs" ("Hard and Soft Facts," p. 430). To be specific, it must entail an *unrestrictedly repeatable present-tense* state of affairs indexed to a time later than the present, where a state of affairs is "unrestrictedly repeatable" just in case it "may obtain, then fail to obtain, then obtain again, indefinitely many times *throughout all of time*" (ibid., p. 423). Now, none of the propositions so far enumerated meets this criterion. The present-tense proposition expressing God's existence can never be false, and a proposition stating that God remembers a certain event becomes true when the event occurs and remains true forever after.

Note, however, that "John drinks a cup of tea at T_1" metaphysically entails
[God believes that John drank a cup of tea exactly n time-units ago] at T_2 (where n time-units = the exact length of time between T_1 and T_2).

The bracketed proposition is true at those times, and only at those times, which are exactly n time-units subsequent to a time at which John is drinking tea—and since John's drinking is unrestrictedly repeatable, so is God's believing this.

communion with himself, it would be inconsistent with his nature for him to annihilate his creation and allow it to fall into nothingness. If this is so, then any proposition entailing the existence of contingent beings (or at least, of created rational spirits) will be non-future-indifferent.

It is clear, then, that if the consistency mentioned in (16) is understood as *metaphysical* consistency, the distinction between hard and soft facts collapses. That consistency, therefore, must be understood as *conceptual* consistency. And in view of the significance that my exposition will attach to conceptual consistency, necessity, and entailment, it may well be that some further account of these notions is called for.

There are at least two classes of conceptually necessary propositions that are relatively unproblematic. There are, first of all, the theorems of formal logic, and there are also propositions that can be reduced to such theorems by the substitution of synonyms. But there is a further important class of examples that are not accounted for in either of these ways. Suppose, for example, that a man stubbornly claims to know something that he at the same time admits to be false. It is clear that this is a *conceptual* mistake, unlike the empirical mistake of someone who takes Kripke's wooden table to be made of ice, or metal, or plastic. The necessary truth that is being denied is not a truth of logic, nor (given the difficulty of defining "knowledge") is it likely to be reducible to one. Nor is the truth "conventional" in any sense but the trivial one according to which all our sentences mean what they do because of our conventions for the use of words. I wish I were able to give a more illuminating account of examples such as this one, but the examples do exist and they must be taken account of by an adequate theory of logic.[14]

And so we have

[14]Those who find conceptual consistency, necessity, and entailment too murky for comfort can obtain an equivalent result by a method developed by John Martin Fischer. He develops a distinction between hard and soft *properties*; soft facts that involve some individual bearing a hard *property* are termed "hard-type soft facts." (For details see John Martin Fischer, "Hard-Type Soft Facts," *Philosophical Review* 95 [1986]: 591–601.)

(H1) An elementary proposition is future-indifferent IFF it is conceptually consistent with there being no times after the present, and also with there being times after the present.

Given this, we can proceed with

(H2) A truth-functional proposition is future-indifferent if each of its constituent propositions is future-indifferent.[15]

It is clear that if a proposition is such that its truth or falsity cannot be affected by anything in the future, the same will be true of that proposition's negation. And if each of two propositions is future-indifferent, so will their conjunction be—and given this, the other truth-functional connectives can be introduced by definition.

(H3) A quantified proposition is future-indifferent IFF each of its possible instances is future-indifferent.

Quantified propositions present a special difficulty, one that is illustrated by (13) and (11) above. The problem is that an apparently innocent-looking quantification may be either true or false in virtue of an instance that refers to the future.[16] Because of this,

---

[15]In the 1989 edition, the connective in (H2) was 'IFF'. But this leads to an inconsistency. Consider: (i) Either it will rain tomorrow, or it will not rain tomorrow. According to the original (H2), (i) is not future-indifferent, because its first disjunct is not future-indifferent. But (i) is conceptually equivalent to (ii) Either it rained yesterday, or it did not rain yesterday. (All tautologies are equivalent.) And since (ii) is future-indifferent, and (i) is equivalent to (ii), it follows from (H4) that (i) is future-indifferent after all; so it both is and is not future-indifferent. Thus, the change of connective. (I am indebted to Lou Goble and Thomas Talbott for pointing out to me this inconsistency.)

[16]An intriguing example is the proposition "All dinosaurs died long ago." Presumably this will be symbolized as

$(x)(Dx \supset x$ died long ago).

Instantiating (with d = Dino), we have

$Dd \supset d$ died long ago.

Clearly, the consequent is future-indifferent. But if we interpret the antecedent as "Dino is a dinosaur," complications arise. The tenseless "is" is equivalent to "is or was or will be," and since the third disjunct is not future-indifferent, neither is the entire disjunction—nor, finally, is the original proposition future-indifferent. A little thought shows that this is as it should be: If "All dinosaurs died long ago" refers to all dinosaurs without temporal restrictions, it could be rendered false by the reappearance of dinosaurs in the future. (Clearly, this is conceptually possible, and it may even be physically possible—if, for example, scientists should recover

Freddoso excludes quantified propositions from being "immediate propositions" (roughly, his counterpart to "true and future-indifferent"),[17] but this move (which Freddoso admits is somewhat counterintuitive) can be avoided as is done in (H3).[18]

(H4) Any proposition that is conceptually equivalent to a future-indifferent proposition is itself future-indifferent.

There is evident, and, along with other benefits, it gives us a way to deal with the contrived predicates discussed above. When confronted with such a predicate, we analyze the predicate and transform the proposition into a more perspicuous (and manageable) form; then we test for future-indifference using (H1) through (H3). This, then, completes our account of future-indifferent propositions; now we are ready for hard facts.

(H5) Any future-indifferent proposition that is true is a hard fact.

No argument will be given for (H5), since it is a common assumption among those who discuss hard and soft facts that true propositions that are "really about the past" are such that it cannot be in anyone's power to render them false. Those compatibilist positions that deny this will be discussed in chapter 7.

(H6) Any conceptually or metaphysically necessary truth is a hard fact.

Evidently, necessary truths are beyond anyone's power to render false.[19] And finally, we have

---

intact dinosaur DNA from fossils.) To avoid this, we must interpret 'Dd' as "Dino *was* a dinosaur" and must read the original proposition as meaning "All dinosaurs *that have ever lived* died long ago."

[17]See, "Accidental Necessity and Logical Determinism," p. 274.

[18]Hoffman and Rosenkrantz, on the other hand, come to grief by admitting quantified propositions as hard facts without the necessary restrictions; see "Hard Facts and Theological Fatalism," p. 435, n. 9.

[19]Thomas Talbott has argued that "with respect to a special class of necessarily true propositions, God does have the (unexercised) power to bring it about that these propositions are false; and similarly, with respect to a special class of necessarily false propositions, he has the (unexercised) power to bring it about that these propositions are true" ("On the Divine Nature and the Nature of Divine Free-

(H7) Any proposition entailed (conceptually or metaphysically) by one or more hard facts is itself a hard fact.

This, again, is evident, and it completes our explication. Given these principles, what conclusions can we draw about the examples given earlier in this section? Clearly, (10) will be future-indifferent whereas (4) will not. (11) also will be future-indifferent, since it conceptually entails nothing about the truth or falsity of the embedded proposition. (12) is equivalent to

(17)   David said yesterday that Sandra will arrive tomorrow, and Sandra will arrive tomorrow.

The first conjunct is future-indifferent, but the second is not, nor is the proposition as a whole. (13) is equivalent to

(18) $\sim(\exists p)((\text{David said yesterday that } p) \ \& \ \sim p)$.

When (18) is instantiated, the first conjunct will be future-indifferent, but for many values of 'p' the second will not. So (13) and (18) are not future-indifferent. In (15) the first disjunct is future-indifferent but the second is not, so (15) is not future-indifferent. It will, however, be a hard fact in virtue of (H7), if the first disjunct is true.

Given the complexity of (H1)-(H7), we cannot claim that the explication that has been given is self-evident or obviously correct. I do claim that it is clear, plausible, and well-motivated, and if deficiencies should be discovered, I am reasonably confident that they can be remedied in ways that preserve the thrust of what has been done here. The problem is inherently complex, and it is desirable that a variety of different attempts should be made to solve it.

---

dom," *Faith and Philosophy* 5 [1988]: 3). Such powers, of course, would be, not only unexercised, but *necessarily* unexercised. Whether it is advisable to speak of "powers" in this connection strikes me as dubious; one wonders what the difference is supposed to be between having a necessarily unexercised power to do something, and lacking such a power. In any case, the "powers" discussed in this book should all be understood as powers whose exercise is (at least) logically possible.

Applying the Distinction

But now it is time to put the distinction between hard and soft facts to work. What we want to know, of course, is whether

(C3) God has always believed that Clarence will have a cheese omelet tomorrow

is a hard fact or a soft fact. If it is hard, then it shares in the necessity of the past, and compatibilism is in deep trouble. If, on the other hand, (C3) should turn out to be a *soft* fact about the past, the victory at this stage goes to compatibilism.

In order to answer this, we need to know what is expressed by the word 'God.' Does it function simply as a nonconnotative proper name, which serves to refer to the bearer but conveys no information about him? Or is 'God' like a title or a common noun in that it expresses something about the nature and status of the divine being? I am strongly inclined to accept the latter view and to say that the word 'God' expresses those properties that are definitionally included in our conception of God. If so, then

(A2) Necessarily, if God has always believed that a certain thing will happen, then that thing will happen

is not only metaphysically necessary but also conceptually necessary. But if that is so, then (C3) conceptually entails

(19) Clarence will have a cheese omelet tomorrow.

But then (C3) cannot be future-indifferent, and the compatibilist appears to have triumphed.

But the compatibilist should not be in too great a hurry to declare himself the winner. Before doing so, he should note that, by parallel reasoning, neither will "God exists" and "God created the universe out of nothing" be future-indifferent, for, God being essentially everlasting, both entail the existence of times after the present. But it is reasonable to suppose that such propositions as these are *soft* facts? The intention of the distinction between soft and hard facts was to distinguish between those propositions that are such that it might be in someone's power to make them false, from those for which this is impossible. But it is absurd—isn't it?—to suggest that anyone, even God, should now have the power to bring it about that God does not exist or that he did not create the universe out of nothing. Do we then need a third category of facts? A colleague suggested to me that besides hard facts and soft facts, there may also be facts sunny-side up. But why stop there? Why not scrambled facts, poached facts, and even facts Benedict?

There is a better way. Consider the name 'Yahweh,' which was used by the ancient Hebrews to refer to their God. They used this name (as a reading of Genesis will confirm) with no thought or connotation of such metaphysical attributes as essential omniscience, essential everlastingness, and the like. For a variety of reasons, this name is not in common use among present-day Jews or Christians, but nothing prevents us from reviving its use for a special purpose. And as we do so, we will take care to avoid importing into the name's significance such metaphysical notions as essential everlastingness. We will use the name, as the ancient Hebrews did, simply as a nonconnotative proper name referring to that individual who in fact was, and is, the God of Abraham, Isaac, and Jacob.

Given this use of the name 'Yahweh,' the proposition "Yahweh exists" is future-indifferent; unlike "God exists," it does not conceptually entail anything about the existence of times later than the present. But by the same token,

(20)   Yahweh has always believed that Clarence will have a cheese omelet tomorrow

is a future-indifferent proposition; unlike (C3), it does not conceptually entail anything about Clarence's breakfast tomorrow, or Clarence's existence tomorrow, or even about whether there will *be* a tomorrow. And since we are assuming that (20) is true, it will also be a hard fact.[20]

[20]An anonymous reviewer for Cornell University Press points out that, following this strategy, almost any proposition can be shown to be a hard fact *if we introduce nonconnotative proper names for times and properties.* For example, let 'worflung' be a nonconnotative proper name for the property of being such that one

Now the truth of (20), by itself, will not make (19) a hard fact. But now consider

(21)   If Yahweh exists, Yahweh is God.

This proposition is not conceptually necessary; its truth is not implied by the meanings of the terms in which it is expressed. And the proposition will not be future-indifferent, because its consequent conceptually entails God's existence. But (21) assuredly is a *metaphysically* necessary truth: it expresses an *essential property* of Yahweh. There is no possible world in which Yahweh exists but is not God; no one, not even God himself and certainly no human being, could bring it about that Yahweh exists but is not God. So although (21) is not a future-indifferent proposition, it is, in virtue of (H6), a hard fact.

And now the denouement becomes clear. As hard facts, we have the following:

(20)   Yahweh has always believed that Clarence will have a cheese omelet tomorrow.
(21)   If Yahweh exists, Yahweh is God.
(A2)   Necessarily, if God has always believed that a certain thing will happen, then that thing will happen.

But of course, (20) and (21) jointly entail

(C3)   God has always believed that Clarence will have a cheese omelet tomorrow.

---

will have written the book *God, Time, and Knowledge* within ten years. Then the proposition "Hasker has worflung," expressed in 1978, was future-indifferent and expressed a hard fact. And as the reviewer states, "logical fatalism looms." (Jonathan Kvanvig has pointed out to me that the same result can be obtained if we introduce proper names for *propositions* [personal communication].)

My response is straightforward: Natural languages, including English, do not *have* nonconnotative proper names for times and properties (the free use of schematic letters in formal logic should not deceive us). And for the purposes of this explication of hard facts, I stipulate that no such proper names for times, properties, and propositions shall be introduced. I do not think this restriction is arbitrary, because I do not think the absence of such names in natural languages is arbitrary. But further pursuit of this topic must await another occasion.

And this, together with (A2), entails

(19)   Clarence will have a cheese omelet tomorrow.

So (19), which is jointly entailed by a set of hard facts, is itself a
hard fact; it is now unpreventable, so that it is utterly impossible
that anyone at all, even God himself, should now have the power
to bring it about that Clarence does not eat that omelet for breakfast tomorrow.

This triumph of incompatibilism, to be sure, has come about as
a result of the specific analysis of the hard fact–soft fact distinction
given above. Because of this, the compatibilist may wonder about
the possibility of developing an alternative analysis according to
which (C3) and (19) will turn out to be soft facts after all. I am
convinced that this is a vain hope. For consider

(22)   Susan believed this morning that Clarence will have a
       cheese omelet tomorrow.

A proposition such as (22) has to qualify as a hard fact about the past
on *any* acceptable analysis of the distinction. As Freddoso has said,

> The past hopes, fears, beliefs, desires, predictions, etc. of historical
> agents are clearly unalterable elements of our past and must be
> counted as part of our history. . . . No world *w* can claim to share
> the same history with our world now if in *w* Chamberlain did not
> fear that Hitler would not keep his word or if in *w* Ernie Banks did
> not hope (and predict) every spring that the Cubs would win the
> pennant.[21]

So any adequate analysis must classify (22) as a hard fact. But the
only relevant difference between (22) and (C3) lies in the replacement of 'Mary' with 'God.' If, however, we employ the name
'Yahweh' instead of 'God,' we arrive at

(20)   Yahweh has always believed that Clarence will have a
       cheese omelet tomorrow,

---

[21]"Accidental Necessity and Logical Determinism," p. 268.

which is similar to (22) in all logically relevant respects, and must like (22) be classified as a hard fact.[22] We conclude, then, that the distinction between hard and soft facts cannot solve the problem of theological fatalism.

But even if the claim that God's beliefs are soft facts must be given up, it would be overly optimistic to expect the compatibilist at this point to fold his tents and steal silently away. For compatibilists have also made claims about powers we have over the past—claims that need not depend on the distinction between hard and soft facts. To these claims we now turn.

[22]Freddoso now agrees with this; he now accepts that facts about God's past beliefs are hard facts about the past (see his Introduction to Molina, *On Divine Foreknowledge (Part IV of the Concordia)*, trans. Alfred J. Freddos [Ithaca, N.Y.: Cornell University Press, 1988], sec. 4.5). His response is rather to deny that the class of hard facts is closed under entailment; that is, he denies (H7) and the power entailment principles. In his own words, he has undergone a "conversion from Ockhamism to Molinism" (ibid.) A bit more will be said about Molinism in the next chapter.

[6]

Counterfactual Power
over the Past

If compatibilism is to be true, we must in some way have power over the past—specifically, over the beliefs God has held in the past. But what sort of power is this? One answer to this, advanced by Alvin Plantinga[1] but since endorsed by a number of other philosophers, is that the power we have over the past is a power that is most accurately expressed in terms of counterfactual propositions—thus, *counterfactual power over the past*. Because this position emerged into prominence in the controversy between Plantinga and Nelson Pike, the first section of this chapter is devoted to an exposition of that discussion and of Plantinga's resulting position.[2] In the second section we examine certain logical principles, known here as *power entailment principles*, which are crucial to the evalua-

---

[1]The notion that power over the past can be expressed counterfactually surfaced in John Turk Sanders's paper "Of God and Freedom" (*Philosophical Review* 75 [1966]), but the influence of this idea seems to have derived mainly from Plantinga's use of it.

[2]Pike's argument is set forth in his article "Divine Omniscience and Voluntary Action," *Philosophical Review* 74 (1965): 27–46; Plantinga's reply is found in *God, Freedom and Evil* (New York: Harper, 1974), pp. 66–73. In quotations from Pike and Plantinga, the original numbering of the propositions is maintained. So that distracting variations can be avoided, all of the formulas in this chapter are set in normal-size type and the style of the schematic letters has been altered to conform to that of the present volume.

tion of Plantinga's position. The third section inquires further concerning the rational acceptability of these principles.

Pike versus Plantinga

In Pike's article "Divine Omniscience and Voluntary Action," a pivotal role is played by the following premise:

(6)   If God existed at T_1 and if God believed at T_1 that Jones
       would do X at T_2, then if it was within Jones' power at T_2
       to refrain from doing X, then (1) it was within Jones'
       power at T_2 to do something that would have brought it
       about that God held a false belief at T_1, or (2) it was within
       Jones' power at T_2 to do something which would have
       brought it about that God did not hold the belief He held at
       T_1, or (3) it was within Jones' power at T_2 to do something
       that would have brought it about that any person who
       believed at T_1 that Jones would do X at T_2 (one of whom
       was, by hypothesis, God) held a false belief and thus was
       not God—that is, that God (who by hypothesis existed at
       T_1) did not exist at T_1.[3]

Pike's argument contains three additional premises, each of which states that the kinds of powers attributed to Jones in subpoints (1)–(3) of (6) are such that no one can have them; thus, he is able to conclude that under the stated conditions it cannot be in Jones's power at T_2 to refrain from doing X. The additional premises are as follows:

(3)   It is not within one's power at a given time to do something having a description that is logically contradictory.
(4)   It is not within one's power at a given time to do something that would bring it about that someone who held a certain belief at a time prior to the time in question did not hold that belief at the time prior to the time in question.

---

[3]"Divine Omniscience and Voluntary Action," p. 34.

(5)   It is not within one's power at a given time to do something that would bring it about that a person who existed
at an earlier time did not exist at that earlier time.[4]

In his response to Pike's argument Plantinga does not challenge
the premises (3)–(5); he agrees that Jones cannot have any of the
powers ruled out by those premises.[5] Plantinga's challenge is directed at (6), which he regards as false on the grounds that subpoints (1)–(3) of (6) do not exhaust the possible ways in which
Jones might have the power at T_2 to refrain from doing X. Pike
himself had admitted, "I do not know how to argue that these are
the only alternatives, but I have been unable to find another."[6]
Plantinga comes to his assistance at this point, pointing out not one
but three additional alternatives—each corresponding to one of the
subpoints (1)–(3)—each of which would enable Jones to have the
power to refrain from doing X at T_2 without violating the constraints imposed by premises (3)–(5). These additional alternatives
are not, however, independent of each other, and for our purposes
it will be sufficient to examine the one that corresponds to sub-
point (2) of (6).
    In discussing (6) Plantinga suggests that it is Pike's view that

(51)   God existed at T_1, and God believed at T_1 that Jones
would do X at T_2, and it was within Jones's power to
refrain from doing X at T_2

entails

(53)   It was within Jones's power at T_2 to do something that
would have brought it about that God did not hold the
belief He did hold at T_1.

---

[4]Ibid., p. 33.
[5]"Premises 3–5 . . . seem correct" (ibid., p. 69).
[6]"Divine Omniscience and Voluntary Action," p. 35.

Plantinga responds: "Here the first problem is one of understand-ing. How are we to take this proposition?" It might, conceivably, mean the same as

(53a) It was within Jones's power at T_2 to do something such that if he had done it, then at T_1 God would have held a certain belief and also *not* held that belief.

Plantinga goes on to say that "(53a) is obviously and resoundingly false, but there is no reason whatever to think that (51) entails it. What (51) entails is rather

(53b) It was within Jones's power at T_2 to do something such that if he had done it, then God would not have held a belief that in fact he did hold.

This follows from (51) but is perfectly innocent."[7]

Now at this point we, as readers of Plantinga, are also con-fronted with a problem of understanding. Since Plantinga has ac-cepted

(4)   It is not within one's power at a given time to do some-thing that would bring it about that someone who held a certain belief at a time prior to the time in question did not hold that belief at the time prior to the time in question,

it would seem that he should also say that (53) is simply *false*, since it attributes to Jones a power that, according to (4), no one can have. In response to an inquiry, Plantinga has clarified his meaning on this point. He writes: "Taken at what I then thought to be the face value interpretation, what (4) says is that a certain state of affairs:

> *that someone who held a belief at a certain time did not hold*
> *that belief at that time*

---

[7]*God, Freedom and Evil*, pp. 70–71.

is such that no one has the power to bring it about."[8] That is, Plantinga, in accepting (4), understood it as

(4′)   It is not within one's power at a given time to do something that would bring it about that someone who held a certain belief at a time prior to the time in question *also* did *not* hold that belief at the time prior to the time in question.

Thus interpreted, of course, (4) is obviously true. But when we give a parallel interpretation to (53), we get (53a), which, as Plantinga says, is "absurd and probably not what Pike meant."[9] It occurred to Plantinga, however, that (53) might instead be interpreted as (53b), which is "perfectly innocent." And of course, if we go back and reinterpret (4) as

(4*)   If someone held a certain belief at a previous time, it is not within one's power to do something such that, were one to do it, that person would not have held that belief at that previous time,

Plantinga would *not* accept this; on the contrary, he holds that we *do* have the kind of power over God's past beliefs that (4*) says we do not have.

Now, the difficulty with all this is that *neither* of Plantinga's interpretations of (53) is adequate or acceptable. (53a) is, in Plantinga's words, "absurd and probably not what Pike meant."[10] But, neither is (53b) adequate. In general,

A brings it about that P

entails, but is not entailed by

A does something such that, were she to do it, "P" would be true.

[8]Personal communication.
[9]Ibid.
[10]I think it is fairly clear that Plantinga's initial interpretation of (4) was mistaken. (4) proclaims something to be impossible, but what? One candidate is

The core idea in the notion of "bringing about" is the notion of something's being the case *in consequence of* what an agent does—but that notion of "consequence" need not be involved at all in counterfactual power. (That is to say, "counterfactual power" with respect to some state of affairs need not involve *power* over that state of affairs at all.) It is impossible that it be the case that there are two events, each of which is *brought about* by the other, but there are many instances of two events, each of which is such that, were it to occur, the other would occur as well.

I believe Plantinga recognizes that, in general, "power to bring about" and "counterfactual power" are not equivalent; in replacing (53) with (53b), he writes,

> I was thinking instead just of the context of Pike's argument: there all I was prepared to agree to was that [Jones] had the power to do something such that if he were to do it, then God would not have believed what in fact he did believe. If Pike meant something stronger than that (when he said that [Jones] could do something that would bring it about that God did not hold the belief he did hold), then I wouldn't accept the premiss—not, at any rate, without further specification as to what this more would be. [11]

But, we may wonder, why is it that Plantinga is uncomfortable with the "bringing about" language? His answer is as follows:

> [My] main difficulty with the expression 'bring it about' is that I am inclined to think it has a strong *causal* association, at least in any case where the context doesn't prevent it. And (as you note) I don't think even God could now have the power to *cause* it to be the case that

---

An agent has it in her power at T_2 to bring it about that: $(\exists x)(x$ believed that P at T_1 and also did not believe that P at T_1).
Another candidate for what (4) rules out is

$(\exists x)(x$ believed that P at T_1, and an agent has it in her power at T_2 to bring it about that x did not believe P at T_1).

Plantinga was aware of both possibilities but opted for the first. The reason I think this was wrong is that it makes no essential use of the *temporal relationships* that are an important part of Pike's (4). (Note the repetition of "a time prior to the time in question.") The fact that T_1 is an *earlier* time than T_2 is immaterial for the first interpretation given, but it is crucial for the second.

[11]Personal communication.

Abraham did not exist, although I think even you and I could now have the power to do something such that if we were to do it, then Abraham would not have existed.[12]

Plantinga's concern here is surely understandable. Still, one may wonder whether two (or three) different questions are being conflated. One question is what it would *mean* to speak of a person's bringing about God's past belief in the way spelled out in (53). A second question is whether (53) really does follow from (51). Yet a third question is whether (53) could possibly be *true*. It would seem that as a matter of proper philosophical procedure we should settle the first two questions—about the *meaning* of (53), and about the *entailment* of (53) by (51)—independently of the third question, about the possible *truth* of (53).

The present question, then, is not whether anyone actually *has* the power specified in (53), but whether (51) *entails* that someone has this power. And this question is not answered by stating that (51) entails that Jones has some *other* power, such as the one specified in (53b). *That* is true enough, but what we really need to know is, *does (51) entail (53), or doesn't it?*

In any case, we are now able to see more clearly what Plantinga is willing to accept with regard to power over God's past beliefs. He is *not* willing to affirm that, if God has always believed a certain thing, it is in our power to *bring about* that God has not always believed that thing. What he *does* affirm is that, if God has always believed a certain thing, it may nevertheless be in our power to *do something, such that were we to do it, God would not have believed that thing*. In stating this power, the counterfactual form is essential: it is *counterfactual power over the past.*

Nor is Jones's power with respect to the past limited to God's past beliefs. A world in which Jones refrained from doing X would necessarily be different from the actual world with respect to God's past beliefs about what Jones would do, but it might well be different in other respects as well. For if God had known that, if placed in the appropriate circumstances, Jones would refrain from doing

[12]Personal communication.

X, he might well have arranged other things differently than they are in the actual world. To take Plantinga's own example:

> It is possible (though no doubt unlikely) that there is something you can do such that if you were to do it, then Abraham would never have existed. For perhaps you will be confronted with a decision of great importance—so important that one of the alternatives is such that if you were to choose *it*, then the course of human history would have been quite different from what in fact it is. Further-more, it is possible that if God had foreseen that you would choose *that* alternative, he would have acted very differently. Perhaps he would have created different persons; perhaps, indeed, he would not have created Abraham. So it is possible that there is an action such that it is within your power to perform it and such that if you were to perform it, then God would not have created Abraham.[13]

So the scope of our power over the past is, potentially at least, very extensive. Yet this is still *counterfactual* power over the past, rather than power to *bring about* the past. As Plantinga says:

> Possibly there is something I can do such that, if I were to do it, then Abraham would not have existed; but it is not possible—is it?—that I now *cause* Abraham not to have existed.[14]

And his subsequent remarks indicate that, in his view, not even God now has it in his power to cause Abraham not to have existed. So much of the past may lie within our power, but it is counterfac-tual power and not power to causally affect the past.

It should be noted here that these latter claims—claims about our power to affect Abraham's existence, and the like—are grounded in the theory of middle knowledge, which we have already seen reason to reject. If God does not have middle knowl-edge, then some of Plantinga's otherwise reasonable-sounding claims about our powers may come into question. But the claim that is central to the argument of the present chapter—the claim

---

[13] "On Ockham's Way Out," *Faith and Philosophy* 3 (1986): 257.
[14]Ibid., p. 258.

that our power over the past is *counterfactual* power rather than power to *bring about* past events—does *not* depend on middle knowledge. So let us try at this point to set out that claim clearly, so as to be able to see what needs to be done in order to resolve the disagreement.

. As we have seen, what Plantinga objects to in Pike's argument is Pike's claim that

> (51) God existed at T_1, and God believed at T_1 that Jones would do X at T_2, and it was within Jones's power to refrain from doing X at T_2

entails

> (53) It was within Jones's power at T_2 to do something that would have brought it about that God did not hold the belief He did hold at T_1.

Plantinga, professing to be perplexed with (53), insists on replacing it with the "perfectly innocent"

> (53b) It was within Jones's power at T_2 to do something such that if he had done it, then God would not have held a belief that in fact he did hold.

Now, is this replacement justified? If it is, then Plantinga would seem to be correct in his assertion that the kind of power over the past required by compatibilism is not the power to *bring about* God's past beliefs but rather the power to do something, such that if we were to do it, God would have held a different belief—that is, the required sort of power is *counterfactual power over the past*. If, on the other hand, the replacement is *not* justified, then Plantinga's position will have to be thoroughly reconsidered.

Power Entailment Principles

It is already evident that the notion of "bringing about" is going to play a crucial role in the present discussion. That being the case, it seems prudent, to say the least, to devote a bit of effort to clarifying this notion and distinguishing it from other related notions.[15] Consider, then, the following three formulas (with the letters designating events):

A causes B.
A brings about B.
A occurs, and if A were to occur, then B would occur.

There is a problem about how to characterize the relation between A and B according to this third formula. Up until this point we have been speaking of "counterfactual power," but now that becomes doubly problematic: First, because we have in these formulas not merely the *power* to bring something about but the *actual* coming to pass of the thing in question. And second, because, as noted above, "counterfactual power" over a thing need not involve *power* over that thing at all. In order to circumvent this, we shall say that there is a *relation of counterfactual dependence* between A and B.

The first thing to be said about our three formulas is that they are arranged in order of decreasing logical strength: If A *causes B*, this entails that A *brings about B*, and if A *brings about B*, this entails that A and B stand in a relation of *counterfactual dependence*.[16] But in neither case does the reverse entailment hold.

That bringing about is different from counterfactual dependence is presumably not in question—it is, after all, this very difference that motivated the move to "counterfactual power" in the first

[15]In both "Foreknowledge and Necessity" (*Faith and Philosophy* 2 [1985]: 121–57) and "A Refutation of Middle Knowledge" (*Noûs* 20 [1986]: 545–57), I took 'bringing about' as an undefined primitive and proceeded to make use of the notion without engaging in a discussion about it. Not surprisingly, this has led to a good deal of confusion and misunderstanding. I am particularly indebted to Thomas Flint ("Hasker's 'Refutation' of Middle Knowledge," unpublished) for making clear to me the need for more explanation at this point.

[16]Actually, if A brings about B, this entails that they stand in a counterfactual relationship that is considerably more complex than is indicated by the third formula; the relationship in question is the one I have attempted to spell out by proposition (16) in chapter 2. But the complications of this need not concern us now.

place. Still, it is worth taking the trouble to point out *how* the two are different. The most important features of bringing about have already been mentioned: If *A* brings about *B*, then we have an *asymmetrical* (and therefore also *irreflexive*) relation in which *B* is a *consequence* of *A*. *It is important to see that none of this is true of the counterfactual dependence relation.* If *A* and *B* stand in the relation of counterfactual dependence, then *A* may be a consequence of *B*, or *B* of *A*, or they may both be a consequence of some third event. (It is because of this that I speak of "the counterfactual dependence relation" rather than saying straight out that *B* counterfactually depends on *A*.) The counterfactual dependence relation is reflexive (it is always true that if *A* were to occur, *A* would occur), and although it is not necessarily symmetrical, it is not asymmetrical either; there are many instances in which it is true both that if *A* were to occur, then *B* would occur, and that if *B* were to occur then *A* would occur.

I believe it is important to emphasize this, because in many cases those who speak in terms of counterfactual dependence seem to read into the relation more than it strictly contains. Counterfactual dependence by itself tells us remarkably little about the nature of the relationship between the events in question. The events *A* and *B* may be identical, or *B* may be entailed by *A*, or *B* may be a causal consequence of *A*, or *B* may be a necessary causal condition for *A*—and there are quite a few other possibilities. It is, I repeat, important to see this; only if we see how little really is involved in counterfactual dependence will we feel the force of the motivation to go beyond counterfactual dependence to something more determinate.

Bringing about, then, is clearly distinct from counterfactual dependence, but is it also distinct from causation? We have already noted Plantinga's inclination to think that 'bring it about' "has a strong *causal* association," and he is certainly not alone in this. Freddoso, indeed, makes the same point more strongly: "I would . . . say that the core idea in the notion of 'bringing about' is something's being *the causal effect of an agent's exercising some causal power.*"[17] For Freddoso, then, "bringing about" just *is* causation, or perhaps a subspecies of causation.

[17]Personal communication.

Plantinga's point need not be wholly rejected: No doubt, in very many cases what "brings about" an event *is* the event's cause, and if this is true, then the existence of an "association" between the two notions is not surprising. But that bringing about is *always* causing simply does not seem to be true. In an important paper Jaegwon Kim argues that "noncausal dependency relations are pervasively present in the web of events, and it is important to understand their nature, their interrelations, and their relation to the causal relation if we are ever to have a clear and complete picture of the ways in which events hang together in the world."[18] One of his examples is particularly striking: The jailor who gave poison to Socrates brought about Socrates's death. In doing this he also brought about Xantippe's becoming a widow. But whereas the connection between the jailor's action and the death is straightforwardly causal, the connection between the death and Xantippe's widowhood does not seem to be causal. One could have *prevented* the death from occurring at that time by taking appropriate countermeasures—say, by knocking the poison out of Socrates's hand, or perhaps by providing an antidote. But given the death, nothing we could have done for Xantippe—no conceivable form of causal isolation, for instance—could have prevented her widowhood. It is not, in Freddoso's words, "the causal effect of an agent's exercising some causal power." Yet between her widowhood and Socrates's death there exists an *asymmetrical relation* in virtue of which the widowhood is a *consequence* of the death; what we have here, then, is a case of bringing about which is not causal.[19]

Kim gives a number of other examples, but most significant for our purposes may be a case he does not examine. If we hold to the omnitemporality of truth, then there seems no alternative to saying that in performing an action today I make it the case that certain propositions were true in the past, that someone who expressed those propositions spoke truly, and the like. It would be perverse to speak of this as causation, thus assimilating these very

---

[18]Jaegwon Kim, "Noncausal Connections," *Noûs* 8 (1974): 41.

[19]One may then be moved to ask: What precisely is it in causal dependence which goes beyond what is present in a bringing about that is not causal? This is one of the questions that Kim places on the agenda but does not answer, and I also have no illuminating answer to give. Once again, causality escapes the net of analysis!

ordinary cases to the highly dubious case of *exerting causal influence*
in the past. Yet the relation between my action and the past truth
of your words is not mere counterfactual dependence, for this, as
we have seen, fails entirely to capture the fact that what you said
was true *because of* what I later did, and not vice versa. Once again,
we have a case of bringing about which is not causal.

With these considerations in view, we are now in a position to
return to the question that ended the previous section: In the context of the Pike-Plantinga argument, does (51) entail (53) or
doesn't it?

Philip Quinn, in a paper discussing this controversy, has suggested a way in which this question might be settled. If the incompatibilist could vindicate a logical principle of a certain type (I call
such principles *power entailment principles*), he could then use it to
justify such inferences as the one from (51) to (53). Quinn himself
proposes two candidates for such a principle, of which the first is

(PEP1) If it is within S's power to bring it about that *P* and if that *P*
entails that Q, then it is within S's power to bring it about
that Q.[20]

(PEP1) is obviously false: Neil Armstrong's being the first human
to walk on the moon entails that $2 + 2 = 4$, but neither Armstrong
nor anyone else has ever had the power to bring it about that this
arithmetical proposition is true. Nor are matters any better for

(PEP2) If it is within S's power to bring it about that *P* and if that *P*
entails that Q and if it is contingent that Q, then it is within
S's power to bring it about that Q.[21]

For Neil Armstrong's being the first human to walk on the moon
entails that there is a moon, but certainly Armstrong never had the
power to bring *that* about. At this point Quinn gives up the search
for a true power entailment principle: he says, "I have been unable

[20]Philip L. Quinn, "Plantinga on Foreknowledge and Freedom," in James E.
Tomberlin and Peter van Inwagen, eds., *Alvin Plantinga*, Profiles vol. 5 (Dordrecht: D. Riedel, 1985), p. 284.
[21]Ibid., p. 285.

to discover such a principle, and I very much doubt that there is one."[22]

The quest for such a principle has been taken up by Thomas Talbott. After reviewing the principle we have labeled (PEP1) and exhibiting its deficiencies, he proposes one of his own:

(PEP3) If (a) it is within S's power to bring it about that "P" is true and (b) it is within S's power to bring it about that "P" is false and (c) "P" entails "Q" and "not-P" entails "not-Q", then it is within S's power to bring it about that "Q" is true.[23]

About this principle Talbott says that it "seems not only true but obviously true. Where "P" and "Q" are logically equivalent, it could hardly be up to me whether or not "P" is true unless it were also up to me whether or not "Q" is true."[24] It seems to me that this is absolutely correct.[25] And since, given Plantinga's assumption that God is a logically necessary, essentially omniscient being, "P" is equivalent to "God has always believed that "P"," it follows that *(PEP3) shows that Plantinga's position is wrong.*

[22]Ibid. (But see n. 26 below.)

[23]Thomas B. Talbott, "On Divine Foreknowledge and Bringing About the Past," *Philosophy and Phenomenological Research* 46 (1986): 458. I have modified Talbott's formulation by enclosing his schematic letters in quotation marks; he uses these letters in such a way that their substituends are not *sentences*, but rather *referring expressions* designating propositions.

[24]Ibid., p. 458.

[25]Both Freddoso (personal communication) and Thomas Flint attack Talbott's comment in support of (PEP3); Flint says:

If two propositions are logically equivalent and I have power over the truth of one of them (i.e., its truth is up to me), then it does seem clear that the truth of the other one is within my power as well; what does not seem clear is that I need to have power in the same sense of "power" over the second as over the first. Suppose I have causal power over the truth of one of two logically equivalent propositions; is it not sufficient that I have counterfactual power over the other? Is that not enough for me to say that each of them is such that its truth is up to me? ("In Defense of Theological Compatibilism," *Faith and Philosophy*, forthcoming).

The answer to this should be clear in the light of our previous discussion of "bringing about." On the one hand, power to bring about need not be *causal* power; on the other hand, the counterfactual dependency relation (and therefore also "counterfactual power") is *not* "enough for me to say that each of them is such that its truth is up to me."

Talbott recognizes this, but he still goes on to look for a stronger principle, because there are valid cases of power entailment that are not instances of (PEP3). For instance, my having the power to draw a triangle certainly entails my having the power to draw a plane figure, in spite of the fact that "I draw a triangle" and "I draw a plane figure" are not equivalent. But a principle to cover this case is indeed available: it is

(PEP4) If (*a*) it is within S's power to bring it about that "*P*" is true, (*b*) "*P*" entails "*Q*," and (*c*) "*Q*" is not a necessary condition of S's having the power to bring it about that "*P*" is true, then it is within S's power to bring it about that "*Q*" is true.[26]

Talbott's proof of this principle is both elegant and conclusive:

> If "*P*" entails "*Q*," then it's within the power of a person S to bring it about that "*P*" is true *only if* at least one of these conditions is met: either "*Q*" is true *or*, if not true, then it's within S's power to bring it about that "*Q*" is true. Suppose, then, that "*P*" entails "*Q*" and it's *not* within S's power to bring it about that "*Q*" is true. It immediately follows that, unless "*Q*" is true, it's not within S's power to bring it about that "*P*" is true either; it follows, in other words, that "*Q*" is a necessary condition of S's having the power to bring it about that "*P*" is true.[27]

It should be noted that, as Talbott says, "the kind of necessary condition specified in (c) is not a logically necessary condition. . . . [F]or those of us who are not omnipotent, not all the necessary conditions of our having the power to do something are logically necessary conditions."[28]

Now, apply this to (51). Is God's having believed at T_1 that Jones would refrain from doing X at T_2 a necessary condition of Jones's having the power to refrain from doing X at T_2? If it is, then it follows immediately that Jones did not have this power.

[26]Talbott, "On Divine Foreknowledge," p. 460.
[27]Ibid., p. 460. Talbott credits William Rowe with assistance in formulating this principle (ibid., p. 460n.).
[28]Ibid., pp. 460–61.

But (51) says that he *did* have such a power, so we are forced to the other alternative: that Jones at T_2 had it in his power to bring it about that God did not hold the belief he did hold at T_1. And this, of course, is just what (53) says. So (51) *does* entail (53); of that there can be no reasonable doubt.

These power entailment principles show that, with respect to our power over God's past beliefs, the distinction between counterfactual power over the past and power to bring about the past collapses: it is a distinction that fails to distinguish. And the defense for compatibilism considered in this chapter, which is based on that distinction, collapses along with it.

Can the Power Entailment Principles Be Proved?

In view of the importance attached to the power entailment principles, it is reasonable to ask whether their truth has been or can be definitively established. I have professed myself satisfied with the reasoning with which Talbott supports his principles, but one might be pardoned for hesitating, especially in view of the ease with which counterexamples can appear from unexpected quarters.[29] (PEP3) and (PEP4) are both rather too complex to be comfortably assessed as self-evident; it would seem desirable, to say the least, that both principles should be incorporated into an axiomatic system in which they could be derived from simpler and more evident premises.

There is merit in this line of thought, yet it is not altogether compelling. Whenever a new branch of logic is being developed, it seems inevitable that discussion will center on particular logical principles—principles that to some will seem self-evident, and to others patently objectionable. (Think, for example, of the discussions concerning the characteristic axiom of S5, the Barcan For-

---

[29]For instance, suppose we omit from (PEP3) the clause "(*b*) it is within S's power to bring it about that "*P*" is false." The resulting principle, though initially plausible, may be subject to counterexamples. Suppose, for instance, that God has promised unconditionally at T_1 that he will perform X at T_2. Then at T_2 God has it in his power to bring about that he does X, but not that he refrains from X, nor does he have it in his power at T_2 to bring it about that at T_1 he promised to do X at T_2.

mula in quantified modal logic, and the principle of conditional excluded middle in counterfactual logic.) The acceptability of such controverted principles is not necessarily determined by their inclusion in a formal system; it tends to be the case, rather, that formal systems are accepted or rejected depending on whether they sanction the "right" principles. So although the development of an axiomatic system for power entailment may be a worthy goal, it is by no means a prerequisite for the rational acceptance of the power entailment principles.

There is also this to be considered: If such a system were to be devised, there is no particular reason to think that its axioms would be a great deal simpler than the principles we now have. What is distinctive about the power entailment principles is that they establish interrelations between a number of different concepts, including possibility, entailment, an agent's bringing about a state of affairs (or the truth of a proposition), an agent's having the power to do this, and—in the case of (PEP4)—the concept of a necessary condition of an agent's having such a power. Now, some of these notions may turn out to be interdefinable, but it is unlikely that all of them will. And an axiomatic system for this part of logic would have to contain an axiom establishing a relationship between all or most of these concepts; it seems unlikely that such an axiom would be especially simple.

Still, some further moves may be possible. Consider the following principle:

(PEP5) If it is in S's power to bring it about that P, and "P" entails "Q" and "Q" is false, then it is in S's power to bring it about that Q.[30]

This principle is somewhat simpler than either of Talbott's, but if it is accepted, then (PEP4) is easily derived. (Indeed, the principle may readily be seen to be implicit in Talbott's argument for

[30]I first formulated this principle during Alvin Plantinga's 1978 NEH seminar, "Evil and Foundationalism," and presented it at the seminar as part of an unpublished paper entitled "Pike vs. Plantinga on Foreknowledge." (It should be noted that this is *not* the principle that in my "Foreknowledge and Necessity" was labeled "(PEP5)"; *that* principle plays no part in the present discussion.)

[PEP4].) I suggest that upon careful consideration it is not at all unreasonable to claim self-evidence for (PEP5). If "*P*" entails "*Q*," then every *P*-world is also a *Q*-world. Now, if "*Q*" is false, and if I cannot bring it about that any *Q*-world is actual (and this is what it is, to be unable to bring it about that *Q*), then how can I possibly have the power to bring it about that some *P*-world (which of course, is also a *Q*-world) is actual?[31] One cannot escape some complexity in formulation, to be sure, but the underlying logical situation is crystal clear.[32]

Yet there is more. By applying a couple of trivial logical transformations to (PEP5), we get

(PEP6)   If "*P*" is true and entails "*Q*," then if it is not in S's power to bring it about that "*P*" is false, it is not in S's power to bring it about that "*Q*" is false.

---

[31]Both Freddoso and David Basinger suggest that (PEP5) be replaced with the following principle:
(PEP5*) If it is in S's power to bring it about that *P*, and "*P*" entails "*Q*" and "*Q*" is false, then it is S's power to do something such that if S were to do it, "*Q*" would be true. (Freddoso, personal communication; Basinger's version is found in "Middle Knowledge and Human Freedom: Some Clarifications," *Faith and Philosophy* 4 [1987]: 334.)
The merit of this is supposed to be that it is more evident than (PEP5) (Freddoso), and that it does the same job as (PEP5) in most contexts (Basinger) without creating difficulties for foreknowledge and middle knowledge.

Unfortunately, (PEP5*) does *not* do the same job as (PEP5) in *any* context. The purpose of (PEP5), as of all the other power entailment principles, is to identify states of affairs that are *necessary conditions* of persons' having the power to do various things. But (PEP5*) entirely fails to perform such a function. Note that the antecedent of (PEP5*) contains the clause, "and "*P*" entails "*Q*." " Given this, for S to have the power to bring it about that *P* just *is* for S to have the power to "do something such that if S were to do it, "*Q*" would be true"; (PEP5*), therefore, fails entirely to specify any *additional* necessary conditions that must be satisfied if S is to have the power to bring it about that *P*. (PEP5*), in fact, reduces to the tautology
(PEP5#) If it is in S's power to bring it about that *P*, and etc. . . . then it is in S's power to bring it about that *P*.
The truth of this need not be doubted. But it can scarcely do the job for which the power entailment principles were designed. (For a bit more on this, see my "Reply to Basinger on Power Entailment," *Faith and Philosophy* 5 [1988]: 87–90.)

[32]I am happy to be able to state that Philip Quinn now accepts this principle (personal communication).

The intuitive rationale for (PEP6) is well stated by Richard Purtill:

> Now it seems as clear as anything in logic can be that the logical
> consequences of what I cannot change are things I cannot change,
> that if A is beyond my control, and B is a logical consequence of A,
> then B is beyond my control. Anyone who doubts this logical
> principle is invited to provide a counter example to it which is
> coherent, much less plausible.[33]

Finally, from (PEP6) we can derive

(PEP7) If "*P*" is true and entails "*Q*," then if it cannot be in any-
        one's power to bring it about that "*P*" is false, it cannot be
        in anyone's power to bring it about that "*Q*" is false.

But (PEP7) is virtually equivalent to

(H7) Any proposition entailed by one or more hard facts is itself
      a hard fact.[34]

This, I think, is evident in its own right; additionally, it can be
supported by the same sort of reasoning that has just been cited
from Purtill.

In view of all this, it seems to me that the power entailment
principles are unassailable. Those who think otherwise are invited
to present cogent logical objections or clear counterexamples,
preferably both.[35] Objections to these principles simply on the
grounds that they have undesired consequences for the foreknowl-

---

[33]Richard L. Purtill, "Fatalism and the Omnitemporality of Truth," *Faith and Philosophy*, 5 (1988): 186.

[34]Strictly speaking, in order to derive (H7) from (PEP7), we need an additional principle stating that any conjunction of two or more hard facts is itself a hard fact. But this is unproblematic.

[35]Freddoso has attempted to do this; he claims that (PEP5) "will be rejected by all those libertarians who believe that there are contingent truths about the absolute future and yet deny that there is any sort of causal power over the past" (Introduction to Molina, *On Divine Foreknowledge (Part IV of the Concordia)*, trans. Alfred J. Freddoso [Ithaca, N.Y.: Cornell University Press, 1988], sec. 5.7). This objection, of course, rests on the misconception that "bringing about" must be causal; enough has already been said about that. Ironically, Freddoso himself argued this

edge controversy do not, it seems to me, merit a great deal of consideration.[36]

---

point very effectively in his paper "Accidental Necessity and Power over the Past" (*Pacific Philosophical Quarterly* 63 [1982]: 54–68). He says:

> Anyone who brings it about that a future-tense proposition has always been true does so by bringing it about that an appropriate present-tense proposition is or will be true. So power over the past is not basic, but is rather parasitic on ordinary causal contribution to what occurs "presently." (p. 67)

In this same paper, Freddoso endorsed a power entailment principle that is quite similar to (PEP3), namely,

> (K) If (i) p is logically equivalent to q and (ii) s has the power to make p true at t, then s has the power to make q true at t (p. 64).

Unfortunately, (K) lacks the clause "(iii) s has the power to make p false at t," and thus is subject to the sort of counterexample mentioned in n. 29 above. But with this emendation, it is an excellent power entailment principle, and it is to be hoped that Freddoso will now reconsider his recantation of it!

[36]Molina holds, in effect, that there is an exception to these principles in the case of God's past knowledge about future contingent events. (See Molina, *On Divine Foreknowledge*, trans. Freddoso, Disp. 52.) He writes:

> Even though it was . . . contingent that God should foreknow that the Antichrist is going to sin at such-and-such a point in time . . . nevertheless, by the very fact that from eternity He did foresee this sin as future, it *now* involves a contradiction for Him not to have foreknown it, both because there is no power over the past and also because no change can befall God. (par. 32; emphasis in original)

God's foreknowledge, then, does partake of the necessity of the past. In spite of this, and in spite of the fact that God's having had this foreknowledge *entails* that the Antichrist does sin, Molina asserts that this sin is "purely contingent," and that it is "unqualifiedly able to obtain and able not to obtain" (par. 34). Molina shows that this conclusion is required by his own theological principles, but I do not think he gives us any help at all in understanding how it might be possible that, of two logically equivalent statements, one is necessary and the other contingent.

[7]

Bringing About the Past

If compatibilism is to be true, we must have power over the past, power to bring about past events and also to prevent past events. But is such power possible? Among the very few philosophers who have considered this question and given an unequivocal affirmative answer must be numbered George Mavrodes.[1] In this chapter I propose to undertake a careful and thorough investigation of Mavrodes's position. I do this not only because of its intrinsic interest, but because I am increasingly convinced that the path he has taken is one that all other compatibilists must come to eventually. Even the distinction between hard and soft facts makes less difference than one might think; as we shall see, those who affirm this distinction are in the end forced to say very much the same sorts of things about our power over the past as are said by Mavrodes, who rejects it. For compatibilism, all other roads lead to this one.

The first section of the chapter is a brief exposition of Mavrodes's view concerning the power we have over the past. The following section deals with the vexed topic of *changing* the past,

---

[1]See George I. Mavrodes, "Is the Past Unpreventable?" *Faith and Philosophy* 1 (1983): 131–46.

and the succeeding section with *affecting* the past. I then consider
carefully the precise meaning that is to be attached to Mavrodes's
claims about our power over the past and conclude with a recon-
sideration of the meaning of *free will* as this is understood by compatibilists.

Mavrodes on Preventing the Past

Do we have power over the past? According to George
Mavrodes, we do indeed. This power is not limited to the counterfactual power over the past discussed in the previous chapter;
rather, it is the power to directly, and indeed causally, bring about
past events. And the past events to which this power extends are
not limited to those involving God's knowledge or belief about
future events; rather, the power in question is quite general, so that
in principle we may be able to bring about or prevent all of the
same kinds of events in the past that we are able to bring about or
prevent in the future.

A qualification is needed here. Mavrodes does not necessarily
want to claim that we *actually have* power over all of these past
events. He is, in fact, quite cautious in his claims about the powers
that we actually have over past events; his point is that we *could*
have such powers, that there is nothing *logically incoherent* in the
idea that we might have them. There may very well be specific
reasons why I cannot (for example) prevent Abraham's birth, just
as there are specific reasons why I cannot swim from San Francisco
to Honolulu. Mavrodes's claim, however, is that there is nothing
logically incoherent in supposing that I might have either of these
powers.

Now, in considering the question of our power over the past, an
important distinction needs to be made. On the one hand, it might
be asserted that we have the power to bring about those past events
that *have in fact occurred*, and to prevent events in the past that *might
have occurred but in fact did not*. To be sure, someone might respond
by asking, "If it has already happened, then why do *you* need to do
something to bring it about?" The answer to this, however, is that
in such a case the event in question has indeed already happened,

but the *reason why* it happened, the *cause* of its happening, is the action that has still to be performed.[2]

Such powers as these would be remarkable enough. But one can imagine yet another sort of power over the past which would be even more remarkable. We have been speaking about the power to bring about past events that have in fact already occurred. But what if there could be a power to bring about past events that *have not* occurred, and to prevent those past events that *have already occurred*? It is one thing to say "*X* has occurred, and the reason it occurred is something I am going to do right now." It is something altogether different to say "*X* has occurred, and there is something I can do right now that would have the effect of *preventing* its occurrence."

Now, which of these two kinds of power over the past is the kind affirmed by Mavrodes? The answer is, he affirms both of them. We do, certainly, have the power to bring about past events that have already occurred and to prevent past events that have not occurred. Do we ever exercise this power? Mavrodes's claim is that we do this every day of our lives. For by performing any free action, I bring it about that God has always believed that I would perform that action, and by freely refraining from an action I prevent God from having believed I would perform it.[3] (It is worth noting that this is the *only* example of power over the past to which Mavrodes definitely commits himself. His view is that, in principle, we may have power over all sorts of events in the past, but he does not claim to know *what* sorts of events these are, or how we might go about exercising this power, if in fact we have it.)

But the power over the past sketched in the last paragraph is *not* sufficient for compatibilism. For on the libertarian view of free

---

[2]There may, indeed, be a motivational problem here—if I *know* that an event has occurred, it may be hard for me to convince myself that there is something I need to do *now* in order to *make* it happen. Because of this, it may be that situations in which a person is motivated to *deliberately attempt* to bring about or prevent something in the past would be limited to those in which the agent *does not know* whether or not the event in question has occurred. Of course, a past event might in fact *be* the causal result of a future event, even if the agent in question does not *deliberately attempt* to bring it about.

[3]Ibid., pp. 144–45.

will, which compatibilists accept, in order to be free with respect to a particular action one must have *both* the power to perform that action *and* the power to refrain from performing it. Now, consider some past belief of God's about an action of mine. According to the kind of power sketched above, I am able to bring it about that God has held this belief (viz., by performing the action in question), and to prevent God from having held some other, incompatible view about what I would do. *But this is not sufficient for free will.* In order to have free will, I must *also* have the power to *refrain* from the action in question and do something else instead. But this entails that I must *now* have the power to *prevent God from holding the belief he has actually held,* and to *bring about that God, in the past, held some belief different from the one he actually did hold!*

Mavrodes sees this clearly, and makes the point with a very striking example: He claims that it might now, in the 1980s, be in someone's power to prevent the coronation of Queen Elizabeth II of England, which occurred in 1953! He goes on to say:

> When I suggest that Elizabeth's queenship may be preventable I do not mean any of the "sensible" interpretations which might, with some straining, be attached to my words. I do not mean, for example, . . . that we might now discover that a mistake had been made in the past—that her apparent coronation was invalid because of a technicality. . . . No, I mean that, assuming that she has been Queen for many years, we might now be able to do something which would bring it about that she has never, up to the present time, been Queen.[4]

Can We Change the Past?

Claims of the sort made here by Mavrodes seem inevitably to call forth a particular response: "You can't change the past!" The claim that someone might have the power to bring it about that Elizabeth never became queen *seems* to be a claim that someone might have power to *change the past*—a power that almost everyone will immediately reject as impossible.

[4]Ibid., p. 139.

Now, just how Mavrodes stands on this question is something we still have to investigate. I believe, however, that the notion of "changing the past" is one that possesses great importance for our inquiry and merits careful study. It is noteworthy that although persons not familiar with the foreknowledge controversy find the terminology of "changing the past" almost irresistible, most writers on the topic hold that such talk is irremediably confused. No, the response comes back, we cannot change the past. But then, neither can we change the future. It cannot be the case that an event E has occurred, and someone subsequently brings it about that E has not occurred. But neither can it be the case that it is true that an event E *will occur*, and someone subsequently brings it about that E never occurs. If someone *prevents* E's occurrence, then it was *never* true that E would occur.[5] So past and future are alike unchangeable. It may be added that we can, *in a sense*, change the future, in that we can perform an action such that the future is changed from what it *would have been* had that action never been performed. But then, it may be possible to change the past in a parallel way—we may be able to perform an action that changes the past from what it *would have been* had that action not been performed. Another way of putting this point is that, although we cannot *change* the future, we are indeed able to *bring about* future events, and we are constantly doing so. To be sure, we cannot *in general* bring about past events, but unless we arbitrarily reject retroactive causation, there is no reason *in principle* why we might not be able to do so at least occasionally. The difference between past and future, then, comes down to the fact that most, if not all, of the causal arrows run from the past to the future rather than from the future to the past.[6]

By talk such as this, then, the notion of "changing the past" is made to seem (at best) a harmless confusion. I believe, however, that it is a mistake thus to dismiss the intuitively important claim "You can't change the past." The problem with the line of thought set out in the previous paragraph lies not so much in what was said there as in what was overlooked. That way of viewing the notion

[5]If someone *brings about* E's occurrence, it will no longer be true that E *will* occur—but this is not the sort of "change in the future" that is in question.
[6]All of the points in this paragraph are made by Mavrodes.

of "changing the past" completely fails, I claim, to grasp the true force and significance of this notion. This failure is not in itself necessarily fatal. The point made by the locution "You can't change the past" can be made in other ways. But something really is lost by failing to appreciate the significance of this locution. The statement "You can't change the past" expresses a powerful intuition, and the failure to grasp the expression correctly carries with it the danger that the intuition itself may be obscured or may lose some of its inherent force. No doubt, what seem to be widespread intuitions may sometimes in the end have to be rejected as confusions—but the recent history of philosophy strongly suggests that we ought to get straight first what the intuition *is*, before we decide to reject it.

But why am I so sure that the common way of treating this locution fails to do it justice? There is one simple fact about these responses which demonstrates conclusively that this way of taking the expression fails to grasp, and indeed runs at cross purposes with, the intuition that the saying is meant to express. That fact is as follows: The point of the responses is to create and emphasize a *symmetry* between the past and the future, whereas the point of the expression as it is ordinarily used is precisely to stress the *asymmetry* between the two. It is pretty clear, then, that if an expression whose purposes is to stress the *difference* between the future and the past is so interpreted that the result is to emphasize their *similarity*, something has gone radically wrong.

Unless, of course, the ordinary belief in the asymmetry of past and future is fundamentally mistaken. But even if we are forced, in the end, to draw this conclusion, we ought to do our best before that to understand what the expression is trying to convey. So let's try to do that. Let us ask ourselves how we can understand the locution about changing the past in such a way as to allow it to have the force its users intend it to have, instead of precisely the opposite force. Or to come at the same point from the opposite direction, what basic mistake is made by the common interpretation, so as to change an affirmation of asymmetry into one of symmetry?

It will be noticed that the interpretation given takes the notion of changing the past (or the future) as having to do with *changing the truth-values of propositions* about the past (or the future). Further, these truth-values are taken, as they normally are in logic, to be *omnitemporal*—if "Jones walks at T_1" is true, it is true at all times whatever (and of course, "Jones *will walk* at T_1" is true at all times prior to T_1, "Jones *walked* at T_1" at all times *after* T_1). But the notion of *changing* an *omnitemporal* truth value is indeed hopelessly confused; in this context the saying that the past cannot be changed makes very little sense.

Now, in spite of the attachment of logicians to omnitemporal truth-values, it is quite clear that the locution we are examining is *misinterpreted* if placed in the context of such truth-values. It should be noted that such locutions as "You can't change the past" (cf. "There's no use crying over spilt milk") are used by a wide variety of persons, many of whom have never heard of propositions or of truth-values and are quite unaware of all they are missing by such sad deprivations. The dairy boy who has let the milk pail get kicked over isn't crying over any *proposition*—it's the spilt milk that bothers him! And although some philosophers may insist that "You can't change the future," it is worth noticing that it is *only* philosophers who say this—and then, only when they are bent on undermining the force of the parallel expression concerning the past. The context in which the ordinary person talks about (not) changing the past is one in which the question of changing the future does not arise at all.

But if "You can't change the past" isn't to be interpreted in the context of omnitemporal truth-values, how shall it be interpreted? I suggest we may take a clue from another common saying: "The future holds unlimited possibilities." What are we to make of *this* saying? Is its meaning merely that the future (like, of course, the past) is largely described in terms of contingent propositions— propositions, then, that though true are possibly false, and whose contradictories, though false, are possibly true? Is *this* what is meant by saying that the future is the realm of possibilities? And if it is, why don't we think of the past, also, as the realm of pos-sibilities? And if this is absurd, as it surely is, how do we get the fly out of this fly-bottle?

The right answer, I suggest, is something like this: When we say that the past is unchangeable, we are thinking of the past as a *concrete totality*, as the sum total of the facts and events that have actually occurred.[7] There is much about this totality that we could wish otherwise; the wish to rewrite the past is as universal as it is futile. And it is just this futility that is eloquently and powerfully expressed by saying that the past cannot be changed. But what, then, of the future? Is the contrast between past and future to be expressed by saying that the future, unlike the past, *can* be changed? I don't think so; the contrast is rather that the future, unlike the past, has not been *made* yet; it exists for the most part only in the form of plans and tendencies. To be sure, these plans and tendencies point in the direction of many things that are "going to happen" *unless prevented*, but in many cases what in this sense is "going to happen"—is *in the process* of happening—*can* all the same be prevented, if we take the right sort of steps in order to do so. *It is often in our power to determine which of two ways the future shall be, but it is never in our power to determine which of two ways the past shall be.* The past and future are in this way fundamentally asymmetrical. Or at least, such is our ordinary view of the matter; whether there are good philosophical reasons for rejecting this ordinary view is a question of great interest.

Before leaving this topic, I have two further points to make. Note first of all that, as explained here, the asymmetry between past and future does *not* depend on whether or not retroactive causation is possible. That is a separate question, one that will be addressed in the next section of this chapter. No doubt, the common view is that such causation is impossible; all the same, the questions are not the same, and (as will become apparent) one could allow the possibility of retrocausation without denying anything in the last paragraph.

The other point requires more extensive development. I have emphasized that the framework of omnitemporal truth-values fundamentally distorts the ordinary meaning of "You can't change the past." Indeed, this framework tends in general to cut across the grain of our natural way of regarding time and temporal processes. The most appropriate framework—the one that most closely par-

---

[7]This may be compared with my claim, in chapter 3, that we must conceive of God's foreknowledge as grasping the *concrete events* of the future, and not merely propositions *about* the future.

allels our ordinary ways of thinking and talking about such matters—would, I maintain, be one in which it is *not* the case that if
Jones walks at T_1, then "Jones will walk at T_1" was true at all
previous times. It would be a framework in which propositions
about contingent future events are not said to be true or false in the
ordinary way.

But how *would* such a framework deal with the future? The
possibility that most readily springs to mind—that of introducing
a third truth-value, "undecided," between "true" and "false"—has
actually the least to recommend it. It is well known that a three-
valued logic—or, indeed, a logic with any finite number of truth-
values greater than two—requires us to abandon some important
principles of ordinary propositional logic. More acceptable is the
system propounded by Arthur Prior, according to which propositions about future events are *false*—that is, when one asserts definitely of a future event either that it *will* or that it *will not* occur,
then, if the occurrence of the event is as yet objectively uncertain
and undecided, the proposition in question is false. This system,
however, is open to what seems to me to be a fairly serious objection. This objection concerns propositions about future events
whose occurrence is almost, but not quite, objectively certain.
Such propositions remain false, on Prior's view, until the exact
moment, often imperceptible to human observation, when the last
possibility of the event's nonoccurrence is eliminated, then sud-
denly they flip-flop to true. There is nothing formally inconsistent
in this, to be sure, but it does seem rather artificial and unnatural.

Better than either of these is the system proposed by Richard
Purtill, according to which propositions about contingent future
events are assigned values *between* 0 and 1 and are treated according
to the probability calculus.[8] Unlike the three-valued system, the
probability calculus with its infinite number of distinct truth-values preserves all the principles of ordinary propositional logic.
Propositions about contingent future events are assigned probability values between 0 and 1 depending on the objective tendency
or propensity for the event to occur. And as the time of occurrence

[8]See Richard L. Purtill, "Fatalism and the Omnitemporality of Truth," *Faith and
Philosophy* 5 (1988): 185–92.

draws closer the probability will normally approach either 1 or 0 as a limit, the limit being reached whenever the event becomes objectively certain.

Such a system, I believe, conforms quite well to our intuitions about temporal processes as well as to our ordinary ways of talking about them.[9] Nevertheless, it will not be adopted in this book, for several reasons. First, because the full development of such a system and the resolution of its inevitable difficulties is a formidable task, one I am not at present prepared to undertake. Second, because in developing and defending such a system one would inevitably make a number of contestable assumptions (e.g., the assumptions concerning probabilities as objectively existing tendencies or propensities); thus, the burden of assumptions to be defended would be substantially increased. But third, and most important, because in adopting such a system one already decides a number of the most crucial issues in the present discussion. For the purpose of the discussion, then, it is much better to employ a more neutral system of logic—in this case, traditional two-valued logic with omnitemporal truth values.[10]

The considerations of this section can be summed up as follows: The claim that "You can't change the past" seems to be one that expresses a powerful intuition—one that is common both to philosophers and to the philosophically unsophisticated. To interpret this claim as the claim that one cannot alter omnitemporal truth values is extremely unfortunate. Such an interpretation is mistaken, first of all, because many of those who make the claim have never heard of omnitemporal truth values and cannot be supposed to be talking about them. But more fundamentally, it is mistaken because the result of this interpretation is to create a symmetry between past and future, when the intuitive point of the expression is precisely the opposite. Omnitemporal truth values are *by defini-*

---

[9]Note that the system does not, as one might think, beg the question against determinism. Rather, determinism, in such a system, is equivalent to the assertion that *all* propositions have truth-values of either 1 or 0.

[10]I therefore do not agree with Purtill that the omnitemporality of truth, together with the unchangeability of the past, entails fatalism. The answer to this contention is found in the distinction between hard and soft facts—a distinction that Purtill considers but rejects for (in my opinion) inadequate reasons.

tion unchangeable, so to interpret the claim in terms of such truth values inevitably trivializes it.

The claim that the past cannot be changed is better interpreted as referring to the past as a *concrete totality of events and processes*; this concrete totality is what it is, and nothing we now do can either add to it or subtract from it. It is in this sense that the past is fixed, unchangeable, and necessary. But if we cannot change the past, can we change the future? The answer is that the concrete totality of future events *does not yet exist*, so the question of *changing* it does not arise. The future is, to a large extent, a realm of *possibilities*, and which of those possibilities get actualized depends to a large extent on what we now do. *It often depends on us now to determine which of two ways the future shall be, but it never depends on us now to determine which of two ways the past shall be.*

This, anyhow, is our ordinary way of regarding the difference between the past and the future. It could be false. Determinists hold that the sense of the "openness" of the future, of the future as containing possibilities that may or may not be realized, is in some ultimate sense an illusion. That could be so, for all we have said here—or, the view we have sketched could be wrong in other ways. All that I am claiming is that there is this ordinary view of the matter, one that is (I think) entitled to a modicum of philosophical respect. At a minimum, philosophers who disagree with it should acknowledge its existence and should not interpret the locutions that express it (such as "You can't change the past") in ways that drain them of their meaning.

Can We Affect the Past?

Compatibilists such as Mavrodes typically lay a great deal of stress on the distinction between *changing* the past and *affecting* the past. The possibility of our changing the past they deny, but they distinguish this from affecting, bringing about, or even causing the past, all of which they proclaim to be entirely possible.

Now, granting the distinction between changing the past and affecting, or bringing about, the past, is the latter possible? It is important for me to stress that *the argument of this chapter in no way depends on the answer to this question.* So far as my argument is concerned, *it may be entirely possible for persons to bring about, and even to cause, past events.* I am therefore under no obligation to argue against this possibility—and in the succeeding argument, the possibility will be conceded.

Having said this, I still need to point out that the claim that it is possible to affect the past is subject to at least two formidable difficulties—difficulties that have not, to my knowledge, been confronted by any of the compatibilists who affirm this possibility. In the present section, then, we examine these difficulties.

The first difficulty may be put simply as follows: How can an event be the causal consequence of, or be brought about by, another event that *does not yet exist?* To be sure, the future event that causes a past event *will exist*—but it does *not* exist at the time when its supposed effect is brought about. One might of course point out that a *past* event that causes something in the present *no longer* exists. But the cases are not parallel. Past events are assumed to have left traces leading up to the present; if, on the other hand, it is literally true that some past event has "disappeared without a trace," such an event can have no consequences in the present or future. But to suppose that future events "cast their shadows before them" and thus have traces in the past (where this does not mean merely that they were foreshadowed by their own causes) is no solution to the problem, which simply reappears in the explanation of the causation of the traces themselves.

This point can be made rather dramatically by imagining oneself in the position of a would-be time traveler—one who (like Julian May's Pliocene exiles[11]) intends to go back into the past with no expectation of ever returning. It is clear when one thinks about it that if I propose to go back to the Pliocene era, I am presupposing that the Pliocene *still exists* to go back to. Otherwise, what would be the difference between going into the past and dying? But if I assume that the past still exists, then quite clearly I am committed to what is called the "B-theory" of time, according to which *all of time exists "simultaneously,"* as a sort of four-dimensional solid in the space-time continuum, with only human consciousness mark-

[11]Julian May, *The Many-Colored Land* and *The Golden Torc* (Garden City, N.Y.: Nelson Doubleday, 1982).

ing the distinction between "now" and "then." If *that* view is accepted, then time travel makes sense, otherwise not.

Now, bringing about the past, unlike time travel, need not involve the transfer of things and persons from the present to the past. But what sense can it make for me to attempt to *affect* the past unless I am assuming that, in some way, it still exists to be affected? William Craig, himself a compatibilist on foreknowledge, nevertheless insists that backward causation is possible only if one accepts the B-theory of time: "Backward causation rests on the assumption that time is a collection of regions among which our present region is not more real than the others. If one denies this conception of time . . . there can be no causal relations across regions of time and hence no backward causation."[12]

It seems to me that this constitutes a real dilemma for the compatibilist who wishes to affirm our ability to affect the past. If she adopts the common-sense view of time (often called the A-theory) according to which the past is gone, the future is not yet, and only the present now exists, then backward causation and bringing about the past are impossible. According to the B-theory, on the other hand, these things may be possible. But even apart from the inherent implausibility of the B-theory, it is quite evident that this theory is inherently fatalistic and thus inconsistent with the libertarian view of free will which the compatibilist affirms.[13]

The other major difficulty with backward causation is that such causation inescapably leads to problems with circular causation and circular explanation.[14] The most dramatic illustration of this I know is Robert Heinlein's tale of a man who journeys to the past, undergoes a sex-change operation, and becomes both of his own

---

[12]William Lane Craig, *The Only Wise God* (Grand Rapids, Mich.: Baker, 1987), p. 80. In the passage quoted Craig is citing with approval the view of Graham Nerlich.

[13]As noted, Craig is a compatibilist yet denies that we can cause or bring about the past. He offers two other possibilities to account for God's foreknowledge, one that God has "innate knowledge" of the past and the other middle knowledge. (See ibid., pp. 119–51.) Unfortunately, both of these suggestions run afoul of the power entailment principles.

[14]These problems are somewhat similar to the problems noted in chapter 3 with the view that God acts, speaks, etc., in the present on the basis of his knowledge of future free actions.

parents![15] This of course is nonsense on stilts, but similar, though less dramatic, scenarios will become possible any time the past effects are not rigorously separated from the causal chain leading to the future cause.

In closing this section let me stress once again that these difficulties form no essential part of my argument and will not be appealed to in what follows. They do, all the same, constitute formidable obstacles for the compatibilist who affirms our power over the past, obstacles that compatibilists have generally failed to address.

What Does It Mean to Bring About the Past?

If we do have power over the past, how is this power to be understood? This I think is the most critical question of all those that the compatibilist must address. In this section we shall consider the question in the context of Mavrodes's position, but in so doing we shall consider alternatives ranging beyond those that Mavrodes himself would accept. The fact is, as it seems to me, that claims about bringing about the past are deeply puzzling and problematical, and the alternative ways of understanding such claims must be exhaustively canvassed in order to be as sure as possible that one has not overlooked something crucial.

We may begin by considering the two kinds of power over the past discussed in the first section of this chapter—power to bring about past events that *have already occurred*, and power to bring about past events that have *not* occurred. The first kind of power, power to bring about past events that *have* occurred, is relatively easy to understand, if one accepts the possibility of backward causation. *For present purposes, this possibility will be conceded.* As promised, we make no further appeal to the difficulties about retrocausation noted in the preceding section. From now on, therefore, we shall assume that the power to bring about past events that have in fact already occurred is philosophically unproblematic.

But what about the power to bring about past events that have *not* occurred? One way of understanding this would be as the

---

[15]Robert Heinlein, "All You Zombies," in *The Best from Fantasy and Science Fiction,* ed. Robert P. Mills (New York: Ace, 1958).

power to bring about *soft facts* that have not occurred. This, of course, is not available to Mavrodes, since he makes no use of the distinction between hard and soft facts. And we have argued that any adequate explication of the distinction will classify facts about what God has believed in the past as hard facts. But even if the compatibilist could arrive at a defensible way of classifying facts about God's past beliefs as soft, it is questionable whether this would do her a great deal of good. All of the clear examples of our power over soft facts have to do with cases in which *one and the same past event* can be correctly described in two different ways, depending on what happens in the future—the *same event* can be either Luther's-birth-502-years-before-Reichenbach-writes or Luther's-birth-502-years-before-Reichenbach-does-not-write. But this sort of thing is of no help to the compatibilist; she has to attribute to Clarence both the power to bring about the event consisting of God's having always believed that Clarence would eat the omelet, *and* the power to bring about the quite different event consisting of God's having always believed just the opposite. She has to maintain, that is, that God has always believed a certain thing and it is in Clarence's power to bring it about that God has *not* always believed that thing. The distinction between hard and soft facts gives us no help in understanding this.

Alvin Plantinga, as we have seen, suggests two possible interpretations for our power to bring about that God held a belief different than the one he did in fact hold. One possibility is that the power in question is the power to bring it about that God held a certain belief and also did *not* hold that belief. That any such power is possible he rightly rejects. The other interpretation, the one Plantinga himself favors, is that the power in question is the power to do something such that, were we to do it, God would not have held the belief he did hold. Now, we may agree that, if compatibilism is true, we must have powers of the sort indicated by Plantinga. But the power entailment principles show that these powers cannot *replace* power to bring about God's past beliefs. What needs to be explained, but *has not* been explained, is how it is possible that *God has always believed a certain thing, and yet it is in someone's power to bring it about that God has not always believed that thing.*

There is another possible way to understand this. Why is it that

Clarence apparently lacks freedom with respect to eating the omelet? The answer is that there is a circumstance that obtains (namely, God's always having believed that Clarence would eat the omelet) which logically *precludes* Clarence's refraining from omelet eating, and since it is not possible for Clarence to *refrain* from eating the omelet, it is also not possible for him to be *free* with respect to eating it.

Now, the precluding circumstances that affect our lives are not by any means limited to God's past beliefs. And perhaps considering how we deal with some other kinds of precluding circumstances will help us to see how Clarence might be free to refrain from eating the omelet even though God has always believed that he would eat it. Suppose, for instance, that I am planning a trip to Romania, and to get the most out of my visit I promise myself that I will take the opportunity to converse with as many Romanians as possible. But there is a snag: I have never learned Romanian. However, a remedy is available; some intensive work at my friendly neighborhood Berlitz school will soon equip me to carry on a passable conversation. It may be helpful to state this situation formally:

(1)   If at T_1 N had never learned Romanian, and it was in N's power to bring it about that at T_2 he could converse freely in Romanian, then it was in N's power to bring it about that whereas it was true at T_1 that N had never learned Romanian, it was no longer true at T_2 that N had never learned Romanian.

(1) is essentially an instance of the power entailment principles (PEP4) and (PEP5), slightly complicated to allow for the different times at which N has or lacks the relevant powers. It should be noted that to have the power in question N must be able to bring it about that a certain past-tense proposition—in this case, "N has never learned Romanian"—is true at one point in time but false at a later point in time. But now consider:

(2)   If at T_1 God had always believed that Clarence would eat an omelet at T_2 and it was in Clarence's power to refrain

from eating the omelet at T_2, then it was in Clarence's
power to bring it about that whereas it was true at T_1 that
God had always believed that Clarence would eat the omelet at T_2, it was no longer true at T_2 that God had always
believed that Clarence would eat the omelet at T_2.

The parallelism between (1) and (2) is rather close and, I believe,
also instructive. In one case, it is N's never having learned Romanian that precludes his conversing in that language; in the other
case it is God's always having believed Clarence would eat the
omelet that precludes his refraining from eating it. In either case, if
the precluding circumstance can be removed (i.e., if the past-tense
proposition that was formerly true can become false), the precluded action may become possible. In the case of N this can
probably be done, but what about Clarence? Here there is a com-
plication that begins to break down the parallelism between (1) and
(2). N's status with regard to the knowledge of Romanian is eminently alterable, unless of course he proves a dunce at language
learning. But, God being infallible, his status with regard to believing that Clarence would eat the omelet is *not* alterable; there
cannot be a time at which God believes this and a later time at
which he does not believe it. So what Clarence must do, if he is to
exercise the power identified in the consequent of (2), is to *eliminate*
the past fact of God's having believed that he would eat the omelet.
But this, clearly enough, would be to *alter the past*—a performance
that is generally mentioned, by compatibilists and others, only in
order to point out its evident absurdity.

However *that* may be, it does seem that if Clarence *could* have the
power specified in the consequent of (2), then he could also have
the power specified in its antecedent, and compatibilism would
have emerged triumphant. So the question arises: Could *this* possibly be the power that is attributed to us by Mavrodes, and other
compatibilists, when they say we have power over God's past
beliefs?

In the case of Mavrodes, one might be tempted to think that he
does attribute such a power to us. How else, one might think, can
one understand his claim that we might even now, many years

after Elizabeth II was crowned queen, be able to "do something which would bring it about that she has never, up to the present time, been Queen"? In a letter, Mavrodes describes most lucidly what it would be like to delete Elizabeth's queenship from the past:

> Elizabeth has been queen of England for many years now. Suppose that I were to do something now whose effect would be that, while she has up to now been queen for many years, from now on she will never have been queen at all or at any time. I believe that it would be perfectly correct, and powerfully communicative, to say that by performing that act I had changed the past.

He observes that some people have an intuition to the effect that such an action is impossible, and proceeds as follows: "I really don't know how widespread that intuition is. But so far as I can tell, *I share it fully myself.* I have no inclination at all to think that I could perform any act which satisfied the description given above."[16] Mavrodes, then, does *not* attribute to Clarence the power described in the consequent of (2); he does not think we can change the past. He very explicitly rules out the power to bring it about that there was "a time at which it was true that *E has occurred*, and a later time at which it was not true that *E has occurred.*"[17]

We seem to have reached an impasse in our attempt to interpret the power we allegedly have to bring about the past. We considered several interpretations of this power proposed by various philosophers and found that each of these interpretations is both unsatisfactory in itself and would be rejected by Mavrodes. We then considered an interpretation suggested by some of Mavrodes's own words, namely, that our power to bring about past events that have not in fact taken place is a power to *change* the past. It seems that *if* Clarence could have such a power, then he would indeed be able to do what he needs to be able to do for compatibilism to be successful. But Mavrodes, as we have seen, emphatically rejects this interpretation of his claim. But now the question becomes acute: *How is this claim to be understood?*

I believe that to answer this we must give further attention to the

[16]Personal communication (emphasis in original).
[17]"Is the Past Unpreventable?" p. 137.

concept of a "power." Up to this point, my discussion has presupposed the concept explained in chapter 4; for convenience of reference, the explanation given there will now be recalled:

> The power in question is the *power to perform a particular act under given circumstances*, and not a *generalized* power to perform acts of a certain kind. (Thus, if Thomas has the skill to perform on the parallel bars, but at T_1 his arms are tied behind his back, we shall say that he *lacks* the power at T_1 to perform on the parallel bars.) In general, if it is in N's power at T to perform A, then there is nothing in the circumstances[18] that obtain at T which *prevents or precludes* N's performing A at T. Here "prevent" applies especially to circumstances that are *causally* incompatible with N's performing A at T, and "preclude" to circumstances that are *logically* incompatible with N's doing so. (The tied hands *prevent* Thomas from performing on the parallel bars; he is *precluded* from marrying Edwina at T by the fact that at that time she is already married to someone else.)

It is apparent that if *this* conception of power is presupposed, then Clarence *cannot* have the power to refrain from eating a cheese omelet. For there is indeed a circumstance that obtains at the time he eats the omelet which is logically inconsistent with his refraining therefrom—the circumstance, namely, that God believes he will *not* refrain. What follows from this is, that *if Clarence is to have power to refrain from eating the omelet, this power cannot be interpreted according to the explanation that has been given.*

How then shall "power" be interpreted? There is a way of speaking about powers according to which a person's powers are thought of *not* primarily as powers to perform a specific action on a specific occasion, but rather as *general* abilities that one has and that remain more or less constant although the possibilities of their exercise come and go. If I ever learn Romanian, I shall have acquired the power to converse in Romanian, although on many occasions my actually doing so may be precluded by there being no other Romanian speakers present. *These* powers—and this is the important point—are *not* powers that one cannot have, on a

---

[18]It will be recalled that the circumstances that obtain at T comprise all and only the hard facts with respect to T.

given occasion, if there are precluding circumstances present. I may perfectly well *have* a power of this sort to do something even though it is either logically or causally impossible that I *exercise* the power under the circumstances that obtain at a particular time. Thus, Thomas may very well have the power to perform on the parallel bars even though at the present moment he cannot do so because his hands are tied. And he certainly has the power to enter into marriage, though his doing so with Edwina is at the moment precluded by her unfortunate union with Dudley.

Now, if we interpret "power" in this way, Mavrodes's claims about what is in our power immediately become clear and make perfectly good sense. (I am inclined to think that this is the *only* way in which they make sense,[19] but it is rash to rule out the possibility that someone might give yet another interpretation. What *is* clear is that they do *not* make sense if interpreted in terms of the explanation of "power" cited above from chapter 4.) How might I now have the power to prevent Elizabeth's coronation? I might have it if (1) there is some action such that, if I performed it in 1983 or later, it would have the effect that Elizabeth would never have become queen, and, (2) I now have all of the abilities, personal qualities, and the like that are requisite for performing such an action. To be sure, (1) presupposes the possibility of backward causation, but we have agreed not to cavil at that. And given that, we are home free. Of course, it is in no way possible that I *will in fact* perform such an action, thus deleting Elizabeth's queenship from our history—*that* is no more possible than that Thomas will enter into a valid marriage with Edwina while she is still married to Dudley, or perform on the parallel bars with his hands tied. But in no case does the preventing or precluding circumstance detract from the power that the person undoubtedly has. Nor, of course, does the fact that God has always believed that Clarence would eat an omelet for breakfast detract from the power that Clarence has to refrain from eating omelets.

With this simple change in our understanding of "power," then, our seemingly intractable problems with understanding Mavrodes's claims vanish instantly. Furthermore, the use of "power"

[19]But see n. 20 below.

thus invoked is in no way outlandish or unusual; if anything, this use of the word is more common than the one explicated in chapter 4. But if so, you may ask, then why did I make such heavy weather about understanding Mavrodes's claims? Was this simply a maneuver to emphasize my cleverness in figuring out the correct interpretation—or perhaps to excuse my slowness in seeing the point?

Not quite. I may, indeed, have been unduly slow in seeing that this is the sense of "power" which is required. But there was a good reason for resisting this conclusion as long as possible, and for considering every other possibility before accepting it. The notion of "power" as general rather than specific *does* provide a solution to the problem of interpreting Mavrodes's claims about power over the past. But this solution has its price, as we shall see in the next section.

What Is the Meaning of Free Will?

In the last section we considered the meaning of the "power over the past" affirmed by Mavrodes. But we were not interested in the notion of power merely for its own sake; rather, this notion was investigated because it plays an essential role in the understanding of *free will*. The section closed by identifying a sense of "power" according to which Mavrodes's claims are intelligible and perhaps (given the possibility of retrocausation) even true. Now we must ask: How does this sense of "power" affect the meaning of free will?

As with the definition of "power," it will be helpful here to recall the definition of free will from chapter 4:

(FW) N is free at T with respect to performing $A =_{df}$ It is in N's
        power at T to perform A, and it is in N's power at T to
        refrain from performing A.

This is, I believe, a quite standard libertarian definition of free will. (Later I will adduce definitions from others in support of the conception of free will here adopted.) But it is important to understand that *the conception of power we have attributed to Mavrodes*, as "*general* abilities which one has and which remain more or less

constant although the possibilities of their exercise come and go,"
*fails to yield a libertarian conception of free will when combined with
(FW)*. For on *that* conception of power, one may, and often does,
have the power to perform *A even when the possibility of exercising
this power is absent*. Indeed, it might well be the case, so far as the
definition (FW) is concerned, that *every* occasion on which it is
possible that one will perform *A* is an occasion on which it is not
possible that one will refrain from doing so, and vice versa—thus,
one might repeatedly be "free with respect to performing *A*" in the
sense of (FW) without its *ever* being the case that both one's performing *A* and one's refraining from doing so are possible.

This is not to say that the conception of power under consideration fails, when combined with (FW), to yield any conception of
free will at all. On the contrary: This combination, when suitably
supplemented, is entirely capable of yielding a *soft determinist* conception of free will—a "Compatibilist" conception in the usual
sense of *that* term, when it has not (as in this book) been preempted
for a narrower use. Some supplementation *is* needed for this, however. On the soft determinist view, one may indeed have it in one's
power to perform an action even though it is impossible that one
actually do so. But it makes a difference *why* it is impossible to
perform the action. Things become rather complex here, as soft
determinists craft and modify their definitions in order to avoid
counterexamples. But the general idea is this: If the reason why it is
impossible that I do *A* in a particular situation lies either in external, physical compulsion or in sheer lack of opportunity, then I do
not in that situation have it in my power to do *A*. If, on the other
hand, I have opportunity and physical compulsion is absent but I
simply have an overwhelmingly strong aversion to doing *A*, then I
do have it in my power to do *A*, and my refraining from *A* counts
as a free choice, *even though it is impossible that I should actually do A*.

We see, then, that the general conception of a power can, when
suitably supplemented and combined with (FW), yield a soft determinist conception of free will. (Without supplementation, it yields
a conception that is even weaker than soft determinism.) But of
course, this is not at all what the compatibilist wants! Compatibilists claim, and intend, to uphold a libertarian conception of free
will and to show that *that* conception is compatible with divine

foreknowledge. Now, one way of defining libertarian free will is the one taken in chapter 4, and cited here, using the notion of "power" as the *power to perform a particular act under given circumstances*. Unfortunately, given *that* notion of power, it seems impossible to make sense of the claims compatibilists make (and must make) about our power over the past. In order to make sense of those claims, we found ourselves forced to adopt the *general* notion of power as a capacity that one has even on occasions when it is not possible for the power to be exercised.[20] And when we combine *that* notion of power with the definition (FW), the result is the unsatisfactory conception of free will just discussed.

Is there, then, *no* possible way to define a libertarian notion of free will, using the general conception of power? It would certainly be premature to conclude this. This conception yields an inadequate idea of free will *when combined with (FW)*, but a simple modification of (FW) gives a much improved result:

(FW') N is free at T with respect to performing $A =_{df}$ It is in N's power at T to perform A and it is possible at T for N to exercise that power, and it is in N's power at T to refrain from performing A, and it is also possible at T for N to exercise *that* power.

At the cost of a little inelegance, therefore, we have a perfectly acceptable definition of libertarian free will, using the general notion of powers as capacities. Unfortunately, however, this result affords little comfort to the compatibilist. For it is evident that *given this definition, the compatibilist cannot affirm libertarian free will.* For the general notion of power as capacity, when supplemented with the stipulation that it must be possible for the power to be exercised on a given occasion, is precisely equivalent to the notion

[20]It is possible that some compatibilist might claim that there is a sense of "power" according to which it refers to a power to perform a particular action on a given occasion, yet such that one may *have* such a power on an occasion even though it is impossible for the power to be *exercised* on that occasion. It seems to me extremely doubtful that there *is* any such sense of "power" either in common or in general philosophical use. But if there is such a sense (or if someone cares to invent it), my remarks will for the most part apply to it just as to the general notion of power discussed in the text.

of power as the power to perform a particular act under given circumstances. And the inability of compatibilism to cope with *that* notion—an inability that was thoroughly detailed in the previous section—is what drove us in the first place to entertain the notion of powers as general capacities.

The situation for compatibilism has now become extremely grave, as indicated by the following thesis: *The compatibilist on fore-knowledge cannot consistently affirm libertarian free will.* If this is true, then incompatibilism is triumphant. Furthermore, it is abundantly clear that compatibilism *is* inconsistent with the idea of free will explicated in chapter 4 and further discussed in the present chapter. The only recourse, then, for the compatibilist is to claim that this notion of free will is excessive—that this is *not* libertarian free will as generally and properly understood. Now, it would be a long day's work to canvass all of the definitions of free will that have been given in the history of philosophy and decide on this basis what "real" libertarianism involves. As a first installment of this task (which, however, I shall leave it to others to complete), I cite three definitions from contemporary philosophers. The first two of the definitions are, respectively, of determinism and indeterminism; this exploits the familiar point that, whatever else a libertarian affirms, the conception of free will he offers is one that is inconsistent with determinism. According to Richard Taylor, "Determinism is the general philosophical thesis which states that for everything that ever happens there are conditions such that, given them, nothing else could happen."[21] And Brand Blanshard says, "By indeterminism I mean the view that there is some event *B* that is not so connected with any previous event *A* that, given *A*, *B* must occur."[22] Finally, I cite Thomas P. Flint, who gives the following "libertarian analysis of freedom": "An agent is truly free with respect to an action only if the situation in which he is placed is logically and causally compatible with both his performing and his not performing the action."[23]

[21]Richard Taylor, "Determinism," *Encyclopedia of Philosophy*, 2: 359.

[22]Brand Blanshard, "The Case for Determinism," in *Determinism and Freedom in the Age of Modern Science*, ed. Sidney Hook (New York: Collier, 1958), p. 20.

[23]Thomas P. Flint, "The Problem of Divine Freedom," *American Philosophical Quarterly* 20 (1983): 255. It should be noted that Flint is himself a libertarian, a compatibilist, and a proponent of middle knowledge.

It is quite clear that, in the light of these definitions, the views of compatibilists such as Mavrodes qualify as a version of determinism rather than indeterminism.

If the compatibilist still hopes to escape from this predicament, it is clear what he must do: *He must present his own definitions of determinism and indeterminism, and show why they are superior to the ones given by Taylor, Blanshard, and Flint.* In general, incompatibilists do not seem eager to undertake this task. Freddoso, however, has made an attempt in this direction which merits our attention. He notes that Molina (with whose position he agrees)

> presupposes the falsity of a principle that libertarians might naturally be inclined to endorse, viz., that an agent P freely performs an action A at time t only if there is a possible world w such that (i) w shares all and only the same *accidentally necessary propositions* with our world at t and (ii) at t in w P refrains from performing A. In opposition to the Ockhamists, Molina holds that God's past beliefs are just as necessary in the sense in question as are any other truths about the past. And, of course, there is no possible world in which God once believed that Peter would sin at t and in which Peter does not in fact sin at t.[24]

It will be noted that the principle rejected by Molina and Freddoso is essentially the same as the libertarian definition of freedom quoted from Flint. But, he goes on, Molina has "what seems to be a wholly adequate alternative" to this principle:

> He can distinguish what is accidentally necessary at a given time from what belongs, strictly speaking, to the causal history of the world at that time, where the world's causal history includes only past exercises of causal power. And . . . he can distinguish the principle just rejected from the benign principle that an agent P freely performs an action A at time t only if P's performing A does not obtain at t by a necessity of nature, where what occurs at a given time by a necessity of nature is a function of the *causal history* of the world at that time. Since Molina holds that God's foreknowledge of

[24]Introduction to Molina, *On Divine Foreknowledge (Part IV of Concordia)*, trans. Alfred J. Freddoso (Ithaca, N.Y.: Cornell University Press, 1988), sec. 4.5.

absolute future contingents is not a cause of anything, he can consistently hold that Peter's sin satisfies this principle.[25]

It seems likely that any attempt by a compatibilist on foreknowledge to define libertarian free will must come out resembling Freddoso's. One is tempted to reply that the definition has been arbitrarily gerrymandered in order to get the result the compatibilist wants, but this would be unfair to Freddoso, who developed his own conception of freedom independently of the foreknowledge controversy.[26] And part of his rationale for the definition will be discussed in the next paragraph. It is clear, however, that a compatibilist such as Molina or Freddoso is claiming that Peter can *have* the power to refrain from sinning *even though it is logically impossible that he should exercise that power under the existing circumstances.* But if one has the "power to do otherwise" only in that sense—the sense in which *having* the power does not guarantee that it is possible for the power to be *used*—then the central idea of libertarianism, as explicated in the definitions cited above from Taylor, Blanshard, and Flint, has been lost. Once again, we see that *the compatibilist on foreknowledge cannot consistently affirm libertarian free will.*

The central idea of the Molinist position, as explicated by Freddoso, seems to be that any determinism that results from divine foreknowledge is not a "serious" determinism, because it is not *causal*. God's foreknowledge, it is generally conceded, does not *cause* human actions or prevent the actions that are not taken, and so it cannot deprive agents of their free will. Now, two answers to this have already been given in chapter 4: First, the incompatibilist arguments given in this book in no way depend on the assumption that God's belief causes human actions, so those arguments cannot be answered by pointing out that it does not. Second, God's foreknowledge might very well *show* an action to be necessary, even if the foreknowledge is not what *makes* it necessary. These answers, I believe, are sufficient. Yet, in view of the frequency with which this objection arises, it may be worth a bit more attention.

[25]Ibid.
[26]See ibid., sec. 2.9.

The compatibilist may be seen as asserting an argument with three premises:

(3) In order for a person to be deprived of free will, she must be caused to act as she does, and causally prevented from acting otherwise.

(4) If God were to foreknow human actions, there would in general[27] be nothing other than the foreknowledge itself that would cause or prevent such actions.

(5) Divine foreknowledge would not itself cause or prevent human actions.

From these she infers

(6) If God were to foreknow human actions, persons would not in general be deprived of free will.

What shall we make of this argument? A first observation is that its premises certainly are *not* known to be true. (This, I submit, places them in strong contrast to the premises of the incompatibilist arguments, which enjoy powerful intuitive support.) (5), to be sure, seems rather plausible, and has been conceded above. Both (3) and (4), on the other hand, are eminently open to question. (3) may seem somewhat plausible, but it is hardly self-evident.[28] And (4) is really pure conjecture—if *anything* is clear from the controversy over free will, it is that the absence of determining causes for an event cannot be determined by simple inspection. So, if there is any force in the arguments for incompatibilism—and there is!—then the proper response to the argument (3)–(6) is simply to reject whichever of its premises seems weakest. If, and only if, the incompatibilist arguments have been *independently* refuted would it be reasonable to accept the argument (3)–(6) as sound.

It may be, however, that the compatibilist will want to insist on

---

[27]I say "in general" because, of course, there might be other causative or preventive factors in particular cases.

[28]Some support for (3) may perhaps be found in the fact that genuine theological fatalists (that is, persons who regard the incompatibilist arguments as not only *valid* but also *sound*) have often posited some factor *other* than divine foreknowledge as that which necessitates human action—say, an efficacious decree of God.

a more specific answer: *Which one* of the premises (3), (4), and (5) is the incompatibilist going to reject? My own inclination is to think that premise (4), resting as it does on a mere unsupported assertion, is most open to question. Taking the incompatibilist arguments to be correct, and adding (3) and (5) as premises, we are entitled to conclude that (4) is false—that *if* God were to foreknow human actions, there *would* be something other than foreknowledge itself that would cause or prevent such actions. If I am further pressed to say what *specifically* would be the cause of human actions if God foreknew them, I reply that the question is inappropriate and I am under no obligation to answer it. My view as a libertarian incompatibilist is that God *does not* foreknow human actions in detail, and I am surely under no obligation to speculate about how things would be in a universe so greatly different from the way I conceive the actual universe to be.[29]

In summary: Compatibilism requires that we have power to bring about past events, including events that have not in fact taken place. But the sense of "power" that is required if these claims are to be coherent is not the sense that is required for libertarian free will. *The compatibilist cannot consistently affirm libertarianism.*

Should we then conclude that Mavrodes, and other compatibilists, are after all soft determinists and not libertarians? Certainly this is not what they want to be and what they claim to be. But would it not be a striking confirmation of the incompatibilist's thesis if compatibilists who affirm our power *over* the past but deny our power to *change* the past find themselves forced implicitly to abandon the libertarian conception of freedom with which the discussion began?

[29]It should perhaps be emphasized that this is *not* the argument for incompatibilism which was rejected in chapter 4, which took as a premise that God is able to foreknow future actions only if sufficient causal conditions for those actions already exist. Rather, this "premise" has itself now been established on the basis of the arguments for incompatibilism, with (3) and (5) as supplementary premises.

[8]

Is "God Is Timeless" Intelligible?

Suppose that the argument for incompatibilism deployed in the last four chapters is successful. Suppose, also, that one is determined to affirm a libertarian view of free will. Does it follow that one must in consistency deny that God has full and detailed knowledge of the future? Perhaps surprisingly, the answer to this question given by the theological tradition is an emphatic No. One must, to be sure, give up the claim that God, *in time,* has *foreknowledge* of contingent events, and in particular of free choices, which are yet to come—that, after all, is what incompatibilism is all about. But this, so the answer goes, is because God is not *in time* at all; rather, God is an eternal, timeless being.[1] And ever since Boethius divine timelessness has been seen, along with other advantages, as a solution for the problem of foreknowledge and free will.

But divine timelessness has fallen on hard times. Probably the most common response to this doctrine in recent philosophy of religion is to dismiss it as incoherent or unintelligible. Sometimes

[1] I do not in general equate "eternal" with "timeless"; those who hold that God undergoes a succession of states are not thereby forced to deny that God is eternal, and they have usually not denied this. But in this and the following chapter I shall for convenience refer to the proponents of divine timelessness as "eternalists" and to their opponents as "temporalists."

the dismissal is offhand, with no reasons given, but in other cases arguments have been presented which demand careful consideration.[2] Several sympathetic expositions and defenses of the doctrine have also appeared in recent years,[3] so our task in the present chapter is to consider these criticisms and defenses of the intelligibility of divine timelessness, in preparation for our assessment of the acceptability of the doctrine in the next chapter. We shall begin by developing a formulation of the doctrine of divine timelessness which is as accurate and careful as possible. Then we shall consider, and answer, a number of objections to the coherence and intelligibility of the doctrine as thus formulated.[4]

Formulating Timelessness

What does it mean to say that God is timelessly eternal? The correct answer to this question is far from obvious, and often the doctrine is misunderstood even by those who claim to accept it.

---

[2]Among the more substantive critiques are William Kneale, "Time and Eternity in Theology," *Proceedings of the Aristotelian Society* (1961), pp. 87–108; Arthur N. Prior, "The Formalities of Omniscience," *Philosophy* 32 (1962): 119–29, reprinted in *Papers on Time and Tense* (Oxford: Oxford University Press, 1968), pp. 26–44; Robert C. Coburn, "Professor Malcolm on God," *Australasian Journal of Philosophy* 41 (1963: 143–62); Norman Kretzmann, "Omniscience and Immutability," *Journal of Philosophy* 63 (1966): 409–421; Nelson Pike, *God and Timelessness* (New York: Schocken, 1970); E. J. Khamara, "Eternity and Omniscience," *Philosophical Quarterly* 24 (1974): 204–219; Nicholas Wolterstorff, "God Everlasting," in *God and the Good*, ed. Clifton J. Orlebeke and Lewis B. Smedes (Grand Rapids, Mich.: Eerdmans, 1975); Richard Swinburne, *The Coherence of Theism* (Oxford: Oxford University Press, 1977), pp. 210–22; Paul Fitzgerald, "Stump and Kretzmann on time and Eternity," *Journal of Philosophy* 82 (1985): 260–69; and Richard A. Creel, *Divine Impassibility* (Cambridge: Cambridge University Press, 1986), pp. 92–96.

[3]Among these should be included Richard L. Purtill, "Foreknowledge and Fatalism," *Religious Studies* 10 (1974): 319–23; R. L. Sturch, "The Problem of the Divine Eternity," *Religious Studies* 10 (1974): 487–93; Paul Helm, "Timelessness and Foreknowledge," *Mind* n.s. 84 (1975): 516–27; Eleonore Stump and Norman Kretzmann, "Eternity," *Journal of Philosophy* 79 (1981): 429–58; William Hasker, "Concerning the Intelligibility of 'God is Timeless'," *New Scholasticism* 57 (1983): 170–95; and David B. Burrell, "God's Eternity," *Faith and Philosophy* 1 (1984): 389–406.

[4]For present purposes I will consider together criticisms that allege the doctrine to be meaningless with those that claim it to be self-contradictory or in contradiction with essential principles of theology.

The doctrine that God is timeless turns out, when properly understood, to be a very strange doctrine indeed. The problem with deviant versions of the theory is not that they are strange, but that they are not strange enough to have a chance of being true.

What criteria must be met by an acceptable version of the doctrine of timelessness? The first criterion is that this is to be a doctrine of *divine* timelessness. That is to say, it must be a doctrine about *God*, in the sense in which that term is understood in the Jewish and Christian faiths: God is the Creator and Sustainer of the universe; he has given the moral law to human beings and desires them to abide by it; he has acted in history to redeem his people; is holy, just, and loving; and so on. A doctrine of timelessness which could not apply to a being with these characteristics would not be a doctrine about *God* and would thus (from the standpoint of those religions) be of minimal interest.

A second criterion may appear less obvious, but I believe it can be justified: an acceptable doctrine of timelessness must provide a solution to the problem of free will and foreknowledge. It is true that not all theologians who have espoused timelessness have put the doctrine to this use, and I am not claiming that this problem was the main reason for the adoption of the theory of timelessness. But Boethius, Anselm, and Aquinas are the central figures of the eternalist tradition, and the fact that all three of them used the doctrine to solve the free will problem justifies my claim that a doctrine that could not be so used would not be faithful to their intentions. Furthermore, this stipulation has significant philosophical advantages in that it places constraints on the doctrine of timelessness that will be of considerable assistance as we seek to develop the best possible formulation.

What exactly is meant—or should reasonably be meant—by asking whether this doctrine is intelligible? As recent philosophy has shown, questions of this sort are difficult to settle without begging the question, and any general criterion of meaningfulness which might be appealed to will probably turn out to be even more dubious than the cases it is called upon to settle. But as a minimum requirement we can say that an intelligible doctrine must be expressible in grammatically well-formed sentences. (I assume that a sentence consists of *words*, as opposed to nonsense syllables, of the language in which it is written.) We may also require that an intelligible doctrine should not be contradictory or otherwise logically impossible. It would seem, furthermore, that a proposition is not understood unless it is possible to give an account of at least some of the nontrivial inferential relationships that hold between it and other relevant propositions. But is this enough? We may be inclined to think that understanding "God is timeless" requires that we have some idea of "what it would be like" for the proposition to be true. But "like" for whom? Things are not supposed to be different for *us* because God is timeless. (That God is timeless is not an empirical proposition.) Is the question, then, what it is like *for God*? If so, the requirement is much too strong. As Thomas Nagel has pointed out, if bats, or Martians, are conscious beings, then there must be "something it is like to be" a bat or a Martian.[5] But there is no guarantee that *human beings* must be able to grasp what it is like to be one of these things.

Perhaps the best we can do, under the circumstances, is to make the notion of intelligibility person-relative in the following way: if a person claims to have a belief that she expresses in well-formed sentences that are free from contradiction, and of whose inferential connections with other sentences she can give an account, her claim to understand the assertion in question is to be (provisionally) accepted. And if someone else professes herself unable to comprehend what is being asserted, this will be taken (pending further argument) merely as an admission of personal incapacity, with no necessary bearing on the general intelligibility of the view in question. It is clear that this approach tends to favor those who find a given assertion to be intelligible, but I think that is proper in such controversies. The inference "I don't understand it, therefore it is unintelligible" is too easy to be good philosophy.[6]

But what sort of timelessness is in question here? Most philosophers will probably admit that it makes sense to speak of the

---

[5]Thomas Nagel, "What Is It Like to Be a Bat?" in *Mortal Questions* (New York: Cambridge, 1979), pp. 165–80.

[6]But is it any better to argue, "I understand it, therefore it is intelligible"? This inference has at least the merit of being valid, but it may tend to beg the question. The correct principle, however, is the following: "I seem to myself to understand it, therefore I have good prima facie reason for regarding it as intelligible."

objects of mathematics as timeless: as Kneale points out,[7] it would be odd to state the truths of arithmetic in past or future tenses, for this would at least suggest the possibility that such truths might be different at different times. In fact, we think that the passage of time is simply irrelevant to mathematical truths: the present tense in "$2 + 2 = 4$" is a timeless present.

But the very facts that make it natural to speak of the timelessness of mathematical objects make the notion of timelessness problematic as applied to God. Mathematical objects, it is sometimes said, are *entia rationis*: their very being consists in their availability as objects of thought. But God's being is *not* supposed to consist merely in the fact that it is possible for us to think of him. Nor can we say that temporal events are irrelevant to God—not at least so long as we represent him as caring for men and women, answering prayer, and acting redemptively in history. And this, as Kneale rightly sees, points us to the crux of the problem. For we are here speaking of a timeless being who is also a *living person*: in Boethius's words, eternity is "the complete and simultaneous possession of endless life."[8] But is this intelligible? Kneale says, "I can attach no meaning to the word 'life' unless I am allowed to suppose that what has life acts . . . [L]ife must at least involve some incidents in time, and . . . to act purposefully is to act with the thought of what will come about after the beginning of the action."[9] In dealing with such matters, the timelessness of abstract entities is of little help, and I think Kneale is within his rights when he demands a further explanation from those who speak of God as timeless.

Before attempting this, however, we turn briefly to our other criterion for an acceptable doctrine of timelessness: such a doctrine must solve the problem of free will and foreknowledge. The merit of this requirement, from the present standpoint, is that it imposes very precise constraints on the sense in which God must be timeless. Stated briefly, the required notion of timelessness is as follows: God exists, but there is no time at which he exists, nor does

---

[7]Kneale, "Time and Eternity," pp. 97–98.

[8]Boethius, *The Consolation of Philosophy*, ed. James J. Buchanan (New York: Frederick Ungar, 1957), Book V, Prose 6.

[9]Kneale, "Time and Eternity," p. 99.

he exist at all times. (The last conjunct guards against a misinterpretation of the second.) This is of course impossible, *unless* God exists as a timeless being. And note that the formula actually makes God timeless in a stronger sense than numbers are: it may be odd to say "5 was a prime number" or "Tomorrow 2 plus 7 will be 9," but we would not be likely to call these assertions false, and certainly it would be wrong to say: "At no time has 5 been a prime number." Yet the eternalist *must* say: "At no time has God ever existed."

But why must he say this? Or why do I say he must say it? The reasoning is straightforward. If God exists at any time, he exists at all times. (God is ingenerable and incorruptible.) If God exists at all times, he knows at all times whatever is true, including future actions of his creatures. And from this it follows, by the standard incompatibilist arguments, that the creatures have no free will. There are, as we have seen, various ways one may attempt to avoid this conclusion, but the solution via the doctrine of timelessness avoids it by denying that God knows what will happen *at some time before it happens*. Rather, God's knowledge is timeless, outside of time altogether.[10] And this is what requires us to say: there is no time at which God exists.[11]

Another, perhaps less jarring, way of stating this point is the following: God has neither temporal extension nor temporal location. Other entities, at any given moment, are located at a certain point in time; their temporal extension covers all of the time during which they exist.[12] Neither of these things is true of God. It is

[10]More will be said on this topic in the next chapter.

[11]Compare Anselm: "In no place or time, then, is this Being properly said to exist." *Monologium*, chap. 22, in *St. Anselm: Basic Writings*, 2d ed., trans. S. N. Deane (La Salle, Ill.: Open Court, 1962), p. 81.

[12]Actually, this is not quite correct. As Dennis C. Holt has pointed out ("Timelessness and the Metaphysics of Temporal Existence," *American Philosophical Quarterly* 18 [1981]: 149–56), it is strictly speaking not objects and persons but rather events and processes that have temporal location, temporal extension, and temporal parts. It is not entirely clear how much difference this makes to the doctrine of timelessness. On the surface, it may seem that all that is required is a trivial restatement, in which not God himself but God's *life* and God's *actions* are said to lack temporal location and extension. But insofar as Holt's point tends to undermine the general symmetry between space and time (on which expositions of timelessness usually depend), it may have wider ramifications. Holt himself uses the point to attack several arguments in support of timelessness given by Anselm.

not that God exists at *all* times; rather, he exists at *no* time, outside of time altogether. To say that God lacks temporal location and extension enables us to mobilize parallels drawn from the relationship between God and space. God is not at *this* place or *that* place, nor yet in all places, though no place is beyond the reach of his power. But when I build a house, I do not thereby create a structure that contains a certain volume of God! God is not in space, space is in God—or, as theologians have said, God is in space in his activity and power, but not in his essence. These ways of speaking about God's relation to space are more strongly entrenched in theology than is the doctrine of timelessness, and so the analogy or symmetry between space and time can be used to explain and support the latter doctrine. (Conversely, the discovery of and emphasis upon disanalogies between space and time tend to weaken support for the doctrine of timelessness.)

But can we conceive of a *living* timeless being? About this Kneale says, "On the face of it, talk about life without a distinction of earlier and later is self-contradictory."[13] Robert C. Coburn argues that a timeless being could not remember, anticipate, reflect, deliberate, decide, intend anything, or act intentionally and concludes from this that a timeless being could not be a person.[14] Nelson Pike, after an extensive discussion, comes more cautiously to the same conclusion.[15] Any attempt to exhibit "God is timeless" as a meaningful assertion must meet this challenge head-on.

Before undertaking this task, we need to consider a little more about the sort of understanding we seek. I think we must give up at the outset any thought of imagining or understanding empathetically "what it is like to be" a timeless person. We will speak of God's experiences in terms drawn from our own experience as finite persons, but no experience of ours is timeless, so in that respect the analogy is not only incomplete but incompletable. Yet the theologians of timelessness have found a basis for analogy even here: according to them, *eternity is more akin to a moment of time than to a temporal process.*[16] That which can exist in a moment of time,

[13]Kneale, "Time and Eternity," p. 107.
[14]"Professor Malcolm on God," pp. 155–56.
[15]*God and Timelessness*, pp. 121–29.
[16]Compare Swinburne: "Another way of putting these points is to say that God

we might say, can also exist in no time at all, whereas in a temporally extended process the distinction of earlier and later is essential. Thus, those attributes of temporal beings which we ascribe to a timeless God must be logically capable of being *momentary* attributes of a temporal being.

And this brings us to the first step of our task, which is to sort out those attributes of ordinary persons which are to be seriously attributed to God, from those which are not. Among the attributes cited by Coburn, even a temporalist might hesitate to say that God "deliberates," since this implies a period of time during which God does not yet know what he will do. The same might be said of "decides," which suggests that the decision is preceded by a state of indecision. It may be that God *wills* and *does* certain things, but that he never *decided* to do them, though certainly whatever he will, he wills decisively. And of course "learning" (not mentioned by Coburn) would also be excluded, in that it implies a previous period of ignorance on God's part.

Remembering and anticipating, on the other hand, might very well be attributes of an everlasting God but cannot be attributes of God if God is timeless. We are driven, then, to search for certain core attributes of persons which the eternalist *does* seriously ascribe to his timeless God. If the eternalist does not take his stand somewhere on this question, he will not be able to save his thesis from the death of a thousand qualifications.

I suggest the following: If "God is timeless" is to be a meaningful assertion, then it must be possible to say of a timeless God that he *knows*, that he *acts*, and that he *responds* to the actions of temporal beings. A doctrine of timelessness which does not allow that God can do at least these things would not be a doctrine of the timelessness of *God* (in the sense in which that word is used in the Jewish and Christian religions), and would thus be of no theological interest. And on the other hand, I think it is reasonable to suppose that if we can meaningfully ascribe to God knowledge,

---

has his own time scale. There is only one instant of time on the scale; and everything which is ever true of God is true of him at that instant" (*The Coherence of Theism*, p. 216). And Boethius: "The now that flows away makes time; the now that stands still makes eternity" (*De Trinitate*, quoted by Aquinas in *Summa Theologiae*, I, 10, 3).

action, and responsiveness, we can also say of him the other things
that must be said to sustain a full-blooded theism.

Of the three, "knowing" is perhaps the least problematic. Pike,
indeed, chides Coburn for neglecting knowing as an eminently
personal attribute that is not so clearly time-bound as those that
Coburn does mention.[17] Knowing is not a time-consuming activity: "How long did it take you to know that?" is meaningless
unless "know" means "learn" or "come to know." And it is not a
necessary truth that whatever I know, I must previously have
learned. To be sure, most of what we know we are not aware of at
a given moment. But this is a limitation of our finitude, which
obviously does not apply to God.

Pike agrees with this, but he still finds the notion of a timeless
knower problematic, for he doubts that a timeless being could act
in such a way as to give us evidence that would warrant our
ascribing knowledge to it. In fact, Pike doubts that a timeless being
could act at all.[18] This will certainly have to be challenged. But it
seems that if action can be ascribed to a timeless God, the attribution of knowledge to him will present few if any additional problems.[19]

What then of action? The personal God of theism must be active,
but what sorts of acts should we consider?[20] I believe it will assist
our considerations if we begin with the simplest, most minimal act
ascribed to God by theology—namely, God's preservation of the
world in being from moment to moment. This is minimal, not in
the sense that it does not take much to accomplish it, but in that it
is a completely *general* action: It is not something God does more in
one place than another, or more in one time than another, or to any
one thing more than another. Schleiermacher, indeed, reduced in

---

[17]*God and Timelessness*, pp. 123–25.

[18]Ibid., pp. 125–27.

[19]E. J. Khamara, to be sure, argues that "Knowledge is . . . like perception . . .
in that, *as ordinarily understood*, they can only be ascribed to agents who are supposed to endure in time" ("Eternity and Omniscience," p. 211). But as an argument against eternalism, this is patently question-begging.

[20]In speaking of God's actions in the plural, I am already departing from the
strict truth, according to the eternalist tradition. God, being simple, performs (and
is) only *one* act; what we, improperly, refer to as his many actions are simply
aspects of that one, simple act.

effect *all* of God's actions to this one, and although most Christians would not agree with the reduction, they could accept that preservation is basic in God's dealing with the world: whatever else God may do with a creature (except annihilate it), he must also and at the same time act to preserve it in being.

But how can we understand preservation as the act of a *timeless* being? Pike considers the notion of divine preservation in the light of several examples, his favorite being the action of a singer in sustaining a musical tone. He rightly points out that in all of the examples the *temporal relation* between the sustaining action and the sustained entity is of the essence (the singer's singing is *temporally extended*, just as is the resulting note).[21] That is to say: The relation between a temporal action and its result is not the same as that between a nontemporal action and *its* result!

Perhaps this is not utterly surprising. But how *are* we to grasp the notion of a timeless action? The traditional answer to this question proceeds by means of the analogy, mentioned earlier, between space and time: our efforts to grasp the notion of a *nontemporal* agent many be facilitated by considering the idea of a *nonspatial* agent.[22] But first, consider some ordinary spatial agents. Modern physics has made familiar the idea that a causal entity is not necessarily either spatially *extended* nor spatially *contiguous* with its effect. And the notion of action at a distance, though occasioning some discomfort, was basic to physics at least from Newton to Einstein. (Of course, it is only the *conceivability* of these ideas, not their physical correctness, that is in question here.)

So a nonextended object can be a cause and can produce effects at spatially remote points. But what of a cause that lacks also spatial *location*? Here we step out of physics and into metaphysics and theology—but we remain, I think, well within the boundaries of intelligibility. (This in any case is what I am going to assume. I do not think there is much hope of being able to explain the timelessness of God to someone for whom, e.g., mind-body dualism is unintelligible.) Cartesian souls do not *exist at* any point in space but they *produce effects* in space, that is to say, in the pineal gland—or in

[21]*God and Timelessness*, pp. 110–18.
[22]For an example of this strategy, see Richard H. Purtill, "Foreknowledge and Fatalism," p. 322–23.

the "liaison brain" (Eccles) that is part of the dominant cerebral hemisphere. And in the case of God, nonspatial causality possesses distinct advantages: a nonspatial agent is *no distance away from*, and thus is *not spatially separated from*, its spatial effect. Thus, God has been compared to the "circle whose center is everywhere and whose circumference is nowhere"; he is closer to us than our own breathing.

If this is intelligible (and I believe that it is), then it shows us how to speak of God also as a timeless being. Just as the nonspatial God can act outside of space so as to produce effects at every point in space, so the timeless God can act outside of time, that is, in eternity, so as to produce effects at every point in time. And just such an action is God's preservation in being of the created, temporal world.[23]

So far, I am in agreement with Schleiermacher, who no doubt would applaud the rebuttal of Pike's objection to the intelligibility of a timeless act that sustains the temporal world. But for Schleiermacher, this is the *only* kind of divine action that can be rendered intelligible. According to him, God cannot do any *particular* thing in the world, such as parting the Red Sea for the children of Israel or creating the heavens and the earth out of nothing. And although this limitation undoubtedly has other roots in Schleiermacher's theology taken as a whole, he seems to regard it also as an inference specifically from the doctrine of God's timelessness:

> The divine omnipotence can never in any way enter as a supplement (so to speak) to the natural causes in their sphere; for then it must like them work temporarily and spatially; and at one time working so, and then again, not so, it would not be self-identical and so would be neither eternal nor omnipotence.[24]

[23]Compare R. L. Sturch: "In the case, then, of the statement 'God sustains the universe', a believer in timeless eternity could presumably say that all he implies is (a) that God wishes the universe to continue in being and (b) that (God being omnipotent) when God wishes something that something happens" ("The Problem of the Divine Eternity," p. 488). The meaning of this is entirely clear, and it in no way implies that God's action is itself temporal.

[24]Friedrich Schleiermacher, *The Christian Faith*, 2d ed., trans. H. R. Mackintosh and J. S. Stewart (Edinburgh: T. & T. Clark, 1956), p. 212. Presumably, this argument is Pike's justification for basing his discussion of "Timelessness and Power" on Schleiermacher. Schleiermacher is certainly no representative of ortho-

There is, however, a confusion in this argument. Schleiermacher seems to suppose that if a spatially and temporally limited event (such as the parting of the Red Sea) is the effect of a divine action, then the action itself must be spatially and temporally limited, and therefore not eternal. But this is inconsistent with the reasoning about preservation. If the divine act partakes of the temporal character of its consequences, then the preservation of the (according to Schleiermacher) spatially and temporally infinite universe must itself be infinitely extended—that is, everlasting rather than timeless. But what we must rather say is this: the *act* of preservation is timeless, whereas its *temporal effect* is of infinite duration. But although a single, timeless divine act *may* produce effects throughout all of time, it *need not* do so: there is no reason why a timeless divine act may not have as its temporal effect a specific, limited event—the parting of the Red Sea, or the raising of Jesus from the dead.

I conclude, then, that it is intelligible to speak of a timeless being as acting, and this not only in the form of general actions (such as preservation) that occur everywhere and at all times indiscriminately, but also in the form of particular actions whose results happen once-for-all and never recur. But it still remains to give an account of the *responsive* action of a timeless being. And it may well seem that this creates a major obstacle. For suppose we admit (as has been argued) that the timeless action of a timeless being could bring about a variety of distinct events occurring at different points in time. Still, it may seem, this is possible only to the extent that the entire temporal sequence unfolds according to a fixed plan—so that it is, as it were, programmed. But if the sequence is to include genuine *response*, the temporal element seems to be reintroduced in a way that cannot easily be eliminated. For in responding to another it is of the essence that one first *acts*, then *waits* for the other

dox or mainstream Christian theology, and Pike realizes that most Christians would not accept his "reduction" of creation and other divine activities to preservation (see Pike, *God and Timelessness*, pp. 110–11). But the passage quoted in the text represents this reduction specifically as an inference from the doctrine of timelessness. Perhaps, then, Schleiermacher is showing us what orthodox eternalists *ought* to say about God's power even if he disagrees with what they actually *do* say.

to react, then acts *responsively*, and so on. There seems to be no way this sequence could be collapsed, as it were, into a single timeless moment.

An interesting response to this problem has been developed by R. L. Sturch and also, independently, by Richard Creel, who affirms that God is "impassible in will."[25] For our statement of the view we turn to Sturch, who cites the story from I Kings 21, in which God first threatens judgment because of Ahab's sin and then postpones it because of Ahab's repentance. He asks: "Is it possible to make sense of this sort of sequence with a timeless God?" and replies:

> In order to do so, I think we must conceive of God's decrees as being normally conditional. (So Moses took them; cf. Deuteronomy 30:15–20.) God must be thought of as, in the very act of creation, laying down what his actions (to us, *re*actions) would be in every possible set of circumstances that his creatures might bring about.

This is followed by a whole series of examples, after which Sturch continues:

> It is arguable that something like this is required by any Christian who takes seriously the saying that 'God is not a man, that he should repent'. If this is so, then whether God be timeless or not, his plans must be thought of somewhat in the way I have been describing. He does not then change, but we do.[26]

Noteworthy here is the phrase "whether God be timeless or not." Nothing about Sturch's view requires that God be timeless, *or even that God should have detailed foreknowledge.* And Creel, in fact, denies both claims, being both a temporalist and an incompatibilist.

Now, I am not sure that I have a conclusive refutation of this view, and yet I find it very difficult to accept. I shall offer two

---

[25]See Sturch, "The Problem of the Divine Eternity," and Creel, *Divine Impassibility*, pp. 14–34.
[26]"The Problem of the Divine Eternity," p. 491.

objections, one that applies both to Creel and to Sturch, and one that applies only to Sturch. The first objection is this: Creel and Sturch picture God as deciding from eternity on a set of *conditional decrees*: items such as, "If Ahab repents I shall postpone judgment, but if he does not, judgment will fall immediately." Now, there is no difficulty in supposing God to issue such decrees. One would suppose, however, that some *further* act of God is required in implementing one decree or the other—God, we may say, has already *decided* what he will do in either case, but he now must *carry out* the decision. But for the Creel-Sturch view to work, there *cannot be* any such further act of God; God himself, we may say, *does nothing differently* whether he postpones judgment or lets it fall immediately. What accounts for the differential response, then, must be some sort of mechanism *built into the creation itself* which will assure that the appropriate response to Ahab occurs.[27] But in the first place, it is difficult if not outright impossible to imagine what such a mechanism might be—and there is, of course, no reason whatever to suspect the existence of any such mechanism, apart from the particular theories of divine action that are being considered. For me, anyway, the postulation of such a mechanism is too high a price to pay for the theories.

The other objection is this: One might expect a theory of divine action developed for the doctrine of timelessness to make more use of the distinctive resources of that doctrine. Consider the following question: Are we to suppose that God, when he issues these conditional decrees, does not know what Ahab's *actual* response to him will be? For Creel, of course, the answer must be that God does *not* know this. But for an eternalist such as Sturch, God *does* know—so, why all these conditional decrees?

This question leads us back to what I think is a better solution of the problem of divine responsive action. We noted earlier that responsive action seems to be inherently temporal: one waits to see what the other will do before deciding on one's next action. We may now add that this is so, *so long as it is not possible for the agent to*

---

[27]Creel actually proposes an illustration in which a scientist constructs a mechanism by which his "responses" to an experimental situation are implemented (*Divine Impassibility*, pp. 23–24).

anticipate the other's response. Consider, for example, a game of chess played by correspondence. Normally, a player sends his move, waits for the response, then sends the next move. But sometimes it happens that the opponent's reply can be anticipated with a high degree of confidence. In this case, as an expedient for saving time and postage, it is a simply matter to include, along with the original move, one's response to the opponent's next move or even series of moves. Thus in the French Defense one might put down: "Pawn to K5; if Pawn to QB4, Pawn to QR3; if Bishop takes Knight (*check*), Pawn takes Bishop." Here by the single act of mailing a postcard one effects an entire series of responses. The requirement of a temporal spread has been eliminated. Of course, the difficulty is in *knowing* what the opponent will do: in the example given, neither of the opponent's moves is strictly forced, and if he chooses another line, the "response" will have been invalidated. God, on the other hand, is supposed to know everything: it will never turn out that he "responded" to a move that we decided not to make.[28]

I believe what has been said here goes some distance towards showing how it is conceivable that a timeless being not only can know but act, and not only act but act responsively. An essential insight that underlies what has been said is that *the temporal characteristics of the effects of divine actions need not characterize the actions themselves.* The act of preserving a temporally extended universe need not itself be temporally extended; the acts by which various specific events are brought about at different times need not themselves be temporally separated; and the act of bringing about responses that occur in time to the actions of temporal beings need not itself be a temporal act.

And by thus vindicating our claim that a timeless God can know, can act, and can respond, we have completed the first phase of our examination of the doctrine. We now proceed to examine some further objections.

Objections to Timelessness

One group of objections, first stated by Arthur Prior and since developed by Norman Kretzmann, Robert Coburn, and Nicholas

---

[28]But doesn't this reintroduce the problem of free will and foreknowledge? I do not think so; for further discussion of this point see the next chapter.

Wolterstorff, claims that a timeless God could not be omniscient. Kretzmann argues that an immutable God cannot be omniscient, because he cannot know what time it is.[29] If God knew, for instance, that it is now 10:45, and then a few minutes later that it is no longer 10:45 but is now 10:51, then God would have changed: at one point God believed the proposition "It is now 10:45," and later on he no longer believed this but instead believed "It is now 10:51." The point is reinforced by Creel: "That God sees things as they are is unnegotiable, and a changing thing can be known as changing only by a knower whose awareness follows along with it. . . . This seems true of God as well as of all other knowers."[30]

Now, it seems to me that Kretzmann and Creel are quite correct: this *does* constitute a change in God. A temporalist, I believe, must just swallow this, and admit that God is *not* immutable in the very strong sense Kretzmann is working with (which seems in any case to be religiously quite irrelevant).[31]

But if God is timeless, the situation is altered. "It is now 10:45" states a relation between the *time of speaking* and a point in our temporal metric. But a timeless God does not speak, listen, or do anything else at any particular time (though God may timelessly bring it about that phenomena occur at some time—say, a voice speaking out of the sky—through which temporal beings will experience God's speaking to them). There just *are* no facts about the temporal relations between a timeless being and temporal beings, because there are no such relations; thus there is nothing there for God or anyone else either to know or to be ignorant of.[32]

Arthur Prior, however, has argued that if God's knowledge is timeless, then it must be limited to those truths that are themselves timeless, and this will leave a great many temporal facts that God cannot know:

> For example, God could not, on the view I am considering, know that the 1960 final examinations at Manchester are now over; for

[29]See "Omniscience and Immutability."
[30]*Divine Impassibility*, p. 88.
[31]The right way to take Kretzmann's argument is to see it as directed against the notion of an absolutely immutable, temporally everlasting God; the doctrine of timelessness does not play a significant role in the article. (This interpretation is confirmed by Stump and Kretzmann, "Eternity," pp. 455–58.)
[32]This point is made clearly by Pike (*God and Timelessness*, pp. 87–95), and also by Paul Helm ("Timelessness and Foreknowledge," p. 522).

this isn't something that He or anyone could know timelessly, because it just isn't true timelessly. It's true now, but it wasn't true a
year ago (I write this on 29th August 1960) and so far as I can see all
that can be said on this subject timelessly is that the finishing-date of
the 1960 final examinations is an earlier one than 29th August, and
this is *not* the thing we know when we know that those examinations are over. I cannot think of any better way of showing this than
one I've used before, namely, the argument that what we know
when we know that the 1960 final examinations are over can't be
just a timeless relation between dates because this isn't the thing
we're *pleased* about when we're pleased that the examinations are
over.[33]

According to Prior, a timeless God could not know that "The
examinations are now over." But that proposition is entailed by
"The finishing-date of the examinations is an earlier one than 29th
August" together with "It is now 29th August." God could timelessly know the first of this pair, but could he know the second? It
is not of course a question of its being 29th August *for God*, but of
whether God can know the thing that Prior knows, when Prior
knows it is the 29th of August. If he cannot, then it seems to follow
that he is not omniscient. It is certain that if God *does* know what
Prior knows, he could not *express* it as Prior does, by saying "It is
now 29th August." But—as Hector-Neri Castañeda has pointed
out[34]—this is not a limitation that is unique to God. On the contrary, the limitation is shared by each one of us, and indeed by
Prior himself, *on any day except the 29th of August.* Consider now
Prior's own case: On 28th August he does not yet know that "It is
now 29th August" for this is not yet true. Nor does he know this
on 30th August, for it is then no longer true. Does it follow that
there is some item of knowledge that Prior has on the 29th but
lacks on the 28th and 30th? This does not seem very plausible.
When Prior said, on 28th August, "Tomorrow is 29th August," or
when he said, on 30th August, "Yesterday was 29th August," it
seems reasonable to suppose that he expressed thereby the *same*

---

[33]"The Formalities of Omniscience," in *Papers on Time and Tense*, p. 29.
[34]"Omniscience and Indexical Reference," *Journal of Philosophy* 64 (1967): 204–
10.

item of knowledge that he expressed on the 29th with "It is now 29th August." God, of course, could not express this item by saying "Yesterday was 29th August," but no doubt he could do so in some other way. One possibility, suggested by Castañeda's discussion, is the following: God expresses the item by saying (or timelessly affirming): "When Prior says 'It is now 29th August,' and . . . [assume other information added so as to identify the occasion uniquely], it is *then* 29th August."[35] No doubt there are other possibilities. It seems clear, however, that Prior has not succeeded in his enterprise of pointing out gaps in God's knowledge.[36]

Even if this is correct, Prior has a parting shot for the eternalist: "In any case it seems an extraordinary way of affirming God's omniscience if a person, when asked what God knows *now*, must say 'Nothing', and when asked what He knew yesterday, must again say 'Nothing', and must yet again say 'Nothing' when asked what God will know tomorrow."[37]

An interesting reply to this has been suggested by Paul Helm: When asked what God knows now, one should reply "Everything," meaning by this that it is correct *now* to say that God knows everything. This ingenious answer shifts the force of the adverb 'now' so that it qualifies, not the time of God's knowing, but only the time at which *we speak* of God's knowledge.[38] But in a sense

[35]Compare Castañeda, "Omniscience and Indexical Reference," pp. 204–208.

[36]Patrick Grim ("Against Omniscience: The Case from Essential Indexicals," *Noûs* 19 [1985]: 151–80) argues ingeniously that it is possible for someone to know the propositions expressed using Castañeda's quasi-indicators, while failing to know what was expressed in the original propositions using indexicals. All of his examples, however, involve subjects who lack certain knowledge about the situation in question, knowledge that God could not possibly lack. So Grim's argument, though perhaps successful in other cases, fails entirely to indicate any gaps in God's knowledge. In denying that Prior possesses any item of knowledge that God lacks, I have left it open whether the *propositions* God knows are the same ones that Prior knows. If they are not, then the doctrine of omniscience cannot be stated by saying that God knows all true propositions, and finding the right way to state it will no doubt be an intriguing exercise. But for present purposes I have no need to decide this point. For further discussion of Prior's and Grim's objections, see Pike (*God and Timelessness*, pp. 92–95), Helm ("Timelessness and Foreknowledge," pp. 517–18), and Jonathan L. Kvanvig, *The Possibility of an All-Knowing God* (New York: St. Martin's Press, 1986), pp. 35–71.

[37]"The Formalities of Omniscience," in *Papers on Time and Tense*, p. 29.

[38]"The question is thus about what a temporal individual judges at a particular time that God knows timelessly. It is equivalent to 'What may God now be said by

Prior's original point remains: if the adverb 'now' is to qualify the time of God's knowing (which is how the question was intended and would ordinarily be understood), then the answer must indeed be "Nothing"—just as we said earlier that the eternalist must hold that there is no time at which God exists.

The general point here is that if the doctrine of timelessness is true, then a great many of the things believers are accustomed to say about God will be strictly and literally false.[39] What is strictly true of God will emerge only after we pass all of our everyday religious statements through the filter of the doctrine of timelessness. But for ordinary religious purposes, there is generally no point in doing this. So we will continue to speak, for instance, of God's having chosen us in Christ "before the foundation of the world," in spite of the fact that it was neither before the foundation of the world nor at any other time that God did this. Only in very special theological contexts will we pause to make the corrections required by the doctrine of timelessness.

Is this cause for concern? Probably the disparity between ordinary religious talk about God and that which (according to the doctrine of timelessness) is required for theological accuracy will occasion some discomfort for most believers when they first become aware of it. But it is not clear that this should alarm anyone. Certainly, the theoretical discourse of physics deviates greatly from our everyday talk about physical objects without in any way implying that that talk is wrong, inappropriate, or out of place. But if we are going to seriously discuss the ultimate nature and structure of physical reality, a different mode of conceptualization is required. It is not immediately obvious that or why a similar situation could not obtain in theology.

We turn now to a further problem for the doctrine of timelessness, one that I have come to regard as the most serious difficulty

you to know (timelessly)?' For a believer in timeless divine omniscience, the answer to this rather bizarre question is that God may be said now to know timelessly exactly what he may be said at any other time to know timelessly" (Helm, "Timelessness and Foreknowledge," pp. 518–19).

[39]The strength of Nicholas Wolterstorff's essay "God Everlasting" lies in his effective marshaling of biblical and theological statements that imply temporal activity on the part of God. Whether the doctrine of timelessness can deal adequately with this language is of course the point at issue.

the doctrine has to face: it may be termed the *problem of the presence of time in eternity*. This problem is suggested in various ways by Prior, by the early Kretzmann, and by Creel, but I will introduce it by way of Stump and Kretzmann and the notion of simultaneity. One of the characteristic affirmations of the doctrine of timelessness is that the whole of eternity is simultaneous with every moment of time. This claim, however, gives rise to one of the simpler objections to the doctrine, as stated for instance by Anthony Kenny: "On St. Thomas' view, my typing of this paper is simultaneous with the whole of eternity. Again, on this view, the great fire of Rome is simultaneous with the whole of eternity. Therefore, while I type these very words, Nero fiddles heartlessly on."[40]

It is to be hoped that by now the reader will not be overly impressed with this objection. Among other things that have been said, the assertion that God does *not* exist at any moment of our time should sufficiently indicate that God cannot be "simultaneous" with temporal things in the flatly literal sense required for Kenny's objection to go through. My own inclination would be to say that the statement about simultaneity is simply a metaphorical way of putting the point that all of time is "present" in the "now" of eternity.

Stump and Kretzmann, however, think they can do better than this in interpreting eternalist talk about simultaneity. Indeed, their notion of *ET-simultaneity* may fairly be called the theoretical centerpiece of their article. As a background for this notion they take the fact, familiar from the physics of relativity, that 'simultaneity' must be defined *relative to a given reference-frame*.[41] But in speaking of the relation of simultaneity which holds between eternal things and temporal things, "we are dealing with two equally real modes of existence, neither of which is reducible to any other mode of existence, [so] the definition must be constructed in terms of *two* reference frames and *two* observers."[42] In view of this, they set up their definition as follows:

[40] *The God of the Philosophers* (Oxford: Oxford University Press, 1979), pp. 38–39. According to Kenny, the same objection was stated by Suarez.
[41] "Eternity," pp. 436–37.
[42] Ibid., p. 439.

Let 'x' and 'y' range over entities and events. Then
(ET) For every x and every y, x and y are ET-simultaneous iff
      (i) either x is eternal and y is temporal, or vice versa; and
    (ii) For some observer, A, in the unique eternal reference frame, x and y are both present—i.e., either x is eternally present and y is observed as temporally present, or vice versa; and
   (iii) for some observer B, in one of the infinitely many temporal reference frames, x and y are both present—i.e., either x is observed as eternally present and y is temporally present, or vice versa.[43]

Stump and Kretzmann point out that according to this definition the relation of ET-simultaneity is neither reflexive nor transitive, so difficulties of the sort urged by Kenny cannot arise. And the notion has other advantages as well, for which the reader is referred to their article. Furthermore, "From a temporal standpoint, the present is ET-simultaneous with the whole infinite extent of an eternal entity's life. From the standpoint of eternity, every time is present, co-occurrent with the whole of infinite atemporal duration."[44]

The notion of ET-simultaneity is an admirable theoretical achievement. As it is stated, however, it leaves unanswered two questions that fairly leap out at one from the printed formula. Or perhaps it is the same question twice over: what are we to make of the clause "x and y are both present" *when one of the relata is temporal and the other is eternal*? For an entity to be temporal, after all, just *is* for that entity's existence to be spread out in a temporal sequence—but in eternity, *nothing* exists in temporal sequence, so *how can a temporal "y" be present in eternity*? Again, to be eternal *means* to exist in a "total present" *without* temporal sequence, whereas time is precisely the medium of temporal succession, so *how can an eternal "x" be present in time*? If there are not good answers to these questions, the notion of ET-simultaneity will collapse.

I believe that Stump and Kretzmann are not unaware of this

[43]Ibid.
[44]Ibid., p. 441.

difficulty, and that their formula contains at least a pointer—one can hardly say more—in the direction of a possible solution. For after each occurrence of the problematic phrase the phrase is glossed as follows:

> (ii) . . . x is eternally present and y is observed as temporally present . . .
>
> (iii) . . . x is observed as eternally present and y is temporally present . . . .

It cannot be accidental that we have in each case the contrast between "*is* present" and "*is observed as* present," with the "observed as" locution attached to the entity that is "alien" to the reference-frame in question. So for the eternal observer the eternal entity *is* present whereas the temporal entity is *observed as* present; for the temporal observer, on the other hand, it is the eternal entity that is *observed as* present and the temporal entity that simply *is* present. And in view of the difficulty noted above, we cannot avoid the suggestion that "observed as" does *not* mean "is observed as, and is in fact," but rather "is observed as, but is *not* in literal fact."[45] As an illustration of this sort of "observed but not actual" presence, one might think of the sorts of interviews that are often conducted on television, where the person interviewed is "observed as" present in the television studio whereas she actually is speaking and being viewed at a remote location.

If we follow this line, we are still left with a double difficulty: How can an eternal entity be observed as present in time? How can a temporal entity be observed as present in eternity? For a variety of reasons, it seems to me that the second of these questions is the more pressing one. (That is why I refer to this as the problem of the presence of time in eternity, rather than vice versa.) Concerning our perception of the eternal God, the eternalist can say something like this: "We have known all along that God in his essence, in his true nature, is not present in time, so that comes as no

---

[45]I wish to emphasize that Stump and Kretzmann do *not* say that this is what they mean; I make the interpretation without their authority. But if this is not what is implied, I think they offer no solution at all for the difficulty under discussion.

surprise. But God makes himself known to us through the temporal effects of his eternal Act. There is no reason to doubt that he is able to do this in a way that is sufficient to meet our spiritual needs and bring us into union with himself. God's revelation may, indeed, fail to give us a fully adequate speculative grasp of God's nature, but that is something we do not need and have no right to expect." Given the other assumptions of the eternalist theory, such an answer seems to me to be reasonably adequate, at least as a first approximation.

But a similar answer concerning God's knowledge of temporal reality would be quite unacceptable. There should be no strong objection to saying that our knowledge of God, though it falls short of the full truth about God, is nevertheless adequate for practical purposes. But to say the same thing about God's knowledge of us is simply out of the question. And so the question is this: How is it possible that God, existing in eternity as a timeless being, has a full and accurate knowledge of temporal realities?

It is at just this point that Richard Creel finds what he takes to be a conclusive refutation of timelessness:

> Isn't it the case . . . that God must be affirmed as a privileged observer . . . that if he is aware of something as actual, then it is actual? . . . Because that which is not actual cannot be known as actual, it follows that, if the future is known as actual by God, then because God cannot be mistaken our belief that the future lies before us must be false, and the occurrence of change must be an illusion. Time becomes the platonic peephole through which we observe things that God knows to have been always in existence. . . . In brief, either a thing is changing or it is not. If God does not know it as changing but we know it as changing, then one of us is mistaken, and it surely is not God.[46]

Somewhat similarly, Kretzmann in 1966 suggested as a possible interpretation of the doctrine of timelessness that "from a God's-eye view there is no time, that the passage of time is a universal human illusion."[47] And Prior complains, "I simply cannot see how

[46]*Divine Impassibility*, p. 96.
[47]"Omniscience and Immutability," p. 415.

the presentness, pastness or futurity of any state of affairs can be in any way relative to the *persons to whom* this state of affairs is known. . . . So I don't understand what is meant by saying that contingent future occurrences are neither contingent nor future *as* God sees them, though I do understand what would be meant if it were said that they are neither contingent nor future *when* God sees them."[48]

The central point in all this is the one made in an earlier quotation from Creel: "That God knows things as they are is unnegotiable."[49] This certainly seems to be true. But I now want to say that it is also ambiguous in a certain way, and for our present purpose the ambiguity is crucial. The quoted sentence, I suggest, can be given two possible meanings, as follows:

(A) The way God knows things to be is the way things really are.

(B) The way in which God knows things (i.e., his *manner* of knowing them) is the same as the way in which they exist.

(A) really is unquestionably, unnegotiably true: it simply does not bear thinking that God "knows" Jason to be a fine fellow, whereas he really is treacherous and deceitful. I suggest, on the other hand, that *(B) must be rejected whether or not we affirm divine timelessness.* One may ask, as Creel does, "If God cannot experience sequentiality, how can he know what it is like to undergo change?"[50] But one may equally ask, "If God doesn't have skin, how does he know what it is like to be hit in the face with a snowball?" The only possible answer, I think, is that we must simply reject the notion that God's experience is somehow inadequate unless he experiences things in the same way we do.

With this as preparation, we can now see what the doctrine of timeless divine knowledge amounts to. From the fact that God knows temporal entities timelessly, does it follow that these en-

[48]"The Formalities of Omniscience," in *Papers on Time and Tense*, pp. 43–44.
[49]*Divine Impassibility*, p. 88.
[50]Personal communication.

tities *really are* timeless rather than temporal? No, it does not. God timelessly knows that the temporal entities *are* temporal; the mode of his knowing them is not the same as the mode of their existence, nor need it be. Should we say, then, that temporal entities have a dual existence *both* in eternity and in time? Even if this could be made intelligible, it is an enormously extravagant metaphysical speculation, and also quite unnecessary. Once again, the mode in which God knows temporal entities need not be the same as the mode in which they exist. How, then, can temporal entities be present in eternity so as to be known there by God? The answer is, that temporal entities *are not* literally present in eternity; since they *are* temporal, and *not* eternal, their literal presence in eternity is impossible. Temporal entities exist in eternity *as represented in the mind of God.* And so, according to Thomas Aquinas, "He sees himself through His essence; and He sees other things *not in themselves, but in Himself,* inasmuch as *His essence contains the similitude of things other than Himself.*"[51]

In taking this position I am forced to part company with a view that has been expressed by William P. Alston. In "Does God Have Beliefs?"[52] he argues that the correct conception of knowledge to apply to God is the "intuitive" conception according to which "knowledge of a fact is simply the immediate awareness of that fact."[53] He recognizes that the intuitive conception of knowledge has received strong criticism as applied to human knowledge but contends that this is "not because we suppose ourselves to have something better, but because it represents too high an aspiration for our condition."[54] But not, of course for God's condition! And he explicitly rules out, in God's case, any "inner mental representation"[55] such as I take the "similitude" or "image" mentioned by Thomas Aquinas to be.[56]

---

[51]*Summa theologiae,* Ia, 14, 6 (emphasis added); cf. also, in the same Article, Reply Obj. 2: "Now those things which are other than God are understood by God, *inasmuch as the essence of God contains their images as above explained*" (emphasis added).

[52]*Religious Studies* 22 (1987): 287–306.

[53]Ibid., p. 294.

[54]Ibid., p. 297.

[55]Ibid., p. 299.

[56]For a different reading of Aquinas, see William Lane Craig, "Was Thomas

Now, the view of God's knowledge as immediate awareness is undoubtedly highly attractive. But if we insist on construing God's knowledge in this way, Creel's argument, cited above, is going to succeed. One can be immediately aware only of what is *present* for one to be aware of; what else, after all, can "immediate" mean? If God is timeless, he can be immediately aware of (supposedly) temporal facts only if these facts *really are* timeless after all. If, on the other hand, the world really is temporal, only a temporal God can be immediately aware of it—and then only of its *present*, not of its past or future.

How then *can* a timeless God know temporal realities? The answer is, he knows them by knowing, in timeless representation, the content of each moment of temporal existence, as well as the order of the moments—an order that he knows to represent temporal sequence, though it cannot be such for him. There is no doubt, however, that many contemporary philosophers will tend to find this inadequate as an account of God's knowledge of temporal things. Some part of this difficulty, however, may be removed if we are careful to avoid wrong connotations for the word 'representation.' The word seems to carry with it automatically associations with 'abstract,' 'schematic,' 'approximate,' and the like, and we have a strong sense that a representation inherently must have less content—must, so to speak, convey less information—than is contained in actual experience of the represented entity. And this is generally true for us, but of course it cannot be true for God. *His* representations, his "similitudes" as Thomas would say, contain precisely *all* of the information content of the actual concrete entity—which means, of course, a great deal *more*

Aquinas a B-Theorist of Time?" *New Scholasticism* 59 (1985): 475–83. Craig quotes several statements from Aquinas about the "presence" of contingent events to God and concludes, "The point here seems to be that this presence is not internal to God, but a real external presence" (p. 481). From this he is led to conclude, for reasons similar to those urged by Creel, that Aquinas was committed to a "B-theory of time" according to which "temporal becoming is merely a subjective feature of consciousness, not the successive actualization of states of affairs" (p. 475). "Nevertheless," Craig writes, "I find it inconceivable that he consciously adhered to such a theory of time. For him becoming was not mind-dependent but real" (p. 483). My interpretation removes this contradiction from Aquinas's view; therefore, I think it preferable to Craig's.

content than could be contained in any *human* experience of the
entity. If God knows by similitudes or representations, this in no
way entails that he lacks information.

Yet there is in most of us a resistance to this theory that will
hardly yield to considerations such as these. Kenny puts it nicely:
"The Psalmist asked, 'Is the inventor of the ear unable to hear? The
creator of the eye unable to see?' These rhetorical questions have
been answered by Christian theologians with a firm, 'Yes, he is
unable.'"[57] Without doubt, modern sentiment here is with the
Psalmist and against the theologians. Yet it must be remembered
that for the medievals it was an excellence and a perfection on
God's part to be incapable of sense perception, and also to be
timeless and thus incapable of sequential experience. Kenny argues
that the medievals have been helped, as regards sense experience,
by the later philosophy of Wittgenstein, who showed that there is
in perception no irreducible cognitive "core" that cannot be com-
municated conceptually.[58] If in spite of this we are unable or un-
willing to overcome our bias in favor of immediate experience, we
shall remain at odds with some of the most fundamental intuitions
that support the doctrine of divine timelessness.

This, then, is the theory concerning God's knowledge which
goes with the doctrine of divine timelessness. I think it is reasonably clear that timelessness does require such a view of God's
knowledge, and also that the view itself is coherent and intelligible.
Whether it is also adequate, whether it is a good view to hold and
as such increases rather than diminishes the acceptability of timelessness itself—these are matters that properly pertain to the topic
of the next chapter.

[57] *The God of the Philosophers*, p. 29.
[58] Ibid., p. 31.

[9]

Is God Timeless?

I believe the considerations of the preceding chapter add up to a fairly strong case for regarding the theory of divine timelessness as intelligible. In spite of strenuous efforts by a number of philosophers, no clear incompatibility has been demonstrated between this theory and established principles of grammar, or logic, or theology. To be sure, the issues are complex, and it may be that in the future some incompatibility will be demonstrated where none has appeared so far. But if someone believes that she understands the claim that God is timeless, nothing that has appeared in the discussion to date need force her to admit that her understanding is illusory.

But should the theory also be accepted as true? For many philosophers the answer to this question may seem obvious. For some, the initial attractiveness and plausibility of the doctrine will have been progressively enhanced as the doctrine was developed to answer or avoid various difficulties, and the resulting theory glows with the luminosity of evident truth. For others, the theory will seem so convoluted, top-heavy, and unintuitive that it collapses of its own weight even without demonstrated inconsistencies. But still other philosophers may find neither of these responses immediately compelling. For philosophers in this third group, some further examination of considerations for and against timelessness seems called for.

Of necessity this chapter cannot claim to be either as comprehensive or as definitive as some of the earlier chapters have attempted to be. The ramifications and connections of divine timelessness stretch over a rather wide area of metaphysics, and the range of possible arguments for and against the theory is similarly large. What I shall attempt to do, then, is merely to summarize some of the more prevalent arguments in favor of divine timelessness and offer a personal assessment. Without doubt, there is much more to be done here, but doing it will have to be left to others. In the first part of the chapter I discuss the topic most relevant to the other themes of this book: the relationship between timelessness and God's knowledge of the future. In the second part I consider several other arguments for timelessness, and in the last section I weigh the arguments and state a conclusion.

Timelessness and God's Knowledge of the Future

In the previous chapter we established as a criterion for the doctrine of timelessness that such a doctrine must provide a solution for the problem of foreknowledge and free will. This stipulation, I believe, can be historically justified. But there are those who contend that this is an inappropriate, because unsatisfiable, criterion—that in spite of claims to the contrary dating back to Boethius, the doctrine of divine timelessness cannot solve the foreknowledge problem. One philosopher who maintains this (though he is sympathetic to the doctrine of timelessness) is Paul Helm. At the conclusion of a generally excellent exposition of the doctrine, he writes: "The notion of foreknowledge expresses a temporal knower's belief or recognition that certain events were known timelessly *before this time*."[1] Now, if the knowledge occurs "before this time," then it has temporal location and is not timeless, and the argument for fatalism will go through. Not surprisingly, Helm concludes: "Hence there cannot be free will, even if God's knowledge of human actions is timeless."[2] Actually, Helm's interpretation is fatal to the doctrine of timelessness even apart from the foreknowl-

[1]"Timelessness and Foreknowledge," *Mind* n.s. 84 (1975): 526; emphasis added.
[2]Ibid., p. 527.

edge problem. If God's timeless (?) knowledge occurs "before this time," then presumably any of God's actions, or any other aspect of God's existence, can also be given a temporal location—and once this is done, the doctrine of divine timelessness has in effect been abandoned.

Alvin Plantinga, though no friend either of the doctrine of timelessness or of incompatibilism, contends that "the claim that God is outside of time is essentially irrelevant to Edwardsian arguments" for fatalism.[3] He reasons as follows:

> Now eighty years ago the sentence
>
> > (5) God knows (eternally) that Paul mows in 1995
>
> expressed the proposition that God knows eternally that Paul mows in 1995 . . . . But if in fact Paul will mow in 1995, then (5) also expressed a truth eighty years ago. So eighty years ago (5) expressed the proposition that Paul will mow in 1995 and expressed a truth; since what is past is now necessary, it is now necessary that eighty years ago (5) expressed that proposition and expressed a truth. But it is necessary in the broadly logical sense that if (5) then expressed that proposition . . . and expressed a truth, then Paul will mow in 1995. It is therefore necessary that Paul will mow then; hence his mowing then is necessary in just the way the past is.[4]

Let us examine this. What Plantinga is claiming, in effect, is that

(1) Eighty years ago the sentence 'God knows (eternally) that Paul mows in 1995' expressed the proposition that God knows eternally that Paul mows in 1995, and this proposition which that sentence expressed was true

is a hard fact about the past. Now, (1) is equivalent to the conjunction,

(2) (a) Eighty years ago the sentence 'God knows (eternally) that Paul mows in 1995' expressed the proposition that

---

[3]"On Ockham's Way Out," *Faith and Philosophy* 3 (1986): 240.
[4]Ibid. I assume that it is due to an inadvertence on Plantinga's part that the reference to God's knowledge is dropped after the first sentence of the passage cited.

God knows eternally that Paul mows in 1995, *and (b)*
God knows eternally that Paul mows in 1995.

Clearly (*a*) is future indifferent, and if true, it is a hard fact, so the conjunction will be future indifferent if and only if the second conjunct is future indifferent. And it is the second conjunct, not the first, that entails Paul's future mowing. We see at once, therefore, that only the second conjunct really counts here; all the references to what a certain sentence expressed eighty years ago are completely unnecessary and irrelevant.

But what about (*b*)? *Is* this conjunct future indifferent? Clearly not, since it entails a fact about 1995. (I am writing this in 1987.) But suppose we were to follow the pattern established in chapter 5 and substitute the name 'Yahweh' for 'God' in (b)? It will be recalled that in establishing the criterion for hard facts we stipulated that propositions affirming a timeless act or event would not be considered candidates for the status of future-indifferent propositions. The purpose of this stipulation was to avoid having to consider, at that point, whether propositions asserting timeless acts should be considered as hard facts. But now this cannot be postponed any longer. *Are* propositions about the eternal acts of God "necessary" in the same way in which the past is necessary?

Let us approach the problem in a slightly different way. Libertarians hold that the future is "open" in a way in which the past is not—that, as of the present moment, it is in many respects *not yet determined* how the future shall be; it may be in one way, or it may be in another. God's timeless eternity, on the other hand, certainly *cannot* be open in this way; *every* fact is determined to be as it is, and not in any other way. And this contrast sets the stage for one of Prior's more profound objections to the theory of timelessness:

> I simply cannot see how the presentness, pastness or futurity of any state of affairs can be in any way relative to the *persons to whom* this state of affairs is known. What makes this quite impossible to stomach is precisely the truth that both Thomas and his objector insist on, namely that the future has an openness to alternatives which the past has not; such openness is just not the sort of thing that can be present for one observer and absent for another—either it exists or it doesn't, and there's an end to it; and so either a thing has already

occurred or it hasn't and there's an end to *that*. . . . So I don't understand what is meant by saying that contingent future occurrences are neither contingent nor future *as* God sees them, though I do understand what would be meant if it were said that they are neither contingent nor future *when* God sees them.[5]

The "openness to alternatives" that characterizes the future is, according to Prior, an objective characteristic of the events themselves and cannot be relative to an observer. Still, the openness does vary relative to *time*; the same event has the openness before it has occurred but loses it afterward. What we apparently need to say, then, is that God timelessly sees the *very same event* as contingent-and-future-before-it-occurs and also as past-and-inalterable-after-it-occurs.

But doesn't this bring us right back to Prior's objection? If God, in eternity, sees an act as already having occurred and therefore as inalterable, how *can* that act remain open and contingent as I consider whether to perform it or not? The solution to this, I believe, can be found in an idea that Prior credits to Anselm:

Anselm observes that the unchanging "presence" which . . . all things have to God, is in some ways less like our own present than our past. Looking back over what *has* happened, we can distinguish what was bound to happen as it did from what could have happened otherwise, though of course none of it can *now*, by the time we look back on it, have happened otherwise. It is in some such way as this that God distinguishes necessities and contingencies even though there is no contingency left in the latter in the form in which they reach His gaze.[6]

Now, if God in his eternity looks upon our time as one would look back on the past, it follows that in a certain respect *we* can view, or rather conceive of, eternity as we conceive of the future! To be sure, the temporal references as such must be eliminated: there *are* *no* temporal relationships between a timeless being and temporal beings. But eternity is like the future, and unlike the past, in that *it*

[5]Arthur N. Prior, "The Formalities of Omniscience," in *Papers on Time and Tense* (Oxford: Oxford University Press, 1968), pp. 43–44.
[6]Ibid., p. 38.

is still open to our influence. And so our question is answered; facts about God's eternal knowledge and activity are *not* hard facts. The eternal life of God is not only the ground but also in certain respects the consequence of the temporal events that it embraces. And so we arrive at the following, to my mind truly remarkable, conclusion: *There are things that God timelessly believes which are such that it is in my power, now, to bring it about that God does not timelessly believe those things.* If, and only if, this proposition is possible, is the doctrine of divine timelessness consistent with libertarian free will.[7]

If this is accepted, the problem of foreknowledge and free will is solved—though, to be sure, it is no longer *fore*knowledge. What additional benefits can be derived from this theory? How does it help us in understanding such matters as prophecy, divine providence, and answers to prayer? The answer to this is simple but may be disappointing: *There are no such benefits at all.* The reason for this was given in chapter 3, in which it was proved that

> *Whether or not there are creatures endowed with libertarian free will, it is impossible that God should use a foreknowledge derived from the actual occurrence of future events to determine his own prior actions in the providential governance of the world.*

If we replace "foreknowledge" in this statement with "timeless knowledge," and understand "future" and "prior" to refer to temporal relations that hold between events in the world but do not apply to God, we have a precise statement of the situation as it results from the theory of divine timelessness. The argument for the proposition cited in no way depends on the temporal relationship between God and the events in question; it is based, rather, on the relationships of dependence and presupposition that hold between the events themselves. The result may seem surprising, but

[7]Freddoso points out (personal communication) that the view set out here is remarkably similar to the "concomitance theory" discussed by Molina, and that my criticisms of the view also closely parallel Molina's. Interested readers should consult the Introduction to Molina, *On Divine Foreknowledge, (Part IV of Concordia),* trans. Alfred J. Freddoso (Ithaca, N.Y.: Cornell University Press, 1988), sec. 3.4, as well as Disputation 51.

the reasoning in support of it is, I believe, entirely cogent; the reader is referred back to chapter 3 for the details. And so we reach the following conclusion: *The doctrine of divine timelessness affords no help whatever in understanding God's providential governance of the world.*

It is at this point that we can see the strategic importance of having a refutation of middle knowledge which is independent of the incompatibilist arguments against foreknowledge. We might, to be sure, have reasoned in this way: Middle knowledge entails foreknowledge; foreknowledge is inconsistent with free will; therefore, middle knowledge is inconsistent with free will. This argument is, in my opinion, not only valid but also sound. But if our objection to middle knowledge were based only on this argument, an opportunity would be left open of which the eternalist could now take advantage. If God is timeless, she might say, then God can timelessly know the counterfactuals of freedom and can base his providential actions in the world on them, rather than being guided only by his timeless vision of the actual future. Thus, she could obtain the powerful advantages for the theory of providence which flow from middle knowledge, while escaping entirely the incompatibilist's strictures against foreknowledge.

But in fact we *do* have a refutation of middle knowledge which is independent of the arguments for incompatibilism—I would claim, in fact, that we have several such refutations. As has been shown in chapter 2, there are no true counterfactuals of freedom— and this argument, also, is independent of God's relationship to time and holds even if God is conceived to be timeless.

The lesson to be drawn from all this is clear. The theory of timelessness does enable us to explain how it is possible that God has comprehensive knowledge of our future and yet we ourselves freely determine what, in certain respects, that future shall be. The theory does *not*, on the other hand, give any help in understanding the topics of providence, prayer, and prophecy.

Timelessness and Metaphysics

For many contemporary philosophers the thought of divine timelessness is most likely to arise in connection with the problem of divine foreknowledge and human freedom. Yet this was not the original motivation for the theory, nor perhaps has it often been held for this reason alone. In this section we shall briefly survey some of the more general metaphysical reasons that have motivated and supported the theory of timelessness. Perhaps the most general of all is a principle that I have heard stated by William P. Alston: Wherever possible, we should subordinate ontological categories to God rather than subsuming God under the categories. When applied to the category of time, this immediately yields the doctrine of divine timelessness.

It is evident that Christian theology would apply Alston's principle with regard to the category of space. Few points in the theistic metaphysic are as clear as that God is not simply a very large object occupying huge amounts of space or even all of it. God must, somehow, *transcend* space—and, given this, one can use the symmetry between space and time to argue for the theory of divine timelessness. This argument has been alluded to in passing in the previous chapter; it is developed with considerable subtlety by Anselm in *Monologium,* chapters 20–24.[8] We shall not discuss Anselm's argument in detail here; suffice it to say that it depends throughout on the space-time parallels.

Still more light is thrown on the metaphysical roots of the doctrine of timelessness if we consider the sources from which the theory originated. In his article "Time and Eternity in Theology,"[9] Kneale traces the origin of the notion of timeless eternity from Pythagorus and Parmenides through Plato and into Christian theology. (Somewhat surprisingly, he does not mention Plotinus.) Though he is, as we have seen, ultimately unsympathetic to the idea of God as timelessly eternal, he notes that "by the end of the fifth century A.D. there was nothing at all strange in the use of Platonic thought for the exposition of Christianity."[10] He cites at length Augustine's passage on eternity from the eleventh book of the *Confessions,* remarking that "it shows not only how the notion of eternity became naturalized in Christian theology, but also how

[8] In *St. Anselm: Basic Writings,* 2d ed., trans. S. N. Deane (La Salle, Ill.: Open Court, 1962), pp. 72–83.
[9] *Proceedings of the Aristotelian Society* (1961), pp. 87–108.
[10] Ibid., p. 94.

it came to be connected with the devotional language of Christian writers."[11]

Stump and Kretzmann likewise trace the lineage of eternity through Parmenides, Plato, and Plotinus, but in addition they give a lucid summary of the thinking that underlies the concept and motivates it:

> Our *experience* of temporal duration gives us an impression of permanence and persistence which an *analysis* of time convinces us is an illusion or at least a distortion. Reflection shows us that, contrary to our familiar but superficial impression, temporal duration is only apparent duration, just what one would expect to find in the realm of becoming. The existence of a typical existent temporal entity, such as a human being, is spread over years of the past, through the present, and into years of the future; but the past is not, the future is not, and the present must be understood as no time at all, a durationless instant, a mere point at which the past is continuous with the future. Such radically evanescent existence cannot be the foundation of existence. Being, the persistent, permanent, utterly immutable actuality that seems required as the bedrock underlying the evanescence of becoming, must be characterized by genuine duration, of which temporal duration is only the flickering image. Genuine duration is fully realized duration—not only extended existence (even *that* is theoretically impossible in time) but also existence *none* of which is already gone and *none* of which is yet to come—and such fully realized duration must be atemporal duration. . . . Eternity, not time, is the mode of existence that admits of fully realized duration.[12]

There is an argument here, though not fully spelled out, based on the "illusion or distortion" involved in our ordinary impression that there is permanence and persistence in temporal existence. Also apparent, however, is a strong *valuational* element in the comparison of time and eternity, signaled by the contrast of "radically evanescent existence" with "persistent, permanent, utterly immutable actuality" and of "genuine duration" with its "flickering im-

[11]Ibid., p. 95.
[12]Eleonore Stump and Norman Kretzmann, "Eternity," *Journal of Philosophy* 79 (1981): 444–45.

age." One is reminded of Kneale's comment on Zeno's arguments against motion, that it is unlikely "that they could even seem cogent to anyone unless he were already in some way emotionally hostile to change."[13]

David Burrell is aware, I believe, that aversion to change as such will have minimal appeal to many contemporary thinkers, and he tries, by following Anselm, to ground the doctrine of divine eternity in a way that does not presuppose such an aversion. God alone exists in the highest degree, and he himself is the very life by which he lives. He is eternal in a way shared with no other being, in that his eternity contains all the past, present, and future of time. God "simply is," and the divine simplicity rules out from God's life the distinction of past, present, and future.[14] "The argumentation," says Burrell, "is simple and direct; it hardly seems beholden to a 'Greek predilection for permanence over change,' though the power of archetypes can never be gainsaid. It is rather a clear perception that what exists of itself *is* in a way in which it is entirely present to itself, and the name given to that mode of being is *eternal*."[15]

This, then, is a brief but representative sampling of the reasons given for the theory of divine timelessness. How should one reasonably assess these reasons? That question is the theme of the final section of this chapter.

Striking a Balance

It is my impression that the current generation of philosophers of religion includes a goodly number of what Richard Purtill has termed "lapsed Boethians."[16] It is interesting to reflect on possible reasons for this. Many of us, I believe, encountered our first philosophically serious theism in the writings of eternalist theologians such as Augustine and Aquinas—not to mention C. S. Lewis! As a result, the eternalist conception of God became incorporated into our thinking and belief at a rather deep level.

---

[13]"Time and Eternity in Theology," p. 88.
[14]See David B. Burrell, "God's Eternity," *Faith and Philosophy* 1 (1984): 390–91.
[15]Ibid., p. 392.
[16]Purtill applies this term as a self-description.

But many of us have also found our philosophical home in the analytical tradition. And it is simply a fact that the habits of thought engendered by that tradition are not particularly congenial to the theory of divine timelessness. It is not so much that specific objections to or incoherencies in the theory have been discovered—though, as we have seen, that has been claimed often enough. But the deeper problem is that the modes of thinking encouraged by our philosophical practice fail to nurture and sustain an outlook that comports well with eternalism. As a result, the doctrine of divine timelessness tends to become an isolated item of belief, segregated from one's other intellectual concerns—in the end, perhaps, to be abandoned altogether.

A possible comment on this is that the current preference for analytical modes of thought is merely a contingent fact about a segment of our philosophical community, and is no more to be given unthinking allegiance than were the Platonic-mystical inclinations of some earlier generations of philosophers. The comment is just, but the problem is inescapable. One can only view the world, and God, from the place where one does in fact stand.

In any case, what is to be made of the arguments? I want to begin by saying that it does not seem to me that the theory of divine timelessness can reasonably be accepted merely as a solution to the problem of foreknowledge and free will. As we have seen, the conceptual structures required for eternalism are complex and difficult, and amount to a conception of the nature of ultimate reality which is fundamentally different than one that might be held by a theist apart from this doctrine. To adopt such an elaborate metaphysic merely as a solution to a problem, even a fairly significant problem, is disproportionate. Speaking in Kuhnian terms, we can say that the problem of foreknowledge is stubborn and may resist solution, but it is insufficient to precipitate a crisis and motivate an entire new paradigm. Eternalism is a deeply metaphysical theory, and it must have metaphysical roots.

Alston's principle—that metaphysical categories should be subordinated to God rather than subsuming God under the categories—has some force. But if it is applied universally, we will be left with nothing that we can say about God at all. What is needed, then, is a reason for applying this principle specifically to the category of time.

Such a reason, of course, is found in the parallelism or symmetry between space and time which is developed extensively by eternalists. But these arguments, though somewhat persuasive, are far from being irresistible. Dennis Holt argues, on the basis of the "tense grammar" developed by A. N. Prior but supported in essentials by Wilfrid Sellars, Nicholas Rescher, and Peter Geach, that our ordinary ways of speaking about space and time indicate an asymmetry between them which undercuts standard eternalist arguments.[17] According to George N. Schlesinger, space and time are necessarily similar in all and only those respects that follow from the fact that each is a *continuum*, although they can and do differ from each other in other respects.[18] If he is correct in this, then it is plausible that he is also right in saying that the mere fact that space and time are both continua does not imply that they are equally fundamental in the metaphysical structure of the world.[19] And I believe there is good evidence from the history of modern philosophy that they are *not* equally fundamental. Descartes has convinced most of us that we can at least conceive of a universe in which space is illusionary; perhaps wisely, he did not attempt to do the same with time. Berkeley's philosophy is often rejected as implausible but is seldom considered unintelligible, but Kant's notion of a noumenal will that exists and acts non-temporally has been a source of deep bewilderment. I conclude, therefore, that the parallelisms between space and time may be useful for eternalism as an expository device but have little or no probative force.

Turning to the more historically oriented arguments, I have to say that I am unconvinced by Burrell's effort to dissociate eternalism from "the Greek predilection for permanence over change." Almost all expositions of the doctrine of timelessness, including Burrell's own, strongly imply that it is *better* for God to experience the world's existence timelessly than temporally, and I doubt that this value dimension can be eliminated from the theory. Burrell's own argument for timelessness, like most others, relies heavily on

---

[17]Dennis C. Holt, "Timelessness and the Metaphysics of Temporal Existence," *American Philosophical Quarterly* 18 (1981): 149–56.
[18]*Aspects of Space and Time* (Indianapolis: Hackett, 1980), pp. 19–21.
[19]Ibid., p. 22.

the doctrine of divine simplicity.[20] But divine simplicity is itself integrally related to the Neoplatonic-Augustinian-Thomistic metaphysical tradition, and this tradition has been very deeply influenced by the perception that change as such is inferior to permanence. That one can at this stage simply delete that value preference and leave the rest of the metaphysic unchanged seems a highly dubious proposition.

In the final analysis, then, I am convinced that the Neoplatonic-Augustinian metaphysic is intimately involved in the doctrine of divine timelessness, which cannot and probably should not survive without it. That is not to deny that the doctrine has been and still is held by some who would not readily embrace this metaphysic, nor would I claim that those who take this stance are irrational in doing so. But I will venture the prediction that over the long haul the doctrine and the metaphysic will stand or fall together—that the theory of timelessness, if its metaphysical tap root is severed, will eventually shrivel and die.

In considering my own response to this matter, I find within myself a deep love and admiration for the Augustinian theology— a love and admiration that tend to be increased by working philo- sophically with its concepts, as in the considerations of the previous chapter. Yet there is in the rest of my philosophical per- spective rather little that would tend to sustain belief in Au- gustine's metaphysic. I do not find permanence to be inherently preferable to change; a workable universe, it seems to me, needs both in full measure. My distinction between matter and spirit is different than Augustine's, and I do not recognize a "great chain of being" in which spiritual beings are inherently, ontologically

---

[20]The doctrine of divine simplicity has probably been the least appreciated as- pect of classical theism but has recently found advocates in William Mann ("Divine Simplicity," *Religious Studies* 21 [1985]: 299–318; "Simplicity and Immutability in God," *International Philosophical Quarterly* 23 [1983]: 451–71; "The Divine At- tributes," *American Philosophical Quarterly* 23 [1983]: 267–76), and in Eleonore Stump and Norman Kretzmann ("Absolute Simplicity," *Faith and Philosophy* 2 [1985]: 353–82). The interpretation of the doctrine given by Mann appears to differ somewhat from Stump and Kretzmann's interpretation, but there is agreement that the doctrine of divine timelessness is a consequence of divine simplicity. For a criticism of certain aspects of Stump and Kretzmann's view, see William Hasker, "Simplicity and Freedom: A Response to Stump and Kretzmann," *Faith and Phi- losophy* 3 [1986]: 192–201.

closer to God than are physical beings. The doctrine of divine simplicity does not have a great deal of appeal for me, and I suspect that if there is a core of truth in that doctrine, it is something much simpler and less pretentious than the traditional theory would suggest. All these matters, perhaps, are merely contingent facts about my own philosophical development. But taken together, they continue to push me in the direction of a negative answer to the question of this chapter.

It should not be forgotten, though it has not been stressed in this chapter, that the doctrine of divine timelessness exacts a considerable price from its adherents. There can be no denying that the conceptual structure of eternalism is difficult; I have defended the doctrine against charges of contradiction and incoherence, but conceptual stresses and strains abound.[21] For me, however, the most difficult aspect of the doctrine to accept is the one that in the preceding chapter was called "the problem of the presence of time in eternity." It seems inescapable, as was there demonstrated, that if God is eternal, he knows us only by contemplating in eternity his own unchangeable "similitudes," "images," or representations of us. But I find this extremely difficult to accept as the truth of the matter. I can tell myself that an eternal God can still cause there to exist in time all of the events that we experience as his historical interventions, as his gracious presence in our lives, and the like. But that God in very truth knows us, and relates to us, only as the eternal representations in his own essence—this is a hard doctrine. I cannot keep myself from thinking, like Alston but unlike Thomas Aquinas, that it is far better if God has "immediate awareness" of facts than if he knows them only as "similitudes" within his own essence. And if, as I have argued against Alston, in order to have immediate awareness of temporal facts, God must himself be temporal, then so be it. To make the other choice leaves too great a distance between the God who is affirmed theologically and the God who is known through Scripture and experience.

In the end, therefore, I find I have no choice but to agree with

---

[21]The point is well illustrated by Richard Swinburne's assertion that the eternalist must "maintain that many words are being used in highly analogical senses" in describing God, whereas the temporalist need not rely so heavily on analogy (*The Coherence of Theism* [Oxford: Oxford University Press, 1977], pp. 221–22.)

Nicholas Wolterstorff: "God the Redeemer cannot be a God eternal. This is so because God the Redeemer is a God who *changes*. And any being which changes is a being among whose states there is temporal succession." "It is not because he is outside of time—eternal, immutable, impassive—that we are to worship and obey God. It is because of what he can and does bring about within time that we mortals are to render him praise and obedience."[22]

[22]"God Everlasting," in *God and the Good,* ed. Clifton J. Orlebeke and Lewis B. Smedes (Grand Rapids, Mich.: Eerdmans, 1975), pp. 182, 203.

God and the Open Future

The truth is what it is, and should be welcomed by men and women of good will wherever it is found. Nevertheless, it can hardly be denied that the results obtained in our study to this point seem largely negative. We first addressed the (apparently) theologically promising theory of middle knowledge and found that it cannot be correct because there are no truths of the sort the theory requires God to know. Our examination of simple foreknowledge led to the realization that such foreknowledge, even if it existed, would contribute nothing at all to our understanding of the divine governance of the world. After a lengthy examination, all of the attempts to eliminate the inconsistency between infallible divine foreknowledge and free will for human beings were seen to fail; the incompatibility is real and must be accepted. The theory of divine timelessness was examined and was held provisionally to be intelligible but was found to be inadequately motivated apart from an abstruse metaphysic that holds little appeal for most contemporary philosophers.

Nevertheless, the considerations developed here do allow, and indeed open the way for, an affirmative, constructive, and (I believe) religiously satisfying conception of God's knowledge of the future and of his providential governance of the world. The first part of this chapter deals with divine knowledge of the future as such, the second explores the implications of this for our understanding of divine providence, and the final section brings into focus the central issue that separates this understanding of God's activity in the world from its rivals.

God's Knowledge of the Future

The central idea concerning God's knowledge of the future which emerges from our reflections can be simply stated: God knows everything about the future which it is logically possible for him to know. A slightly more formal definition of divine omniscience may be adapted from premise (C2) in chapter 4:

(DO) God is omniscient $=_{df}$ It is impossible that God should at any time believe what is false, or fail to know any true proposition such that his knowing that proposition at that time is logically possible.

Earlier I argued that such a definition as (DO) ought to be uncontroversial, unless of course one wants to maintain that there are truths that are known by God even though it is logically impossible that he know them! Jonathan Kvanvig, however, has sharply criticized the notion that God could be called omniscient if there are truths he does not know. Kvanvig's criticisms are directed at Swinburne,[1] but they apply equally to the conception developed here. He says:

There is . . . a quite severe paradox generated if this line of reasoning is allowed. Since human knowledge does not require infallibility, humans can know what some of the future free actions will be. God cannot, since his knowledge requires infallibility. Thus, an individual can be God and hence omniscient on Swinburne's view even if that individual knows less about a particular domain than mere humans. Such an implication is surely too adverse to sensibility to detain us even for a moment.[2]

[1] See Richard Swinburne, *The Coherence of Theism* (Oxford: Oxford University Press, 1977), pp. 171–72.

[2] Jonathan L. Kvanvig, *The Possibility of an All-Knowing God* (New York: St. Martin's Press, 1986), p. 18.

I have no wish to further injure Kvanvig's sensibility, but if a few moments can be spared for consideration, the paradox can be made to disappear. God's knowledge concerning the future includes all of the future outcomes that are objectively possible, *as well as* knowledge of the objective likelihood that each outcome will occur, and in cases where one choice is overwhelmingly likely (though not as yet absolutely certain) to be made, God will know that also. So God's awareness of the future contains a great deal *more* than does what we call *our* "knowledge" of future free actions, though it is still not good enough to count as knowledge *for God*.

It is evident that this conception of omniscience as subject to logical limitations is influenced by the parallel considerations that have influenced many philosophers to accept logical limitations on divine omnipotence. Kvanvig, however, discounts the analogy:

> The analogy intended to support a limited doctrine of omniscience is between feasible tasks and knowable truths and between unfeasible tasks and unknowable truths; but the analogy is crucially defective. Whereas an unknowable truth is still a truth, an unfeasible task is not a task at all. . . . A good analogy here is the response one might make to a child who claimed to be drawing a square circle. We might say, "You may be drawing something, but it is not a square circle, for there aren't and can't be any such things."[3]

Now, Kvanvig's point works nicely as regards square circles, but there are other things that it is generally thought that God cannot do which cannot be thus dismissed. If, as Kvanvig agrees, God is essentially morally perfect, then presumably lying to the American people about their government's foreign policy is something God cannot do, but that is hardly because this is "not a task at all"! Will Kvanvig scoff at the claim that such a being could be omnipotent and yet be able to do "less about a particular domain than mere humans"?

It will no doubt have been noticed that the conclusions we have reached agree, on an important point, with the conception of God's knowledge developed in process theology. This is undeniably the case, but of course our arguments, in attesting the correct-

[3]Ibid., p. 22.

ness of process theology's view on one point, by no means show that theology to be right on other points of contention. Nor, for that matter, do these arguments show process theology to be wrong. But on what I take to be the most central point of disagreement, namely, God's ontological self-sufficiency and independence from the world, I stand squarely with the classical theism of John Mason:

> Thou wast, O God, and thou wast blest,
>   Before the world began;
> Of thine eternity possessed
>   Before time's hour glass ran.
> Thou needest none thy praise to sing,
>   As if thy joy could fade;
> Could'st thou have needed anything,
>   Thou couldst have nothing made.[4]

Our concern in these pages, however, is with God's relationship to the future, both in knowing and in controlling it. (For God as for us, it is *only* the future that can be controlled—with regard to the present and the past, it is always already too late.) Here a difference emerges with Hartshorne, at least, in that we would affirm God's comprehensive and exact knowledge of the *possibilities* of the future[5]—and, as has already been said, of the gradually changing *likelihood* of each of those possibilities' being realized. And as the probability of a choice's being made in a certain way gradually increases toward certainty, God knows *that* also; often, no doubt, before the finite agent herself is aware of it. "Even before a word is on my tongue, lo, O LORD, thou knowest it altogether" (Psalm 139:4).

But we are concerned not only with God's *knowledge* of the

---

[4]John Mason, "Thou wast, O God, and thou wast blest," in *Hymnal for Colleges and Schools*, ed. E. Harold Geer (New Haven, Conn.: Yale University Press, 1956), no. 110.

[5]According to Hartshorne, possibilities are as such inherently vague and indeterminate, and can only be known as such. For an excellent discussion of Hartshorne's view as well as a defense of the classical view of God's comprehensive and exact knowledge of possibilities, see Richard A. Creel, *Divine Impassibility* (Cambridge: Cambridge University Press, 1986), chap. 3.

future but with his *action* in the world based on that knowledge—
and in that regard, the resources of the essentially classical theism
here espoused differ radically from those available to process theism. To these matters we now turn.

Providence, Prayer, and Prophecy

As was pointed out as early as chapters 2 and 3, the greatest
importance of foreknowledge is not foreknowledge itself but the
implications it has for our understanding of God's activity in the
world. This claim, I would maintain, is easily verified both from
the writings of theologians and from the perceptions of ordinary,
theologically unsophisticated believers. Drawing out the implications for the divine activity of the view here developed is not
particularly difficult. What may prove difficult, or even impossible, is the task of convincing those who are attracted to another
view of divine action that this view is adequate. Here, as elsewhere, I forbear trying to show in detail how the views espoused
are implied by or consistent with the biblical text. For a general
perspective on the problem, however, I will cite some words of
Clark Pinnock: "The Bible seems to be pretheoretical in its approach to the relationship between divine sovereignty and human
freedom. Some passages can be read to support God's determining
all things. Others, with equal strength, stress the significant freedom of human beings. A tension is allowed to stand in the biblical
text; a definitive resolution is nowhere attempted."[6] I believe there
is wisdom in this statement. If anyone doubts that there are force-
ful texts on both sides, then probably she just has not read the
Bible very much, or at any rate not the works of the Calvinist and
Arminian theologians who take those texts as battle standards. If
she acknowledges the tension but thinks there *is* a definitive resolution in the biblical text itself, then most likely she *has* read the
theologians, on one side only of the controversy! But if Pinnock's
statement is correct, as I believe it is, then it is *up to us* to construct a

---

[6]"God Limits His Knowledge," in *Predestination and Free Will: Four Views of
Divine Sovereignty and Human Freedom*, ed. David Basinger and Randall Basinger
(Downers Grove, Ill.: InterVarsity Press, 1986), p. 143.

consistent position on the question, and to do it on the basis of biblical data without claiming that the text clearly or unambiguously supports the conclusion we have reached.

To be sure, the Christian tradition is closer to consensus in affirming comprehensive divine foreknowledge than it is with respect to predestination and human freedom. But again, it is not as though scriptural texts pointing in a different direction were lacking. Again I cite Pinnock:

> According to the Bible, God anticipates the future in a way analogous to our own experience. God tests Abraham to see what the patriarch will do, and then says through his messenger, "Now I know that you fear God" (Gen 22:12). God threatens Ninevah with destruction, and then calls it off when they repent (Jon 3:10). I do not receive the impression from the Bible that the future is all sewn up and foreknown. The future is envisaged as a realm in which significant decisions can still be made which can change the course of history.[7]

The difficulty is, of course, that "readers almost never . . . [read] the biblical story with this view in mind."[8] We have been strongly conditioned, most of us, to dismiss what was said to Abraham as "anthropomorphic" and to affirm texts that suggest a more comprehensive foreknowledge as the literal metaphysical truth. But why so? It is not because one thing is said *in the Bible* more clearly or emphatically than the other. But the "hermeneutical circle" within which we have encountered these texts constantly turns us around and tells us to face in a particular direction—a direction that may, when all is said and done, be more toward Athens than toward Jerusalem! What I am suggesting here is that the "dehellenization of Christian theology" that Wolterstorff celebrates in his own repudiation of divine timelessness may have just a small step further to take.[9]

But what *are* the implications for divine action of this view of

---

[7]Ibid., p. 157.
[8]Ibid.
[9]Nicholas Wolterstorff, "God Everlasting," in *God and the Good*, ed. Clifton J. Orlebeke and Lewis B. Smedes (Grand Rapids, Mich.: Eerdmans, 1975), p. 183.

God's knowledge? To begin with, God has complete, detailed, and utterly intimate knowledge of the entirety of the past and the present. He also, of course, knows the inward constitution, tendencies, and powers of each entity in the fullest measure. And, finally, he has full knowledge of his own purposes, and of how they may best be carried out. Everything God does is informed by the totality of this knowledge; the guidance he gives, if he chooses to give it, is wisdom pure and unalloyed. Knowing what he knows, God may sometimes know also that the uninterrupted course of natural action and human responses will best serve his deep purposes. He may, on the other hand, know that for his purpose to go forward there is need for his own direct touch and influence, whether recognized or unrecognized, on this or that human personality. Or finally, he may see that for his purpose best to be fulfilled what is called for is his immediate, purposeful intervention in the processes of nature—in other words, a miracle. Whatever God needs to do, he has the power to do; whatever he sees is best to do happens forthwith. And if we trust him, we can also trust his purposes, for they culminate in the Kingdom of God, which is our happiness and *shalom*.

And now I ask, is this not enough? If God is like this, is he not worthy of our most entire devotion? And if we hesitate to agree to this, is the hesitation because a God so described would truly be unworthy, or is it because of our attachment to a theory?

There is, I admit, one conceivable, or at least imaginable, resource that is lacking to God so described. God in this view cannot, as C. S. Lewis thought he did, know in advance by direct vision precisely what will occur and *prearrange* concomitant circumstances so as to meet the needs of the occasion. He cannot, for instance, know the sequence of free actions that led up to the encirclement at Dunkirk, and *on the basis of that knowledge* prearrange the weather patterns to allow for the successful evacuation of the Allied forces. It has already been argued that this conception of providential action is incoherent. But leaving that aside, why should it be thought that such a view of divine action is somehow *better* than the one put forward two paragraphs back? Just how is God disadvantaged, if he cannot act as Lewis describes? It is not as though his resources are strained to the limit, so that if he fails to anticipate exactly what will happen (like a commander who fails to reinforce the exact point at which the enemy will attack), he will fail to accomplish his ends. Such a finicky eking out of meager resources to attain the optimum results just is not appropriate to divine governance, so there is no reason to regret its being impossible.

Perhaps I can, after all, think of one reason that for some might suggest at least an imaginative preferability of this mode of divine providence. Suppose that, though not denying the miraculous in principle, one is sufficiently impressed by the modern prejudice against it to feel that, in a rationally respectable account of the faith, divine miraculous interventions ought to be kept as narrowly confined as possible. Then it may seem that Lewis's account of prearranged circumstances is better than either a direct claim about God's frequent miraculous interventions or the admission that God seldom, if ever, does anything *specific* about the problem situations that arise in everyday life.

It should be noted, however, that this really economizes on miracle only if the prearrangement takes place *right at the beginning of creation*. If God intervened, say, five months or five years in advance in order to get the sort of weather he wanted at Dunkirk, that would be just as much a miracle (though perhaps not as noticeable) as if he had quieted the waves instantly on the day of the evacuation. But the notion that all these prearrangements took place at the beginning of creation simply will not bear examination; other considerations aside, we now know with virtual certainty that physical processes are *not* strictly deterministic, and thus the quantum indeterminacy would preclude information's being carried forward with the required degree of exactitude.

What has been said about providence in general applies in particular to answers to prayer, and there is no reason to suppose that the lack of exact, fully detailed foreknowledge is more of a handicap in one case than in the other. It is worth noticing, by the way, that Christ said, "your Father knows what you *need* before you ask him" (Matthew 6:8; emphasis added), and not that he knows what we *ask* before we ask him! There is certainly no clear biblical warrant for the notion that God answers specific prayers before they are offered, or for the idea that we should pray for what already lies in the past.[10]

Without doubt, many persons will see biblical prophecy as the most serious obstacle to acceptance of the view here set forth. Simply put, if God does not *know* what the future will be like, how can he *tell* us what it will be like? The difficulty is real but not insuperable. First, it should be noted that there is a very broad scholarly consensus that the main agenda for the biblical prophets was not prognosticating the future, but rather witnessing to the people concerning God's purposes and requirements and seeking to recall them to obedience. And this purpose clearly is often uppermost even when coming events are the explicit subject of the discourse. A striking text that bears this out, and also has important implications for our topic, is Jeremiah 18:7–10:

> If at any time I declare concerning a nation or a kingdom, that I will pluck up and break down and destroy it, and if that nation, concerning which I have spoken, turns from its evil, I will repent of the evil that I intended to do to it. And if at any time I declare concerning a nation or a kingdom that I will build and plant it, and if it does evil in my sight, not listening to my voice, then I will repent of the good which I had intended to do to it.

Here we are told that prophecies are to be interpreted as conditional *even when this is not explicitly stated*. But of course, a conditional prophecy requires no detailed foreknowledge of what will actually happen; the purpose, in many cases, is that what is foretold may *not* happen.

Clearly, not every biblical prophecy concerning the future is conditional, though a great many of them are. A second important category, however, must include *predictions based on foresight drawn from existing trends and tendencies*. Even with our own grossly inade-

---

[10]This is admitted by William Lane Craig, *The Only Wise God* (Grand Rapids, Mich.: Baker, 1987), pp. 87–88; Craig, however, defends the philosophical coherence of such prayers. It should be noted that, on the view I am defending, God could know about a believer's *disposition* to pray concerning a certain matter and could respond on the basis of that disposition in advance of any specific prayer's being offered.

quate knowledge of such trends and tendencies, we invest enormous amounts of energy trying to make forecasts in this way; evidently God with his perfect knowledge could do it much better. To take a simple example: Jesus was able to predict Peter's betrayal because he knew something about Peter which Peter himself did not know, namely, that Peter, though brave enough in a fight even against the odds (as in the Garden of Gethsemane), lacked the specific sort of courage as well as the faith needed to acknowledge his allegiance in a threatening situation where physical resistance was impossible.

Finally, however, there is a most important category of prophecies, namely, of *things that are foreknown because it is God's purpose to bring them about.* With regard to the major events of redemptive history this is evident: God did not *foresee* the death and resurrection of his Son; he declared them as going to happen, because he fully intended to bring them about. But the same interpretation may be given even to somewhat less momentous events. There is a striking passage on this in Geach's *Providence and Evil*:

> God is the supreme Grand Master who has everything under his control. Some of the players are consciously helping his plan, other are trying to hinder it; whatever the finite players do, God's plan will be executed; though various lines of God's play will answer to various moves of the finite players. God cannot be surprised or thwarted or cheated or disappointed. God, like some grand master of chess, can carry out his plan even if he has announced it beforehand. "On that square," says the Grand Master, "I will promote my pawn to Queen and deliver checkmate to my adversary": and it is even so. No line of play that finite players may think of can force God to improvise: his knowledge of the game already embraces all the possible variant lines of play, theirs does not.[11]

The rhetoric is strong; the example (at least) overstated. An amateur at chess playing a grand master may have no choice about winning or losing, but he has a great deal more choice about *how*

[11]Peter Geach, *Providence and Evil* (Cambridge: Cambridge University Press, 1977), p. 58. Geach's book as a whole can be read as an exhibition of an understanding of divine providence which is consistent with the views adopted here.

he will lose than Geach allows.[12] Still, Geach is not claiming that God's purpose and superior strategy enable him to foresee *everything* that will happen: "Various lines of God's play will answer to various moves of the finite players." The central point is that God is able to carry out his overall plan despite whatever resistance may be offered by human beings.

It should not be overlooked, furthermore, that God has at his disposal a great many more different ways to influence the course of events than does a chess master. God is perfectly capable of making someone an "offer he can't refuse"; many accounts of conversion (for example) suggest that he has done just that. Some ways in which God might control the course of events might strike us as manipulative, but this is not necessarily so, so long as a person is not influenced to act in a way inconsistent with his own major intention and motivations. When God "hardened Pharaoh's heart" (whatever exactly that involved), he by no means gave to Pharaoh a temper and inclination that were foreign to him; at most, he gave him a stronger disposition to do what he was already inclined to do: defy God, and make things difficult for the Israelites. Here, as elsewhere, the specifics are for us unknowable, but one thing is abundantly clear: *God's capacity to control the detailed course of events is limited only by his self-restraint, not by any inability to do so.* And as broad as is the scope of God's ability to control events, so also is the possibility for prophecy based on God's intention so to do.

These, then, are the resources for understanding biblical prophecy consonant with the understanding of omniscience here set forward. Some prophecies are conditional on the actions of human beings; others are predictions based on existing trends and tendencies; still others are announcements of what God himself intends to bring about. Do these categories enable one to deal with the phenomena of the biblical text? I believe that they do, but the matter cannot be pursued further here. The reader is invited to investigate the matter for herself, using the best commentaries and technical aids as well as the Scriptures themselves.

[12]Anthony Kenny makes this point: see *The God of the Philosophers* (Oxford: Oxford University Press, 1979), p. 59.

Does God Take Risks?

It is evident that the view of God's governance of the world here proposed differs from others that are commonly held. But wherein precisely does the difference lie? I believe it can be formulated in a simple, yet crucial, question: *Does God take risks?* Or, to put the matter more precisely, we may ask: *Does God make decisions that depend for their outcomes on the responses of free creatures in which the decisions themselves are not informed by knowledge of the outcomes?* If he does, then creating and governing a world is for God a risky business. That this is so is evidently an implication of the views here adopted, and it is equally evident that it would be rejected by some Christian thinkers—those, for example, who hold to a theory of predestination according to which everything that occurs is determined solely by God's sovereign decree.

But though the importance of the question about God's risk taking will be widely recognized, the bearing on this question of the positions discussed in this book is often misunderstood. Here the argument developed in chapter 3 is crucially important: *Simple foreknowledge and timeless knowledge have no bearing on the question whether or not God takes risks.* It is true that on these views God's knowledge of the future is complete and comprehensive, either before all time or outside of time in God's eternity. But on either of these views *God's knowledge of future events is derived from the actual occurrence of those events,* and thus in the order of explanation it is *subsequent to* the decisions on God's part which lead to the events' occurring. The reasoning for this conclusion is entirely clear and straightforward, and only inattention can have led to its being so widely overlooked.[13]

[13]It has not been entirely overlooked; consider the following from William Lane Craig:

> Divine foreknowledge without prior middle knowledge would be exceedingly strange. Without middle knowledge, God would find himself, so to speak, with knowledge of the future but without any logically prior planning of that future. To see the point imagine that logically prior to the divine decision to create a world, God has only natural knowledge. If creatures are going to be genuinely free, then God's creation of the world is a blind act without any idea of how things will actually be. True, he knows at that prior moment all possible worlds, but he has virtually no idea which world he will

Short of absolute predestination, the only theory known to me that eliminates risk taking on God's part is the theory of middle knowledge. For on this theory God's knowledge of the future is *not* derived from the actual occurrence of the future events, but rather from the knowledge of the counterfactuals of freedom together with God's knowledge concerning which states of affairs he will actualize. But the knowledge of the counterfactuals is prior, in the order of explanation, to God's decisions about what to create, so that these decisions are indeed informed by full and complete knowledge of the respective outcomes of any possible choice God might make. The element of risk is eliminated entirely.

By this time the reader is well aware of my opinion that the philosophical prospects for middle knowledge are dim. To maintain the viability of this theory, one would have to defeat the arguments against middle knowledge in chapter 2, as well as the arguments for incompatibilism deployed in chapters 4 through 7. Since I believe those arguments to be sound, I do not think that attempts to answer or evade them will be successful. But our purpose in this final chapter is not to rehearse these arguments from earlier in the book, but rather to address a quite different question: What sort of theory of divine providence should we *want* to have? Is it *better* if God takes risks with the world, or if he does not? Where do the interests of faith really lie in this matter?

From a certain standpoint it may seem evident that a risk-free world is preferable to one in which God takes risks. A world in which God's creative and providential action is guided by middle knowledge is a world in which nothing can ever turn out in the slightest respect differently than God intended. It is in a sense a

---

in fact create, since he does not know how free creatures would act if he created them. All he knows are the possibilities, which are infinite in number. In a sense, what God knows in the logical moment after the decision to create must come as a total surprise to him. (*The Only Wise God*, pp. 134–35)

My reply to this would be that *whether or not* God has simple foreknowledge, we should conceive of his decisions about what to do as being made progressively, in stages, with the action at each point directed to the situation as it results from God's earlier decisions. The final result, then, would hardly be the "sudden shock" depicted by Craig! But his statement does nicely capture the uselessness of simple foreknowledge. Once again, I direct the reader's attention to the important article by David Basinger, "Middle Knowledge and Classical Christian Thought," *Religious Studies* 22 (1986): 407–22.

world that provides absolute security for the believer, similar to that which is often felt to be the greatest benefit of the doctrine of predestination. It is not for nothing that William Craig states, "Given middle knowledge, the apparent contradiction between God's sovereignty, which seems to crush human freedom, and human freedom, which seems to break God's sovereignty, is resolved. In his infinite intelligence, God is able to plan a world in which his designs are achieved by creatures acting freely."[14]

Still, the need for this kind of theory is open to question. Might not the demand for a wholly risk-free divine plan be another example of a genuine religious need that has been, so to speak, subjected to metaphysical inflation and made to underwrite requirements that go beyond any legitimate need? Proponents of middle knowledge themselves would say this about the Calvinistic doctrine of sovereignty, and another example may well be the doctrines of absolute divine immutability and timelessness. Faith needs the assurance that God's character is absolutely reliable and that his purposes will hold true, but this need can be met without the excesses of the classical theory of absolute immutability. Similarly, we have argued above that the believer has every reason to trust God and to commit herself to him unreservedly, quite apart from theories that guarantee that God's plan is risk-free.

There are, on the other hand, reasons for questioning whether a risk-free providence is even desirable. Those who admire risk taking and experimentalism in human life may feel that the richness of God's life is diminished if we deny these attributes to him. And, on the other hand, the significance and value of human creativity may seem diminished if our most ennobling achievements are just the expected printouts from the divine programming. But perhaps the most serious difficulty here is one that also plagues Calvinistic doctrines of predestination: If we accentuate God's absolute control over everything that happens, we are forced to attribute to him the same control over evil events and actions as over good. On the theory of middle knowledge we can *never* say that some act of God's failed of its intended purpose, no matter how disastrous the outcome may be.[15] We cannot avoid saying, then, that God specif-

---

[14]*The Only Wise God*, p. 135.
[15]Freddoso objects to this; he says, "The theory of middle knowledge most

ically chose for Hitler to become leader of the Third Reich and instigator of the Holocaust. To be sure, the proponent of middle knowledge, unlike the defender of absolute predestination, will say that it was through Hitler's *free will* that he became what he was—but the fact will remain that God, fully knowing Hitler's counterfactuals and the use he would make of his free will, chose that he should come into existence and should be confronted with precisely those situations that led to such incalculable evil.

These considerations can be brought into a clearer light if we consider the implications for our topic of two recent theodicies. Neither theodicist explicitly takes a position on the questions of foreknowledge and middle knowledge, but this will not hinder us from using their theories as exemplars and test cases for the understanding of divine providence.

The first of the two theodicies to be considered is found in Eleonore Stump's paper "The Problem of Evil."[16] Stump's theodicy in its entirety is quite complex, but her most striking claim is made in the context of a discussion of the suffering of children. She says:

> With considerable diffidence . . . I want to suggest that Christian doctrine is committed to the claim that a child's suffering is outweighed by the good for the child which can result from that suffering. . . . It seems to me that a perfectly good entity who was also omniscient and omnipotent must govern the evil resulting from the misuse of significant freedom in such a way that the sufferings of any particular person are outweighed by the good which the suffer-

emphatically does *not* entail that God *intends* whatever happens; it leaves ample room for God's *permitting* things to happen in a way that goes against his intentions" (personal communication). I question, however, whether the theory really does leave room for anything to happen that is not intended by God. To be sure, not everything that happens need be *desired* by God; in that sense we could perhaps say that God's *primary intention* embraces only the good that occurs and not the evil. But God has deliberately and with full knowledge chosen that *these good purposes shall be fulfilled through a plan that entails the actual occurrence (not just the possibility) of specific evils,* and once God has made this choice it is absolutely impossible that either God or anyone else will act so as to avert those evils. Must we not then say that he *intends* to achieve these goods by means of a process that involves those evils?

[16]Eleonore Stump, "The Problem of Evil," *Faith and Philosophy* 2 (1985): 392–423.

ing produces *for that person*; otherwise, we might justifiably expect a
good God somehow to prevent that *particular suffering*, either by
intervening (in one way or another) to protect the victim, while still
allowing the perpetrator his freedom, or by curtailing freedom in
some select cases.[17]

It may occur to the reader that this claim is so strong as to be
extremely implausible.[18] Rather than pursue this, however, let us
consider the implications of Stump's theory for our understanding
of divine providence. It is evident at once that for the theodicy to
work there must be a very high degree of planning and coordina-
tion on God's part so as to insure that all of the apparently random
events in the world's history work together to achieve his goal.
(Remember that it is not a question of *some particular* evil having a
good result for the sufferer; *every* instance of serious evil must be
for the good of the sufferer.) And this, in turn, requires a high level
of *control* over the course of events on God's part. Since Stump is a
determined libertarian, this cannot come by way of absolute predestination, but one would think that for her scheme to work God
must have *at least* as much control as would be afforded by middle
knowledge. Yet middle knowledge, if it exists, would also create a
serious problem for Stump,[19] for the following reason: In the majority of cases the principal benefit that flows from suffering is that
of bringing the sufferer closer to God, of increasing the person's
chances of union with God and ultimate salvation.[20] Yet it would
appear that in many cases this is unavailing; in spite of the best God
can do to persuade us to return to himself, we have it in our power,
and some of us exercise that power, to resist to the end.[21] Now,
what are we to say about the justification for the sufferings of those

---

[17]Ibid., p. 411.

[18]For discussion of this point, as well as other aspects of Stump's theodicy, see
my "Suffering, Soul-Making, and Salvation," *International Philosophical Quarterly*
28 (1988): 3–19.

[19]Eleonore Stump has acknowledged this point in discussion.

[20]Stump, "The Problem of Evil," pp. 406–415.

[21]It is worth noting, however, that middle knowledge lends itself rather readily
to a belief in universal salvation: God may simply have chosen not to instantiate
those essences concerning which he foresaw that, if instantiated, their instantia-
tions would finally resist his grace.

who are ultimately impenitent? What I think Stump clearly wants to say[22] is that God has done his best for them and that if even his best has failed to overcome their stubborn resistance, that is not his fault. But on the assumption of middle knowledge, it becomes extremely difficult to say this. For on that assumption, God chose to inflict the suffering *in the full light of the knowledge that it would be unavailing* and would bring the sufferer no spiritual benefit. The notion that one could then still say that the infliction of suffering is justified by the benefit to the sufferer is, to say the least, extremely puzzling.

We see, then, that Stump's theodicy is left in something of a quandary. For the theodicy to work, God must exercise a very close supervision over the affairs of the world—a supervision that, one might plausibly suppose, requires *at least* the degree of control which would be made possible by middle knowledge. But if God *does* possess middle knowledge, then he chooses in some cases to inflict suffering in the full knowledge that such suffering will be unavailing, and the central idea of the theodicy is in jeopardy.

The other theodicy to be considered is found in Michael Peterson's book *Evil and the Christian God*.[23] Peterson's theodicy, like Stump's, is rather complex; it incorporates elements of the free-will defense, of the natural-law defense for natural evil, and of the soul-making theodicy, along with still other ideas. But it contrasts most sharply with Stump's in its treatment of *gratuitous evil*, evil that is not a necessary condition of some greater good or of the prevention of some greater evil. Peterson's discussion of this topic is focused on the *principle of meticulous providence*, which is defined as follows:

(MP) An omnipotent, omniscient, wholly good God would prevent or eliminate the existence of really gratuitous or pointless evils.[24]

The term "meticulous providence" strikes me as a felicitous bit of terminology; though it is defined strictly in terms of the preven-

[22]Cf. Stump, "The Problem of Evil," pp. 411–12.
[23]Michael Peterson, *Evil and the Christian God* (Grand Rapids, Mich.: Baker, 1982).
[24]Ibid., p. 76.

tion or elimination of gratuitous evils, it suggests the very close, "meticulous" supervision of earthly affairs which would evidently be necessary if God is to insure that *no single instance of evil* is permitted to occur unless as a means to a greater good or the prevention of a greater evil.

Although Peterson does not discuss this point, I think it can readily be seen that there is a close connection between the ideas of meticulous providence and middle knowledge; so close, indeed, that meticulous providence *without* middle knowledge is difficult to conceive. Suppose, for instance, that some person is engaged in making a rather crucial decision, one that will result in great good if taken in a certain way, and great evil if taken in another way. If God lacks middle knowledge, then it would seem that God must simply take his chances and abide by the result. As we have already seen, simple foreknowledge of the outcome will do him no good, for the outcome can be foreknown only on the assumption that it does in fact occur, so that it is then "too late" for the wrong choice, however disastrous, to be prevented. Only middle knowledge would enable God to foresee the disastrous consequences that *would* ensue *if* the decision were allowed to be made, and thereby either to prevent the choice or to alter the circumstances so that those consequences would be averted.

Now, Stump's theodicy, as we have seen, incorporates a principle even stronger than (MP); she requires, not just that each instance of suffering be the necessary means to a greater good, but that it be the means to such a good *for the sufferer himself.* Peterson, in contrast, argues forcefully that (MP) should be rejected. He says:

> As long as the theist understands his theological position to entail that there are no gratuitous evils, and as long as his efforts to show that there are none fall markedly shy of complete success, his conceptual commitments will always be in tension with ordinary experience of evil in the world. Theism will be forever plagued by a systematically insoluble problem. . . . Relinquishing the theological premise [viz., (MP)] . . . offers at least two important benefits to the theist who wrestles with the problem of gratuitous evil. First, accepting the existence of some gratuitous evil is more consonant with our common experience than is the position which denies gratuitous evil *a priori.* Second, rejecting the principle of meticulous

providence opens the way for a deeper and more profound apprehension of God than that widely accepted principle allows.[25]

It should be noted that in denying that God prevents all gratuitous evils, Peterson is not claiming that God permits evils to
occur *for no reason whatever*. The central idea, rather, is that God
adopts certain *overall strategies* in his dealing with the world; these
strategies are justified in that they enable the creation of great and
significant goods, but they also permit the occurrence of *individual
instances* of evil which are, as such, pure loss and *not* a means to any
greater good.[26]

Peterson's case for his claim that the rejection of (MP) "opens
the way for a deeper and more profound apprehension of God" is
too rich and complex to summarize here. Something of the spirit
of his enterprise, however, is conveyed by the following quotation:

> If the conception of human free will is taken to involve the possibil-
> ity of bringing about really gratuitous evil (specifically, moral evil),
> then God cannot completely prevent or eliminate gratuitous evil
> without severely diminishing free will. That would be logically
> impossible. At stake here is not merely the ability of humans to
> choose among options, but the ability to choose among significant
> kinds of options: between goods and evils, even the highest goods
> and most terrible evils. Thus, free will is most significant—and
> most fitting for the special sort of creature man is—if it includes the
> potential for utterly damnable choices and actions. This is part of
> the inherent risk in God's program for man.[27]

The reference to "risk" in the last sentence underscores my point
about the relationship between this theodicy and middle knowledge: The theodicy that denies (MP) is a theodicy of divine risk
taking, and risk taking is incompatible with middle knowledge.

At this point I wish to state some conclusions that are suggested
(certainly they have not been rigorously established) by the forego-
ing reflections. Peterson's theodicy entails that God takes risks in

[25]Ibid., p. 89
[26]For more on this, see my "Suffering, Soul-Making, and Salvation."
[27]Peterson, *Evil and the Christian God*, p. 104.

governing the world; thus it entails that God does not have middle knowledge. This theodicy, and the understanding of divine providence which it involves, are clearly acceptable as judged by the canons of orthodox, mainstream Christian theology. It follows that the denial of middle knowledge, and the attribution of risk taking to God, are theologically acceptable. I believe, indeed, that a considerably stronger conclusion is warranted. The type of theodicy advocated by Peterson is not only *acceptable*; it is, in my view, clearly *preferable* to the type advocated by Stump, or indeed to any theodicy that accepts (MP). So the *best* Christian theodicy will deny middle knowledge and will affirm forcefully that *God the Creator and Redeemer is a risk taker!*

Conclusion

It is time to place the results of this chapter in perspective. I make no claim to have proved, through these reflections on divine action in the world, that the view of God's knowledge here advocated is the correct one and that other views are unsatisfactory. That burden of proof must be carried by the arguments in the previous chapters; it is by their success or failure that my work must be evaluated. Nor have I proved here that the conception of divine action encapsulated in the statement that God takes risks is the correct one, though some hints have been given as to how such a case could be made. Rather, my effort here has been to exhibit a conception of divine action which is consonant with the view of divine knowledge for which I have argued, and which satisfies the needs of Christian theology and Christian experience. To the extent to which that has been successfully done, it should help to relieve some of the religious and theological resistance to my arguments. And if this resistance can be alleviated, I am confident that the arguments will emerge victorious.

Index

Cornell Studies in the Philosophy of Religion

A Series Edited by

William P. Alston